fresh from the
vegan
slow cooker

Other books by Robin Robertson

fresh from the
vegan
slow cooker

200
Ultra-Convenient,
Super-Tasty,
Completely
Animal-Free
Recipes

ROBIN ROBERTSON

THE HARVARD COMMON PRESS
BOSTON, MASSACHUSETTS

The Harvard Common Press
535 Albany Street
Boston, Massachusetts 02118
www.harvardcommonpress.com

Printed in the United States of America
Printed on acid-free paper

Library of Congress Cataloging-in-Publication Data
Robertson, Robin (Robin G.)
  Fresh from the vegan slow cooker : 200 ultra-convenient, super-tasty, completely animal-free recipes / Robin Robertson. -- 1st ed.
      p. cm.
  Includes index.
  ISBN 978-1-55832-790-0 (alk. paper)
  1. Vegan cooking. 2. Vegetarian cooking. 3. Electric cooking, Slow. 4. One-dish meals. 5. Cookbooks.
  I. Title.
  TX837.R624928 2012
  641.5'636--dc23
                                                  2012004605

Special bulk-order discounts are available on this and other Harvard Common Press books. Companies and organizations may purchase books for premiums or resale, or may arrange a custom edition, by contacting the Marketing Director at the address above.

Cover recipe: Seitan *Ropa Vieja*, page 132

Back cover recipes: Sunday Supper Strata, page 155; Moroccan Tempeh and Chickpeas with Prunes and Apricots, page 160

Cover design by Night & Day Design
Text design by Jill Weber
Cover photography and prop styling by Sabra Krock; food styling by Carrie Purcell

10 9 8 7 6 5 4 3 2 1

Dedicated to compassionate people everywhere

who love animals and don't eat them

Acknowledgments

Many thanks to the wonderful recipe testers who slow-cooked their way through all of the recipes in this book, giving me invaluable feedback along the way: Amanda Sacco, Andrea Zeichner, Barbara Bryan, Dave Melmer, Debbie Cowherd, Heather Galaxy, Jill Paschal, Joan Farkas, Jocelyn Kimmel, Jonathan and Nancy Shanes, Julie Smallwood, Lea Jacobson, Lori Maffei, Lyndsay Orwig, Melissa Chapman, Melissa West, Sabrina Butkera, Terri Merritts, and Vegan Aide. Your careful and enthusiastic testing made my job much easier.

Special appreciation goes to my husband, Jon Robertson, for always being there for me.

I'm also grateful to Bruce Shaw and everyone at The Harvard Common Press for their part in making this book a reality, with special thanks to editor Valerie Cimino and copyeditor Karen Wise for being so great to work with. Thanks also to my longtime agent, Stacey Glick of Dystel & Goderich Literary Management.

Contents

Introduction

The irresistible appeal of a slow cooker is its convenience and simplicity. Turn it on, and it cooks dinner while you do other things. You have no pot to watch. It doesn't burn or spill over. Just set it and let it do its work. Next thing you know, your kitchen smells heavenly, and you feel like your personal chef did all the work.

Slow cookers first appeared in the 1970s, and you could get one in harvest gold, avocado green, or maybe decorated with orange flowers. Back then, the Crock-Pot (as the Rival Company, which is now a brand of Sunbeam Products, trademarked it) was mostly favored for cooking tough cuts of meat. The Crock-Pot left the limelight for a while, but in 2002, when I wrote my first slow cooker cookbook (*Fresh from the Vegetarian Slow Cooker*, The Harvard Common Press, 2004), slow cookers were enjoying a comeback. The goal of my first slow cooker book was to show how versatile slow cookers are for vegetarian cooking—they can be used to prepare everything from breakfast to dessert.

Fast forward 10 years from writing that first book, and the popularity of slow cookers shows no sign of waning. In addition, more people are enjoying a plant-based diet than ever before. Since that first slow cooker cookbook was published, I've written many other titles, but I never stopped developing new recipes, discovering new techniques, and exploring new ideas for vegan slow cooking. As I've explored new ways to use the slow cooker for plant-based meals, I've been continually amazed at the effectiveness of slow cookers for vegan recipes. Over the years, I have developed scores of new recipes and explored the world's cuisines to discover more creative ways to prepare food using the slow cooker method. What I came up with was enough to fill another book.

I'm pleased and proud, therefore, to present this new book to you. It contains more than 200 recipes using only plant-based ingredients. While I've included much of the general information and some of the basic recipes from the first book, this new volume contains mostly new recipes and lots of new tips and pointers for making the most of your slow cooker experience. I've worked hard to make the recipes accessible using most sizes of slow cookers. In addition to being 100 percent plant-based, many of the recipes are also gluten-free, soy-free, or low in fat.

We all know that a slow cooker is ideal for cooking beans, soups, and stews, but as you explore the pages of *Fresh from the Vegan Slow Cooker*, you'll discover a whole new slow-cooking world. The slow cooker can be used to make braised vegetable dishes, comforting casseroles, luxurious risottos, and fun dips and snacks. It can even be used to "bake" potatoes, breads, pâtés, and desserts.

With chapters on everything from appetizers to main dishes, desserts, and beverages, there's something for everyone's breakfast, lunch, and dinner. My new book picks up where my previous book left off and elevates vegan slow cooking to a higher level. I love to cook in my slow cooker, and I hope that after you try some of these recipes, you will too.

Slow Cooker Basics

There is something almost primal about slow cooking that warms the soul. Perhaps this feeling is rooted in our ancestral iron-pot traditions around the hearth. Cooking food in closed ceramic vessels dates back at least to Roman times and is still done throughout the world, from the Moroccan *tagine* and the Italian *fagioliera* to the Pan-Asian clay pots (in Chinese, *shāguo* or *bàozai*; in Japanese, *donabe*). There is growing interest in another, even lower-tech method called "retained heat" or "haybox" cooking, in which food is brought to a boil and then allowed to continue cooking inside an insulated container.

The first modern electric slow cooker was originally developed for bean cooking. The "Beanery," made by Naxon Utilities Corporation, was redubbed the Crock-Pot by the Rival Manufacturing Company after it bought Naxon in 1971. This revolutionary kitchen appliance was marketed to working women as a way to make a home-cooked meal while they were at work, and they quickly put it to use in preparing pot roasts and other meat-centric dishes. A phenomenal hit at the time, the Crock-Pot fad faded, only to enjoy a resurgence some 30 years later. Since those early days, more than 80 million slow cookers have been sold, with more than 350 models and counting, from basic manual cookers limited to the two Low or High settings to fully programmable units with a variety of settings.

Why Use a Slow Cooker?

If you have been using a slow cooker in your kitchen with any regularity, then you know that there are many answers to that question.

For many years, I used my '70s-era slow cooker for cooking beans or bean soups. However, when I got my first high-tech slow cooker, I was inspired to look beyond bean basics and began experimenting with all of the ingredients I love. To my delight, I discovered that the slow cooker cooked a seitan pot roast just as well as it had cooked traditional roasts, and it easily cooked many of my other favorite vegan dishes.

Most slow cooker enthusiasts would agree that convenience, economy, and great taste are what keep them coming back to their slow cookers time and again. When you cook in a slow cooker, the longer cooking times allow the flavors of the ingredients to meld into a deep complexity that is often unparalleled in other cooking methods. Slow cooking can be more nutritious, too, since the long cooking time allows the nutrients to concentrate in the food as it draws more flavor out of the ingredients. When you factor in the convenience quotient, you've got a kitchen helper worthy of the name.

Think about it: You simply assemble your ingredients in the slow cooker, turn it on, and that's it—several hours later, dinner is served. But the benefits don't stop there. For added convenience, your meal can be served directly from the ceramic pot in which it was cooked. In addition, the removable ceramic insert can be refrigerated, so you can prepare your ingredients the night before and refrigerate them overnight right in the insert so it's all ready to cook the next day. Slow cooking can be a terrific solution for busy people who are trying to eat healthier and for anyone who wants an easy way to eat more deliciously.

At the heart of slow cooking lies a paradox: Your food takes longer to cook, but it gives you more free time. I find it more liberating to get dinner cooking in a slow cooker than I do preparing even the quickest meal at the last minute, especially when I'm tired and hungry. Slow cooking can help you to eat more well-balanced and economical meals on the nights when you're running late or too exhausted to cook. The reason is that those are the nights when you're tempted to order takeout, or eat junk food or a packaged convenience food. Simply by planning ahead, slow cooking can reward you with the ultimate convenience food.

Because of how well slow cookers cook many bean, grain, and vegetable dishes, the appliances are especially useful for preparing vegan meals. While some people may prefer using a pressure cooker for beans and other long-cooking recipes, I find the slow cooker more convenient since you can leave it un-attended—something you wouldn't do with a pressure cooker or any stovetop cooking method. So even though meals prepared in a slow cooker take longer to cook, they can end up saving you time.

10 Great Things to Know About Your Slow Cooker

1. It's a convenient way to prepare healthy home-cooked meals.

2. It allows you to cook and serve in the same vessel, so it saves on cleanup time.

3. It can have dinner ready and waiting for you at the end of the day.

4. The slow, gentle cooking adds depth of flavor to foods.

5. It keeps the kitchen cool on hot days.

6. It's an ideal way to cook beans and seitan from scratch.

7. It doubles as a chafing dish or hot punch bowl at parties.

8. It's economical because it both uses less energy than oven cooking and makes great leftovers.

9. It can be used as a mini-oven to slow-bake cakes, casseroles, potatoes, and more.

10. It frees up stovetop burners when cooking for parties or for a crowd on holidays.

The flavor factor is also a good reason to use the slow cooker. Dishes that have been simmered for hours in a slow cooker taste better than the same recipe prepared quickly on top of the stove. The extended, gentle cooking time in a covered ceramic pot allows the flavors of the ingredients to fully bloom, mingle, and intensify. Using a slow cooker allows you to enjoy the intense flavors of hearty soups, stews, and other recipes without having to be tethered to a hot stove.

In addition, a slow cooker doesn't heat up the kitchen the way other cooking methods do, which is a great relief when you're cooking on hot days. Finally, the slow cooker uses less energy than other cooking methods, so you save money on utilities. And speaking of saving money, the slow cooker also makes it easy to cook larger quantities of food that can then be portioned and frozen. This is much preferable to relying on frozen convenience foods, which are more expensive.

While your main dish is simmering in the slow cooker, you also have more time to be creative with your side dishes, salads, or other accompaniments. Food doesn't burn when left unattended because the heating coils in slow cookers cook food gently and evenly from the bottom and sides. The lid keeps the heat and moisture inside. While the benefits of slow cooking make it ideal for when you're not home, it's also a great relief to busy stay-at-home moms and those who work at home and don't have the time to linger in the kitchen.

Versatility is another great reason to slow-cook. Thanks to the wide variety of sizes now available, slow cookers can be used to make anything from appetizers to desserts. A slow cooker can also be a great help when company's coming, allowing you to keep the soup or main dish warm while you entertain your guests.

Using a slow cooker also lets you free up other cooking surfaces. This can be especially handy for holiday meals. If you're serving a buffet meal, you can place the slow cooker right on the table. It will keep the food at the proper serving temperature for hours while you enjoy the party. Slow-cooked dishes are also great for potlucks and other gatherings. Just prepare your dish in the slow cooker, bring along the entire unit (some come with their own carrying cases), and plug it in when you arrive at your destination to keep your dish warm for serving.

All Shapes and Sizes

The original Crock-Pot came in only one size (3½ to 4 quarts), one shape (round), and a few colors that now seem awful, such as harvest gold and avocado green. The stoneware crock was not removable, and the temperature settings were manual and limited to either High or Low. How things have changed!

Today there are many slow-cooker brands available, including the original Crock-Pot made by Rival (now a brand of Sunbeam Products) and similar units made by companies such as Proctor Silex, West Bend, All-Clad, and others. The removable ceramic inserts of most slow cookers are dishwasher-, oven-, and microwave-safe, but they typically cannot be used directly on the stovetop. One exception is the Hamilton Beach Stovetop-Safe Slow Cooker, which is designed to go from stovetop to slow cooker, allowing you to brown and cook in the same vessel.

You can find slow cookers in sizes ranging from 1 to 7 quarts. They are available in round or oval shapes with removable crockery inserts. The most popular sizes are the 4-quart (medium-size) and the 6-quart (large). The bigger models of slow cooker are great for large quantities of food and also to hold racks and pans for "baking" inside a slow cooker. Smaller 1- to 1½-quart slow cookers are ideal for dips, hot drinks, and other party food, but they are impractical for most everyday cooking. Only two or three recipes for dips in this book call for the small cooker.

If you can buy only one slow cooker (and your household consists of more than one person), I recommend that you buy a larger model—at least 5 to 6 quarts. This will allow you more flexibility, because most recipes calling for a 4-quart model can easily be made in the larger one, often with no adjustment to the recipe. The bigger slow cooker also enables you to make larger volume recipes, which you can then portion and freeze for further convenience. In addition, certain recipes (such as breads and desserts) call for a small (7-inch) springform or other pan to be inserted in the cooker, and you will need a larger model to accomplish this. Even though I'm usually cooking for only two people, I most often use my 6-quart slow cooker so that I can freeze plenty of leftovers.

Recent innovations in slow cookers include a 3-in-1 unit that features three different size crocks that fit into the same base, offering lots of flexibility. There are also models, such as the one described above, that have inserts that can be used on the stovetop as well as in the oven or freezer. This type of cooker is especially handy for browning onions and other ingredients on the stovetop before cooking in the slow cooker. In addition, there are "multi-cookers," so named because they can be used for deep-frying and other types of cooking. However, bear in mind that multi-cookers are not true slow cookers because their heating elements are located only in the base of the unit for more direct heat from the bottom (as opposed to the sides, as in a slow cooker), which may result in scorching if left unattended. There are also slow cookers that have inserts with a non-stick finish.

While some slow cookers have basic manual High and Low settings, other cookers are completely programmable with integrated timers to start and stop the cooking, as well as a "Keep Warm" setting to keep the food at a constant serving temperature once the allotted cooking time is over. You can also plug your cooker into a kitchen timer that you can set to switch on or off at a designated time, allowing for more peace of mind if you're late getting home.

Slow Cookers Used for Testing These Recipes

More than 20 people tested the recipes for this book, using various brands and sizes of slow cookers, including several Rival Crock-Pots, a number of Hamilton Beach/Proctor Silex slow cookers, a few West Bend Crockery Cookers, a Betty Crocker slow cooker, a Cuisinart programmable slow cooker, and more. Some of the testers noticed, as I have, that their cookers have various quirks—some cook faster or slower than others, and some have a "hot spot" on one side. For that reason, most of the recipes in this book include a range of cooking times that you may need to adjust according to your own slow cooker's "temperament."

If you think that having one slow cooker is great, then you may find that having two is even better. I regularly use both 4-quart and 6-quart models, and I sometimes use both sizes at once. As many slow-cooker fans have discovered, there is frequently a need for both. Sometimes you may need a large one for the main dish and a smaller one for a side dish, soup, or dessert. I have a total of three slow cookers in different sizes: one small (1½-quart)

Crockery Care Caveats

The slow cooker is an easy-to-use appliance, but there are guidelines that should be followed in order to keep your slow cooker (and the food cooked in it) in tip-top shape.

- Avoid using frozen ingredients in slow cooker recipes, as they will slow down the heating process dramatically. Thaw all frozen items first or else the cooking time will be way off.

- Do not put cold ingredients into a hot slow cooker. It can crack the ceramic insert.

- Let the ceramic insert cool completely before removing and washing it. A sudden change in temperature (such as immersing a hot insert in cool dishwater) can cause it to crack.

- Do not immerse the outer housing of an electric slow cooker unit in water. Instead, unplug the appliance and wipe the inside and outside clean with a damp cloth or sponge.

- Read the manufacturer's instructions for specific information regarding the care and cleaning of your slow cooker.

round, one medium-size (4-quart) round, and one large (6-quart) oval. They all get a lot of use, especially during one of my marathon cooking days when I prepare food for the following week and cook up some staples such as beans to portion and freeze for future use. Even if it's just to take advantage of the various recipes that are best prepared in one size or another, you may want to consider buying a second cooker.

It's Easy to Become a Slow-Cooking Expert

Since food cooked in a slow cooker virtually "cooks itself," this type of cooking is simple and stress-free. By keeping a few basic tips in mind, you can become a slow-cooking expert in no time.

INGREDIENT VOLUME VERSUS SLOW COOKER SIZE

Each recipe in this book specifies a recommended slow cooker size. However, since the amount of the ingredients determines the volume, it is important to pay attention to how full your cooker is after adding all of your ingredients.

For example, since the range of what constitutes a "small" onion or a "large" potato may vary, you may find that the volume of ingredients in your cooker is too close to the top. Especially if you are preparing a soup or stew, there is a risk that the contents may bubble up and over onto your kitchen counter. You will need to assess this as you are preparing the recipe, keeping in mind that slow cookers perform best when at least half full but no more than three-quarters full.

RECIPE COOKING TIMES

When slow cookers first came on the market, the appeal to the working woman was the fact that most recipes listed an 8- to 10-hour cooking time—long enough for the dish to cook all day while she was at work. While this cooking time may be correct for certain recipes, particularly meat-centric ones, the fact is that many of them don't take as long to cook as once thought. This is especially true for a variety of vegan ingredients, including seitan, tofu, and vegan sausage.

In developing the recipes for this book, my testers and I found that many recipes are actually ready to eat much sooner than the traditional 8 hours, although some recipes do hold up well when left to cook for an additional hour or so. The forgiving nature of slow-cooker cooking times is one of the great features of the appliance.

I've done my best to provide realistic times for when dishes may actually be done while stressing that you may often tack on an additional hour or so for the food to cook without compromising flavor or texture. Most recipes will also be fine for a while beyond the cooking time when held at the Keep Warm setting.

If this still doesn't allow you enough time to get home and turn off the slow cooker (and if your slow cooker doesn't have a built-in timer), the solution is to purchase an inexpensive appliance timer to use with your cooker. Simply set the timer to start cooking up to 2 hours later. That way you can enjoy the convenience of shorter-cooking recipes if you're away from home all day.

If you're short on time in the morning, one of the easiest solutions is to prepare your ingredients and load your slow cooker insert the night before, then refrigerate the crock overnight. The next morning, you can then put the insert in the slow cooker and set the cooking time in just seconds.

HIGH ALTITUDES

If you are cooking at a high elevation (over 3,000 feet), you may find that food cooked in a slow cooker takes somewhat longer to get done than the cooking times recommended in this cookbook. To compensate, you can cook all recipes on High, although you will probably also need to cook your food a little longer as well. Once you calibrate the cooking time for your location, make a note of the changes for future use.

Slow Cooker Points and Pointers

1. While slow cookers are designed for even heating, some have "hot spots." So, for all but very "soupy" recipes, it's a good idea to oil the insert of your slow cooker or spray it with nonstick cooking spray. If you have a slow cooker with a nonstick insert, oiling or spraying may not be needed.

2. Many recipes achieve a better flavor if some of the ingredients (specifically onions, garlic, and spices) are cooked for a few minutes before adding them to the slow cooker. Since some people won't want to dirty a skillet to do this, such recipes include the option of using the microwave for this step.

3. It's a fact that all slow cookers cook at different temperatures: sometimes slightly different, sometimes dramatically different. For this reason, you will notice a fairly wide time range for doneness—usually plus or minus 2 hours. For the most part, recipes will be cooked on Low, since many people want to be able to set it in the morning and forget it until dinnertime. A High cooking time choice is sometimes also provided. If the cooking time in your own slow cooker varies dramatically from those listed in this book, make a note of it in order to "calibrate" future recipes for your own slow cooker.

Tips for Slow-Cooking Success

Slow cooking is simple, but you can still make mistakes by not knowing some basic do's and don'ts. Follow these simple rules—and their exceptions—and you can transform what would have been so-so slow cooker meals into meals that are nothing short of sensational.

Try not to lift the lid when cooking. Doing so will reduce the cooking temperature considerably and cause your dish to take longer to cook. It is estimated that each time you lift the lid, you lose 20 minutes of cooking time. However, some rules are made to be broken, and sometimes you just need to lift the lid. *Exceptions to this rule include* the need to add certain ingredients before the end of cooking time or the need to stir a particular dish. For the most part, you should be able to check on what you're cooking by looking through the clear glass lid. If you do want to lift the lid to stir, check for doneness, or adjust seasonings,

4. If there's too much liquid left in the cooker at the end of cooking time, remove the lid and turn the heat to High to evaporate some of it. Conversely, if there's not enough liquid, add a little more and let it warm up and blend with the other flavors.

5. Hard vegetables, such as onions and carrots, added raw to soups and braises will soften just fine because of the amount of liquid they are cooking in. However, if these same vegetables are added raw to stews, they will remain hard long after the rest of the ingredients are cooked because there is not as much liquid for them to cook in. When using hard vegetables in a stew dish, it is best to sauté them first to soften them.

6. The smaller or thinner you cut or slice ingredients, the more quickly they will cook.

7. For easy cleanup, consider using Reynolds Slow Cooker Liners, made specifically for use in slow cookers on both High and Low settings.

8. With a few exceptions, you will achieve optimal results if the slow cooker is between one-half and three-quarters full. The majority of recipes in this book can be made in most medium-size to large slow cookers (4 to 6 quarts).

just do so as quickly as possibly—and be aware that you may need to tack on a little extra cooking time.

Always fill your slow cooker at least half full. Avoid filling it more than three-quarters full to keep it from spilling over while simmering. *Exceptions to this rule include* recipes that call for "steam-baking," such as cheesecake on a trivet, stuffed vegetables, baked potatoes, or other such recipes. Special instructions are provided for recipes that require this step.

One size fits most. As a general rule, most of these recipes can be made in 4- to 6-quart slow cookers because they contain enough volume that they require no adjustment. For example, approximately 3 quarts of total ingredient volume will fill a 4-quart model three-quarters full (the maximum recommended volume), and the same amount of ingredients will fill a 6-quart cooker one-half full (the minimum recommended volume).

Sometimes partial cooking is required. Some recipes call for partially cooking or browning some ingredients, such as onions and garlic, on the stovetop before placing them in the slow cooker. The short amount of time this extra step takes can make a big difference in the taste, texture, and appearance of the dish. In many cases, this step can be done in a microwave or even directly in the slow cooker, when the purpose is to bloom the flavor or soften the ingredients as opposed to browning them.

Save the best for last. Some recipes that use quick-cooking or delicate ingredients, such as fresh herbs or spinach, will call for these ingredients to be added at or near the end of the cooking time. This attention to detail will pay off when you taste the finished dish.

Adapt your own recipes. Because the lid remains on throughout most slow-cooked recipes, the liquids do not evaporate the way they do in similar stovetop recipes. Because of this, when converting your own recipes for the slow cooker, you may need to reduce the total amount of liquid called for. If you find that you have too much liquid near the end of the cooking time, remove the lid and cook on High for an additional 30 to 40 minutes to reduce the excess liquid, or simply drain off some of the liquid before serving.

Always presoak dried beans. This will help with digestibility and make your slow-cooked beans tender in less time. I also offer options for using canned beans in the recipes.

Dried beans prefer an "acid-free" zone. When cooking dried beans, don't add tomatoes or other acidic ingredients until after the beans have softened; otherwise they will take longer to cook and may remain tough. Once the beans are cooked, drain and discard the cooking liquid before using the beans in a recipe. This will improve their digestibility.

Add pasta or rice. There are two ways to add pasta or rice to slow-cooked recipes. You can either add uncooked pasta or rice during the final hour of cooking time, or cook the rice or pasta separately on the stovetop and add it to the dish just prior to serving. The latter is my preference because it gives you more control and assures the proper texture. Rice or pasta cooked directly in the slow cooker often turns out too mushy or starchy. In addition, cooking either one in the cooker will soak up much of the recipe's liquid and change the texture of the finished dish. (Converted rice works well when added raw to a slow cooker recipe, as does Arborio rice. If you prefer brown rice, long-grain brown basmati works best. Still, you may want to cook it separately on top of the stove, unless a soft-textured rice is acceptable in a particular recipe.)

The Microwave: An Optional Step for Extra Flavor

As I've mentioned, my recipes occasionally contain instructions to brown or sauté some of the ingredients before adding them to the slow cooker. This is done for several reasons—usually to get the most flavor or most appealing color from certain ingredients or, in the case of particularly hard vegetables, to jump-start the cooking process. For that reason, you'll find that many recipes in this book begin with first sautéing onions (and other ingredients) for a few minutes for best results.

To me, that extra step and that extra pan to wash is a small price to pay for superior flavor. However, I understand that time is at a premium for many of you, and many people simply don't want to wash an extra pan when slow cooking. Rather than omit the step entirely, I've included a compromise solution: Use your microwave!

Instead of sautéing onions and garlic and other ingredients in a skillet, you can simply "sweat" them in a covered microwave-safe bowl for a few minutes in the microwave to soften them and bring out their flavor. This also works for giving extra-hard ingredients, such as carrots, a head start so that they get done cooking at the same time as the softer vegetables in a recipe. The microwave option lets you avoid washing an extra pan, since you can then simply put the bowl in the dishwasher. This is also a good choice if you wish to avoid the oil used in sautéing the ingredients, since you can omit the oil and add a little water to the vegetables in the microwave. If you prefer not to use a microwave but want to avoid sautéing in oil, you can instead sauté the vegetables in a few tablespoons of water for a few minutes before adding to the slow cooker.

Another way to give certain ingredients a head start is to place them in the slow cooker, cover, and turn it on High while you prep the rest of the ingredients. The amount of time this will take depends on the size and volume of the vegetables being used. For example, 1 tablespoon of minced garlic may take only 15 min-

utes to soften and allow the flavor to bloom, while ½ cup of chopped onion can take up to 30 minutes, so this shortcut is practical only if you plan to be in the kitchen doing other things anyway.

If you plan to turn on the slow cooker in the morning before leaving the house, you might want to do any advance prep the night before.

NOTE: A final option is to simply skip all preliminary steps and just load the crock with the ingredients, and let it cook in the slow cooker from start to finish.

LAST-MINUTE ADDITIONS

The microwave can also come in handy near the end of cooking a recipe. You can use the microwave to cook delicate vegetables, such as spinach, for a last-minute addition to a slow-cooked dish. Just place washed spinach (or other delicate greens) in a microwave-safe bowl, cover, and wilt them in the microwave for a couple of minutes. Then drain off any liquid.

Other delicate ingredients are best added near the end of cooking, or at serving time, so that their flavors don't dissipate and they don't overcook. Cooked pasta or rice should be added close to the end of the cooking time so they do not become mushy. Fresh herbs are a good example of ingredients that lose their flavor if added too soon. Just as the flavor of fresh herbs dissipates if added at the beginning of the cooking time, the flavor of dried herbs can concentrate or turn bitter, so they need to be used in judicious quantities. You can always add more near the end of the cooking time, after checking the dish for flavor balance.

If You Need to Extend the Cooking Time

For those with especially long workdays, having dinner ready when you get home is a dream come true. However, many slow-cooker recipes are done in 6 to 8 hours, when you need it to be more like 9 to 10 hours. Here are three ways to extend the cooking time:

1. Choose a slow cooker that has a built-in timer to allow the cooker to turn on after you've gone to work. On the other end of the cooking time, it can also switch over to the Keep Warm setting, if needed.

2. A less expensive solution is to buy a small appliance kitchen timer (available at hardware stores). When you plug your cooker into a kitchen timer, you can set it to start up to 2 hours after you leave the house.

3. For a really low-tech solution, simply prepare your ingredients the night before and place them in the slow cooker insert, then refrigerate it overnight. Before you leave in the morning, place the cold insert in the cooker and turn it on Low. It will take an extra 30 to 45 minutes for your recipe to cook from the cold state, so you can extend the cooking time that much further. If your cooker has an automatic Keep Warm setting, it will keep your dinner warm for you until you get home. (Remember not to leave food on this setting for longer than 2 hours.)

Cooking-Time Variables

Some slow-cooker brands and models cook a bit faster (hotter) than others, while others cook more slowly. For that reason, you may need to monitor the cooking times of the first recipes you try so that you can calibrate your particular slow cooker. Other cooking-time variables include the actual temperature of the food you start with—Is it at room temperature or cold from the refrigerator?—and the size of the pieces of food being cooked.

If you begin slow cooking with cold ingredients, they will take longer to cook than if they were at room temperature. If both the food and slow cooker insert are cold (as would be the case if you assemble your ingredients in the cooker insert the night before and refrigerate it until morning), the cooking time will be longer still. Be sure to factor in some extra time (30 to 45 minutes) for things to warm up when estimating your cooking time. You can use this to your advantage if you will be away from home all day.

Slow-Cooker Timing Factors

The amount of time it will take for food to cook in your slow cooker depends on more than just how long you cook it and whether you set it on High or Low. Here are some other factors that can affect the cooking time:

- **The type and model of slow cooker.** One cooker's Low setting may be several degrees hotter than another cooker's Low setting. I have discovered that one of my slow cookers cooks "faster" (or hotter) than the others, and another cooks more slowly than normal, so I plan accordingly.

- **The temperature of the ingredients when you add them to the slow cooker.** If your ingredients are at room temperature or hotter, they will cook faster than if the ingredients (or the entire ceramic cooking insert) just came out of the refrigerator.

- **The size of the pieces of vegetables and other ingredients you are using.** This may be a no-brainer, but the smaller/thinner the pieces of your ingredients, the faster they will cook.

- **The amount of liquid in the pot and its temperature.** Less liquid takes less time to heat up. In addition, if you use hot or boiling liquid, it will shorten the cooking time.

The original reason that slow cookers became so popular was because of their ability to cook dinner all day while we were at work. From that perspective, recipes that take about 8 hours to cook have special appeal. For recipes to finish around the 8-hour mark, they will generally need to be cooked on Low (200°F). If you cook the same recipe on High (300°F), the food will be ready in about half the time.

Whenever possible, I cook on Low rather than High because I think that the slower, gentler cooking coaxes more flavor from the ingredients. Unless otherwise specified, most recipes in this book use the Low setting, although you may use the High setting if you're pressed for time or simply prefer your food to cook faster.

While some recipes require every bit of an 8-hour spread, many recipes will actually be quite ready to eat after about 6 hours, and some even less. Wherever possible, I've listed the cooking times in 2-hour spreads, to compensate for the heat variables in individual slow cookers, and also to indicate the particular time window when a recipe may be done. In many cases, if you're going to be a little later than the designated time, many recipes will hold just fine for a little while longer. Some slow cookers have a built-in function that will allow them to cook for 6 or 8 hours, for example, then automatically switch to the Keep Warm setting. This kind of cooker is great for people who don't arrive home at the same time each day. For food safety reasons, once your food is cooked, you should not let it sit on the Keep Warm setting for longer than 2 hours. If your schedule requires a longer time frame, I suggest you use an appliance timer with your cooker and set it to start cooking up to 2 hours after you leave the house.

Ways to Thicken Liquids

Because the food is essentially sealed inside the slow cooker while it is being cooked, there tends to be a lot of moisture produced that doesn't have an opportunity to evaporate, as in other cooking methods. In some cases, such as brothy soups, this extra liquid may be fine, but in some recipes, such as stews, you may prefer to thicken the liquid so it is more of a sauce. There are a number of ways to thicken the liquid in a slow-cooked dish. Here are the most common:

Mashed vegetables: After the food is cooked, mash a couple of chunks of cooked potato (you may want to add a few extra chunks to a recipe for this purpose) and stir it into the liquid. The addition of cooked rice can absorb some of the liquid as well.

Pureed vegetables: Scoop out a cup (or more) of the cooked vegetables and puree them in a blender or food processor, then stir back the puree into the slow cooker.

Cornstarch slurry: Blend 1 tablespoon cornstarch with 2 tablespoons cold water (to thicken 1 cup of liquid). Set the slow cooker on High and stir the cornstarch mixture into the hot liquid. Put the lid back on the cooker and cook for about 10 minutes longer.

Beurre manié: Set the slow cooker on High and stir 2 tablespoons *beurre manié* (page 28) into the hot liquid. Put the lid back on the cooker and cook for about 10 minutes longer.

Reduction: Set the slow cooker on High, remove the lid, and let the food simmer until the volume of liquid reduces.

Vegan sour cream or cream cheese: At the end of the cooking time, blend 2 tablespoons vegan sour cream (page 57) or vegan cream cheese (page 31) with ½ cup of the hot liquid from the slow cooker to temper it and make it smooth. Stir the mixture back into the slow cooker liquid.

Arrowroot: Blend 1 tablespoon arrowroot with 2 tablespoons cold water (to thicken 2 cups of liquid). Set the slow cooker on High and stir the arrowroot mixture into the hot liquid. Put the lid back on the cooker and cook for about 10 minutes longer.

Roux: Melt 2 tablespoons vegan butter in a small pan, then stir in 2 tablespoons flour and stir for a minute or two. Pour in about ½ cup of the liquid from the slow cooker, then set the cooker on High and stir the roux mixture back into the hot liquid. Put the lid back on the cooker and cook for about 10 minutes longer.

Tapioca starch: Blend 1 tablespoon tapioca starch with 2 tablespoons cold water (to thicken 2 cups of liquid). Set the slow cooker on High and stir the tapioca mixture into the hot liquid. Put the lid back on the cooker and cook for about 10 minutes longer.

Slow-Cooking Vegan Ingredients

Since this is a vegan cookbook, you obviously won't find the typical slow cooker recipes using cheap cuts of meat. Instead, you will find recipes that use a variety of beans, grains, and more vegetables than you ever imagined could be prepared in a slow cooker. In addition, there are recipes that use tofu, tempeh, seitan (also known as wheat meat), and other versatile ingredients such as vegan sausage and TVP (textured vegetable protein). Here is a brief overview of the some of the ingredients used in this book.

TOFU

Tofu has become so mainstream that most people who use it are familiar with the two basic types and the various textures in which it can be purchased. "Regular" tofu, also known as "Chinese bean curd," is sold refrigerated in 14- to 16-ounce tubs. "Silken" or "Japanese-style" tofu is most often sold in 12-ounce aseptic containers. Both regular and silken tofu are available in varying textures, ranging from soft to extra-firm; the softer the tofu, the more water it contains. Generally speaking, silken tofu is softer and creamier than regular tofu and is best suited to making sauces and desserts. Tofu in all its forms has come to be readily available in supermarkets these days, in addition to natural food and international grocery stores.

Because of the delicate texture of tofu, it does not usually hold up well in slow-cooker recipes unless added right at the end of the cooking time, although I have included recipes for braised tofu that allow for slabs of extra-firm tofu to cook in a small amount of liquid. Generally, however, tofu is most successful in slow-cooker recipes where the tofu is mixed with other ingredients, as in a terrine, lasagna, stuffing, or dessert. Recipes calling for regular tofu will simply list "tofu" (usually firm or extra-firm). If silken tofu is required, it will be listed as such.

Regular tofu may be stored unopened in the refrigerator until you need it (in accordance with the expiration date on its package). Once tofu is opened, use it as soon as possible. It will keep for 3 to 5 days in the refrigerator if covered in fresh water in a tightly sealed container.

Because tofu is packed in water, it is important to drain it before using or it may add extra moisture into your recipe. After draining the tofu, you should blot it to remove even more moisture. To do this, cut the tofu into slabs and arrange them on a baking pan lined with two or three layers of paper towels. Cover the tofu with additional paper towels and blot. If you wish to remove even more moisture from tofu, you can press it. To do this, follow the steps for blotting tofu, then place a second baking pan on top of the top layer of paper towels. Place some heavy canned goods on top of the pan and allow the tofu to sit for an hour or so. Removing excess liquid will result in a firmer texture and allow the tofu to better absorb the surrounding flavors in your recipe.

TEMPEH

With its sturdy texture and ability to absorb surrounding flavors, tempeh is ideal for cooking in a slow cooker. Made from fermented soybeans that are compressed into a cake, tempeh has a chewy, meat-like texture and is especially suited to stews and braised dishes in the slow cooker. Tempeh can be sliced, diced, cubed, or grated. If you prefer a more mellow-flavored tempeh, you should steam it for at least 15 minutes before using it in a recipe. To make it more visually appealing, you can sauté the tempeh in a little oil before adding it to the slow cooker to turn it a crisp golden brown, although that step is a personal choice.

Look for tempeh in the refrigerated or frozen section of natural food stores, Asian markets, and larger supermarkets, where it can be found in 8-ounce packages. Increasingly, you can find versions made with a mix of soybeans and grains, or even from other beans such as black beans. Tempeh can be stored in the refrigerator or freezer. If left unopened, tempeh will keep for several weeks or months (in accordance with the expiration date). Once opened, it is best to use it within 4 days.

SEITAN

Seitan (pronounced *say-TAN*) is made from the protein part of wheat known as gluten. The meaty texture and appearance of seitan make it a versatile ingredient that is ideal for slow cooking because it absorbs the surrounding flavors as it cooks and its texture holds up during long cooking. You can use diced seitan in stews and soups, shredded or ground seitan in chili, or sliced seitan braised in wine or vegetable stock. Larger pieces can be cooked as a roast.

Although precooked seitan is available in natural food stores and Asian markets, it is much more economical and versatile to make your own using vital wheat gluten, and it can typically be used from its raw, freshly made state. A recipe for homemade seitan can be found on page 136. It's best to make a large amount at once and freeze it in usable portions. If you do buy precooked commercial seitan, be sure to drain and rinse it before using, since it is often sold in a marinade that may not be compatible with your recipe.

PACKAGED MEAT ALTERNATIVES

Several varieties of packaged meat alternatives can be found in the frozen food department of natural food stores and well-stocked supermarkets. These products have the flavor and appearance of cooked meat and include vegan sausage links and burger crumbles. These products are convenient and versatile, and many have a good flavor and texture. Because they are precooked, it is best to add them near the end of cooking time in slow-cooker recipes, since they can fall apart if overcooked.

Some ingredients, such as vegan sausage links, should be browned in a skillet before using, while others, such as burger crumbles, do not require browning. I prefer to make my own vegan sausage and other such ingredients in order to avoid processed foods as much as possible. A recipe for homemade sausage links is provided on page 157.

TEXTURED VEGETABLE PROTEIN (TVP)

Textured vegetable protein (TVP) or textured soy protein (TSP) is an inexpensive dry product used as a meat substitute. It is made from soy flour that is cooked under pressure and then extruded to make different sizes and shapes. TVP is available in granules, chunks, and strips. The granules can be used to make vegan burgers, sausage, meatballs, and meatloaf. They can also be added to chili and pasta sauces in the same way as ground meat. The chunks and strips are ideal for stews. TVP has no cholesterol, is low in fat and sodium, and is an excellent source of protein and fiber. It is easily rehydrated for use in soups, stews, and casseroles. It can be added to certain recipes (especially brothy ones) in its dry state, and it will reconstitute while cooking. To reconstitute TVP, combine 1 cup TVP with a scant 1 cup boiling liquid to yield about 1⅓ cups. Two cups of reconstituted granules or chunks is equal to about 1 pound of cooked seitan or other meat alternative.

SOY CURLS

Butler Soy Curls are similar to textured soy protein, but they are superior in texture and less processed. Soy Curls are made from whole non-GMO soybeans. The product is high in fiber and protein and contains no additives or preservatives. It is very tender when reconstituted and ideal for adding to stews in the slow cooker. Soy Curls are available online and in some natural food stores.

OTHER INGREDIENTS

Most of the ingredients used in this book can be found in well-stocked supermarkets. These days, many supermarkets have a good natural food section and international grocery aisles where you can find good-quality soy sauce, rice noodles, agave nectar, and so on. Nondairy milk and vegan cream cheese are commonplace in many stores, although a few ingredients, such as miso paste, nutritional yeast, and vital wheat gluten, may require a trip to a natural food store. If you can't find a particular ingredient where you live, do an online search and chances are you can easily find what you're looking for.

This book also includes several "not from the crock" recipes for homemade versions of certain ingredients that are used in other recipes throughout the book, including vegan cream cheese (page 31), sour cream (page 57), and creamy cheesy sauce (page 123).

Wide World of Beans

Since bean cooking was the intended use of the first slow cookers, it almost goes without saying that beans are a natural fit for the slow-cooking method. That said, however, there is a distinction to be made between "cooking beans" and "cooking with beans." Because beans take longer to cook than, for example, most vegetables, I prefer to use beans that have already been cooked in most of my recipes in order to avoid overcooking the vegetables. Another reason for using precooked beans in recipes is that it allows me to drain off the cooking liquid after cooking beans, making them more digestible.

In Chapter 5 you will find a recipe for Basic Beans, along with variations. Cooking beans from the dried state in the slow cooker is both easy and economical. I like to cook large batches of different kind of beans and portion them into containers and freeze them to use later in recipes. If you prefer your beans firm rather than soft, you can slow-cook your beans until they are just tender but still quite firm, and then allow them to cook the rest of the way in the various recipes you will be using them in.

While many of us enjoy cooking a variety of different beans, it's a safe bet that most of us have barely scratched the surface in terms of what types are available. Believe it or not, there are more than 13,000 different beans and legumes in the world—that's a lot of beans!

BEAN COOKING

There are some general guidelines to follow when cooking beans in a slow cooker. Bear in mind that dried beans expand when soaked and cooked. One cup of dried beans yields 2 to 3 cups cooked.

As a general rule, you can cook 1 cup of presoaked beans in 4 cups of water. You should use 6 cups of water for 2 cups of presoaked beans. For 1 pound dried beans, you will need 8 to 10 cups water.

The beans should stay submerged in the water while cooking, so you should check on them about 1 hour before they are scheduled to be done and add some boiling water if needed. Otherwise, the beans that are not submerged may still be hard when the cooking time is over.

Once cooked, the beans should cool in the slow cooker in their own liquid. You can then transfer the cooked beans into 1- to 2-cup containers, using a slotted spoon, then refrigerate or freeze until needed.

Most beans are done cooking in a slow cooker after 3 to 4 hours on High or 8 to 10 hours on Low, although some may take longer depending on the age and variety of bean, and others are done much sooner. With the exception of lentils and split peas, which do not require soaking, beans benefit from presoaking to shorten the cooking time and make them more digestible.

Bean Slow-Cooking Times

Here is a list of cooking times (on High) for presoaked dried beans. The times may vary depending on factors such as altitude and the age of the beans.

Black beans: 3 hours

Black-eyed peas: 3½ hours

Cannellini beans: 3 hours (boil 15 minutes before slow-cooking)

Chickpeas: 4 hours

Great Northern beans: 2½ to 3 hours

Kidney beans: 3 hours (boil 15 minutes before slow-cooking)

Lentils: 1½ to 2 hours (no need to presoak)

Navy beans: 2½ to 3 hours

Pinto beans: 3 hours

Split peas: 2½ hours (no need to presoak)

NOTE: Uncooked kidney beans (including cannellini beans) contain a natural toxin (lectin phytohaemagglutinin) that must be destroyed by cooking. To do this, it is very important that you boil raw kidney beans in water for at least 10 to 15 minutes before cooking in the slow cooker, since the temperature of slow cooking alone may not be hot enough to destroy the toxin.

You may sometimes want to make a recipe using cooked beans but you don't happen to have any stashed in the freezer and there's no time to cook them from scratch. In those instances, let canned beans come to the rescue, and that's another reason most recipes call for "cooked" beans—allowing you the choice of using cooked-from-scratch beans or canned beans. When a recipe calls for 1½ cups of cooked beans, for example, you can use one 15-ounce can of drained beans. Use two cans of beans when a recipe calls for 3 cups, and so on.

Here are some ratios of dried, cooked, and canned beans to help in your planning:

- 1 pound dried beans = 2 cups dried beans = 6 cups cooked beans = 4 (15-ounce) cans of beans

- 1 (15-ounce) can of beans = ½ cup dried beans = 1½ cups cooked beans

Bean Cooking Tips

- A convenient way to prepare dried beans to use in recipes is to cook the beans in your slow cooker overnight on Low. They will be done by morning and ready for you to use in recipes.

- A small piece of kombu sea vegetable added to the pot while the beans cook will help tenderize the beans while adding flavor and nutrients.

- Dried herbs should be added to beans during the final 30 minutes of cooking time. However, it is best to add fresh herbs after the beans are cooked for the best flavor.

- To keep cooked beans from drying out, cool them in their cooking liquid.

- For improved digestibility, be sure to drain the bean cooking liquid first before using the cooked beans in a recipe.

- For convenience, cook a large amount of beans, portion them into airtight containers, and store them in the refrigerator for up to 1 week or in the freezer for up to 6 months.

HOW TO SALT-SOAK BEANS

In recent years, many cooks have become enlightened about the relationship between beans and salt. Despite previous convictions to the contrary, it is now thought that "salt-soaking" your beans before cooking can actually help the beans cook faster.

Quick Method: In a large pot or heatproof bowl, combine 1 pound dried beans (rinsed and picked over), 2 tablespoons salt, and 2 quarts boiling water. Stir to dissolve the salt. Set aside at room temperature for 1 hour, then drain the beans, discard the soaking liquid, and rinse the beans before cooking.

Overnight Method: In a large pot or bowl, combine 1 pound dried beans (rinsed and picked over), 2 tablespoons salt, and 4 quarts cold water, stirring to dissolve the salt. Cover and set aside at room temperature for 8 hours, then drain the beans, discard the soaking liquid, and rinse the beans before cooking.

Something for Everyone

In the same way that I developed these recipes to be accessible to most types and sizes of slow cookers, I also wanted them to be accessible to as many people as possible, regardless of any dietary restrictions.

Many of the recipes in this book are naturally low-fat or even fat-free, while others are either gluten-free or soy-free, or both. Notes in the outer margins indicate which recipes are gluten-free and/or soy-free, or can easily be made so. Although there will invariably be exceptions that are not conducive to substitutions, if a particular recipe is not already in line with your dietary preferences, here are some easy ways to make it so:

Gluten-free: Use wheat-free versions of ingredients such as soy sauce, pasta, and flours. For recipes that call for seitan, substitute tempeh or beans, depending on the type of recipe.

Soy-free: Use almond milk instead of soy milk; use soy-free vegan butter. For recipes that call for tofu or tempeh, substitute beans or seitan, depending on the type of recipe. And see the recipe on page 35 for a homemade soy-free sauce that you can use anytime soy sauce (or Worcestershire sauce) is called for.

Fat-free or low-fat: Some recipes call for a small amount of oil (usually 2 teaspoons) for advance sautéing of some ingredients. This use of oil in such recipes is optional in order to accommodate people who prefer to cook without oil. You can, instead, reduce the fat in recipes by spraying a skillet or pan with nonstick cooking spray or using a nonstick skillet. In addition, two other options for cooking without oil are provided in such recipes:

1. Water-sauté: Simply sauté the ingredients in water instead of oil.

2. Microwave: Microwave the ingredients (with a little water instead of oil) for a couple of minutes in a covered microwave-safe bowl instead of sautéing them.

To eliminate fat from recipes such as cakes or breads, you can substitute any of the following for the oil in an equal volume: nondairy milk, unsweetened applesauce (or other pureed vegetable or fruit, depending on the recipe), ground flaxseed mixed with water, or pureed beans.

How to Use This Book

Some of the recipes in this book are inspired by traditional global recipes, while others are based on favorite recipes that I adapted for the slow cooker. I've been pleased to discover that, in addition to the usual soups, stews, bean dishes, and chili, the slow cooker can be used to braise vegetables, make risotto, "bake" breads and desserts, and cook delectable appetizers and snacks.

Some of the more foundational recipes, such as the basic bean cooking recipes, are similar to ones you may recall from my earlier cookbook, *Fresh from the Vegetarian Slow Cooker*. However, even within such basic recipes, you'll find new information, tips, and methods, such as the salt-soaking method for beans, information on new slow-cooker models, and using the microwave to get more flavor from certain ingredients. And while most of the recipes themselves are new creations, the few carryovers have been updated, revised, or otherwise improved.

The various sizes, shapes, and different heat levels of slow cookers make the standardizing of cooking directions somewhat challenging. However, in order to accommodate the broadest range of slow cookers, I've done my best to develop recipes that can be made in most sizes. In each recipe, you will find the optimal size listed—that is, the best-size cooker for the job—with many recipes calling for a size range of 4 to 6 quarts. In those instances, the ingredients should fit somewhere between the maximum recommended capacity for a 4-quart cooker and the minimum recommended capacity for a 6-quart cooker. Many recipes in this book specify a 4- to 5-quart slow cooker, but in most cases, the recipe will also work fine in a 5½- to 6-quart or even a 7-quart model, with little or no adjustment.

In terms of recipe yields, most recipes are designed to make 4 to 6 servings. Of course, a serving size can mean different things when you factor in big eaters, child-friendly portions, and second helpings. In my house, I purposely make large quantities of certain dishes so that I can portion and freeze leftovers.

I can't stress enough that you need to get to know your own slow cooker to familiarize yourself with how long different foods will actually take to cook in it. Once you do, you'll find that your slow cooker is the best kitchen helper you could ever want. I hope you enjoy preparing these recipes as much as I've enjoyed developing them.

Snacks and Appetizers

I f you've used your slow cooker only to make soup or chili, you may be excited to discover that it can also make snacks and appetizers, including dips, spreads, spiced nuts, and party mixes.

The versatile slow cooker can also double as a food warmer or chafing dish when you're having a get-together. Just set the food out in the cooker on the Keep Warm setting, and your guests can serve themselves. Larger slow cookers can even be employed as "steam cookers" to make luscious pâtés and terrines.

Featuring appetizer and snack recipes ranging from a luscious Savory Mediterranean Cheesecake to the crisp and crunchy Life of the Party Mix, this chapter has you covered.

Spicy Tomato Queso Dip 25

Warm and Creamy Artichoke-Spinach Dip 26

Smokin' Chipotle Bean Dip 26

Golden Summer Caponata Bruschetta 27

Sherried Mushroom Crostini 29

Savory Mediterranean Cheesecake 30

Upcountry Pâté 32

Chickpea, Artichoke, and Mushroom Pâté 34

Artisanal Sweet and Spicy Wiener Balls 36

Southern-Style Sugar and Spice Pecans 37

Seven-Spice Cashews 38

Life of the Party Mix 39

Oregon Trail Mix 40

Spicy Tomato Queso Dip

This is a quick and delicious dip that assembles easily. It also lends itself to variations. For example, you can add crumbled vegan sausage or stir in some black beans. Serve with tortilla chips. To make it gluten-free, be sure to use a certified gluten-free oat flour or substitute your favorite gluten-free flour.

1 (14.5-ounce) can diced tomatoes with green chiles, drained
½ cup nutritional yeast
3 tablespoons oat flour
1 teaspoon yellow mustard
1 teaspoon onion powder
1 teaspoon garlic powder
½ teaspoon ground cumin
½ teaspoon chili powder
½ teaspoon salt
1 cup plain unsweetened nondairy milk
1 tablespoon fresh lemon juice

MAKES ABOUT 2 CUPS

SLOW COOKER SIZE:
1½-QUART

COOK TIME:
2 HOURS ON LOW

GLUTEN-FREE

SOY-FREE

1. Puree the tomatoes in a blender or food processor until smooth. Add the nutritional yeast, flour, mustard, onion and garlic powders, cumin, chili powder, and salt, and blend until smooth.

2. Lightly oil the insert of the slow cooker or spray it with cooking spray, and transfer the queso mixture to the cooker. Stir in the nondairy milk until well incorporated. Cover and cook on Low, stirring occasionally, for 2 hours, or until the mixture is thick and hot. If the mixture isn't thick after 2 hours, turn the setting to High, remove the lid, and cook for 20 to 30 minutes longer.

3. When ready to serve, spoon about ⅓ cup of the queso into a small bowl, stir in the lemon juice, then stir the mixture back into the slow cooker. Taste and adjust the seasonings, if needed.

Warm and Creamy Artichoke-Spinach Dip

Now you can enjoy a vegan version of the popular spinach and artichoke dip. This one is made with vegan cream cheese for a creamy, warm dip that can be cooked and served right from a small slow cooker. Serve this addictively delicious dip with your favorite crackers or lightly toasted baguette slices.

MAKES ABOUT 3½ CUPS

SLOW COOKER SIZE:
1½- TO 2-QUART

COOK TIME:
2 HOURS ON LOW

GLUTEN-FREE

1 (10-ounce) package frozen chopped spinach, thawed and well drained
2 (8-ounce) jars marinated artichoke hearts, drained and chopped
1 cup vegan cream cheese, purchased or homemade (page 31), at room temperature
3 scallions, minced
⅓ cup nutritional yeast
1 tablespoon fresh lemon juice
½ teaspoon Tabasco sauce
½ teaspoon salt

Lightly oil the slow cooker insert or spray it with cooking spray. Add all of the ingredients to the cooker and mix well to combine. Spread the mixture evenly in the cooker. Cover and cook on Low for 2 hours. Serve warm from the slow cooker.

Smokin' Chipotle Bean Dip

This bean dip is smokin' hot thanks to the addition of chipotle chiles. This is a great dip for casual get-togethers because you can cook and serve it in the same small slow cooker. Serve with tortilla chips for dipping.

1½ to 2 cups cooked pinto beans, mashed, or 1 (15-ounce) can beans, rinsed, drained, and mashed
¾ cup tomato salsa, purchased or homemade
¼ cup water

1 tablespoon minced chipotle chiles in adobo, or to taste

1 teaspoon chili powder

½ cup shredded vegan cheddar cheese (optional; Daiya works well in this)

Salt

MAKES ABOUT 3 CUPS

SLOW COOKER SIZE:
1½-QUART

COOK TIME:
3 TO 4 HOURS ON LOW

GLUTEN-FREE

SOY-FREE

1. Lightly oil the slow cooker insert or spray it with cooking spray. Combine the mashed beans, salsa, water, chipotle chiles, and chili powder in the slow cooker. Stir to mix well. Cover and cook on Low until the dip is hot and the flavors are well blended, 3 to 4 hours.

2. Just before serving, remove the lid and stir in the vegan cheese, if using, and season to taste with salt. Serve warm from the slow cooker.

Golden Summer Caponata Bruschetta

Reserve this version of caponata for late summer months, when fresh produce is plentiful and you want something delicious to enjoy with a glass of wine but don't want to heat up the kitchen. This caponata delivers the goods with a golden hue courtesy of yellow tomatoes and bell peppers. Enjoy it as a bruschetta as in this recipe, or serve it without bread as a side dish or a pasta topping. Best served at room temperature, caponata should be made well ahead of when you need it so that the flavors have a chance to meld. Use a gluten-free bread to make this gluten-free.

1 large yellow onion, minced

1 celery rib, minced

1 medium-size eggplant (about 1 pound), peeled and cut into ¼-inch cubes

1 yellow bell pepper, seeded and chopped

4 garlic cloves, chopped

3 large ripe yellow tomatoes, chopped

¼ cup golden raisins

3 tablespoons white wine vinegar

1 teaspoon dried basil

SERVES 6

SLOW COOKER SIZE:
5- TO 6-QUART

COOK TIME:
6 HOURS ON LOW

GLUTEN-FREE OPTION

SOY-FREE

½ teaspoon dried oregano

1 teaspoon salt

¼ teaspoon freshly ground black pepper

1 cup green olives, pitted and coarsely chopped

1 to 2 tablespoons capers, rinsed and drained

2 tablespoons chopped fresh flat-leaf parsley or basil

1 loaf French or Italian bread, cut into ½-inch-thick slices

1. Combine the onion, celery, eggplant, bell pepper, garlic, tomatoes, raisins, vinegar, basil, oregano, salt, and pepper in the slow cooker. Stir to mix well. Cover and cook on Low until the vegetables are soft but still hold some shape, about 6 hours.

2. Stir in the olives, capers, and parsley. Taste and adjust the seasonings. Transfer the caponata to a bowl and let cool to room temperature.

3. Preheat the broiler. Arrange the bread in a single layer on a baking sheet and broil until just toasted, watching carefully so the bread doesn't burn. Remove from the oven and turn the bread slices over, then return to the oven to lightly toast the other side. Serve the toasted bread immediately with the caponata.

Beurre Manié

A classic French thickening ingredient, *beurre manié* is made by combining equal parts flour and soft butter. It's an ideal way to thicken thin sauces at the end of the cooking time, making it well suited to slow cooker stews. It freezes well and can be made in whatever batch size you like. I like to make a large batch in my food processor and then divide it into 1-tablespoon portions and freeze it, so that I have it ready when I need it. You can also keep a few portions in your refrigerator, where it keeps well for about 1 week.

To make *beurre manié*, combine equal parts flour and softened vegan butter (such as Earth Balance) in a food processor or mixing bowl, then pulse or mash with a fork until the mixture is incorporated. Divide the mixture into 1-tablespoon portions, wrap each portion in plastic wrap, and transfer them to a container or zipper-top plastic bag and refrigerate or freeze until needed. Use about 1 tablespoon of *beurre manié* to thicken 1 cup of liquid. Note: For a soy-free *beurre manié*, use a soy-free vegan butter.

Sherried Mushroom Crostini

The fragrance of sherry and thyme signals the luscious flavor of these mushrooms. In addition to making a great crostini topping, the mushrooms are also delicious over cooked pasta. To make this gluten-free, use a gluten-free bread and omit the optional *beurre manié* or use a gluten-free flour to make it.

2 teaspoons olive oil (optional)
3 large shallots, minced
1½ pounds white or cremini mushrooms, sliced
3 tablespoons dry sherry
1½ teaspoons minced fresh thyme leaves or ¾ teaspoon dried thyme
¼ cup vegetable broth
Salt and freshly ground black pepper
¼ cup plain unsweetened nondairy milk
1 tablespoon *beurre manié* (page 28; optional)
1 French baguette, cut into ½-inch rounds

SERVES 4 TO 6

SLOW COOKER SIZE:
4-QUART

COOK TIME:
4 HOURS ON LOW

GLUTEN-FREE OPTION

SOY-FREE

1. For the best flavor, heat the oil in a small skillet over medium-high heat. Add the shallots and sauté until softened, about 3 minutes. Alternatively, omit the oil and sauté the shallots in a few tablespoons of water or place them in a microwave-safe bowl with a little water, cover, and microwave for 1 minute. Transfer the shallots to the slow cooker. Add the mushrooms, 2 tablespoons of the sherry, half of the thyme, the broth, and salt and pepper to taste. Cover and cook on Low until the mushrooms are soft, about 4 hours.

2. Preheat the broiler. Arrange the baguette rounds in a single layer on a baking sheet and broil until just toasted, watching carefully so the bread doesn't burn. Remove from the oven and turn the rounds over, then return to the oven to lightly toast the other side.

3. Use a slotted spoon to transfer the mushrooms to a serving bowl. Stir the nondairy milk into the cooker, then taste and adjust the seasonings. If you want to thicken the sauce, turn the slow cooker to High, add the *beurre manié*, and stir until thickened. Add the remaining 1 tablespoon sherry and the remaining thyme. Taste and adjust the seasonings and pour over the mushrooms. Serve with the toasted bread rounds.

Savory Mediterranean Cheesecake

The cheesecake takes a savory turn in this sophisticated appetizer made with vegan cream cheese and Mediterranean flavors, including sun-dried tomatoes and kalamata olives. It is at once cool and creamy, a bit tangy, a little garlicky, and deliciously herby. For the best flavor, serve and enjoy this at room temperature. Offer crackers or toasted bread rounds for spreading. To make this gluten-free, use gluten-free bread crumbs (or grind up gluten-free pretzels).

SERVES 8 TO 12

SLOW COOKER SIZE:
6-QUART

COOK TIME:
4 HOURS ON LOW

GLUTEN-FREE OPTION

¼ cup dried bread crumbs

1 cup raw cashews, soaked overnight and well drained

3 garlic cloves, crushed

1 teaspoon salt

1 cup vegan cream cheese, purchased or homemade (recipe follows)

8 ounces silken tofu

2 tablespoons chopped oil-packed sun-dried tomatoes

2 tablespoons chopped pitted kalamata olives

2 tablespoons minced fresh basil

2 tablespoons minced fresh flat-leaf parsley

1 tablespoon cornstarch or tapioca starch

1 teaspoon minced fresh oregano or ½ teaspoon dried oregano

¼ teaspoon cayenne pepper

Crushed toasted pine nuts, minced fresh flat-leaf parsley or basil, and/or halved or quartered cherry tomatoes, for garnish

1. Lightly oil a 7-inch springform pan or spray it with cooking spray. Sprinkle the bread crumbs evenly in the bottom of the pan.

2. In a food processor, combine the cashews, garlic, and salt, and process until it forms a paste. Add the cream cheese and tofu and process until smooth. Add the tomatoes, olives, basil, parsley, cornstarch, oregano, and cayenne, and process until well combined. Scrape the mixture evenly into the prepared pan. Place the springform pan on of a sheet of aluminum foil and bring up the sides of the foil to prevent leakage. Cover the top of the springform pan tightly with aluminum foil, piercing the foil in several places on top to allow the steam to vent.

3. Place a rack, trivet, or a ring of crumpled aluminum foil in the bottom of the slow cooker insert. Pour about 1 inch of hot water into the bottom of the insert. Place the foil-covered springform pan on the rack, cover the cooker, and cook on Low for 4 hours.

4. Remove the pan from the cooker, take off the foil, and set aside to cool. When it is completely cool, cover and refrigerate for at least 3 hours or overnight. It should be completely chilled before removing from the pan.

5. To serve, remove the sides of the pan, using a knife to loosen it around the edges if necessary. Garnish with the pine nuts, minced herb, and/or cherry tomatoes.

VEGAN CREAM CHEESE

Made with cashews and tofu, this homemade vegan cream cheese can be used in any recipe calling for vegan cream cheese.

1 cup raw cashews, soaked for 4 hours and drained

2 tablespoons fresh lemon juice

1 tablespoon apple cider vinegar

1 teaspoon agave nectar

1 teaspoon white miso paste

½ teaspoon salt

6 ounces firm silken tofu

MAKES ABOUT 2 CUPS

Combine the cashews, lemon juice, vinegar, agave, miso, and salt in a food processor or high-speed blender and process until smooth. Add the tofu and process until completely smooth and well blended. Transfer to an airtight container and refrigerate until needed.

Upcountry Pâté

The hearty flavor of this country-style pâté improves if you make it ahead of time and refrigerate it overnight. The optional brandy adds a nice flavor, so try to include it if you can. This recipe requires a small loaf pan or springform pan that can fit inside your slow cooker. Crushed nuts and a sprig of a fresh herb make a nice garnish. For a soy-free version, omit the soy sauce and use a soy-free sauce (purchased or homemade, page 35) or add some soy-free vegetable broth base or additional salt.

SERVES 6 TO 8

SLOW COOKER SIZE:
6-QUART

COOK TIME:
4 HOURS ON LOW

SOY-FREE OPTION

1 cup unsalted sunflower seeds, soaked overnight and well drained

¾ cup walnut pieces

1 small yellow onion, chopped

3 garlic cloves, chopped

1 small Yukon Gold potato (5 to 6 ounces), peeled and chopped

1½ cups cooked brown lentils, well drained

½ cup nutritional yeast

⅓ cup whole-grain flour

2 tablespoons vital wheat gluten

1 tablespoon olive oil

2 tablespoons soy sauce

2 tablespoons brandy (optional)

2 tablespoons chopped fresh flat-leaf parsley

1 teaspoon sweet paprika

1 teaspoon dried thyme

1 teaspoon salt

½ teaspoon freshly ground black pepper

½ teaspoon ground sage

⅛ teaspoon ground allspice

⅛ teaspoon cayenne pepper

1. Combine the sunflower seeds and walnuts in a food processor and blend until smooth. Sauté the onion and garlic in a skillet in a small amount of oil or water until softened, or combine them in a microwave-safe bowl, cover, and microwave for 2 to 3 minutes. Transfer the onion and garlic to the food processor along with the potato and lentils. Pulse a few times until just combined.

2. Add all of the remaining ingredients to the food processor and process until just combined. Do not overprocess. Taste and adjust the seasonings, adding more salt if needed.

3. Lightly oil a small loaf pan or 7-inch springform pan, depending on the shape of your slow cooker. Fill the pan with the mixture, packing it evenly and smoothing the top. If using a springform pan, place the pan on a sheet of aluminum foil and bring up the sides of the foil to prevent leakage. Cover tightly with aluminum foil, piercing the foil in several places to allow the steam to vent.

4. Place a rack, trivet, or a ring of crumpled aluminum foil in the bottom of the cooker insert. Pour about 1 inch of hot water into the bottom of the cooker. Place the foil-covered pan on the rack, cover the cooker, and cook on Low for 4 hours.

5. Remove the pan from the slow cooker, take off the foil, and set aside to cool. When it is completely cool, cover and refrigerate for at least 3 hours or overnight.

6. To serve, run a knife around the edge of the pan to loosen, then transfer to a serving plate. Serve cool or at room temperature.

Chickpea, Artichoke, and Mushroom Pâté

This recipe calls for a small loaf pan or springform pan—whichever will fit inside your slow cooker. The pâté can be served as is with crackers for spreading or sliced and plated as a first course.

SERVES 6 TO 8

SLOW COOKER SIZE:
6- TO 7-QUART

COOK TIME:
4 TO 5 HOURS ON LOW

GLUTEN-FREE

2 teaspoons olive oil (optional)

3 garlic cloves, chopped

1 cup chopped mushrooms of your choice

2 cups canned or thawed frozen artichoke hearts, drained

½ cup raw cashews, soaked overnight and drained

1 cup crumbled extra-firm tofu

1½ cups cooked chickpeas (page 104) or 1 (15-ounce) can chickpeas, rinsed and drained

1 tablespoon fresh lemon juice

1 tablespoon minced fresh basil or 1 teaspoon dried basil

Salt and freshly ground black pepper

Paprika, for garnish

Shredded fresh basil leaves, for garnish

1. For the best flavor, heat the oil in a large skillet over medium heat. Add the garlic and cook, stirring, until fragrant, about 30 seconds. Add the mushrooms and cook until softened, about 3 minutes. Stir in the artichokes and cook until the moisture evaporates. Alternatively, omit the oil and sauté these ingredients in a few tablespoons of water or combine them in a microwave-safe bowl with a little water, cover, and microwave for 1 to 2 minutes. Drain off any liquid.

2. In a food processor, combine the drained cashews and tofu and process until smooth and well blended. Add the artichoke mixture, chickpeas, lemon juice, basil, and salt and pepper to taste. Process until smooth. Taste and adjust the seasonings, if needed.

3. Lightly oil a small loaf pan or 7-inch springform pan (depending on the shape of your slow cooker) or spray it with cooking spray. Spoon the pâté mixture inside, packing it evenly and smoothing the top. If using a springform pan, place the pan on of a sheet of aluminum foil and bring up the sides of the foil to prevent leakage. Cover tightly with aluminum foil, piercing the foil in several places to allow the steam to vent.

4. Place a rack, trivet, or a ring of crumpled aluminum foil in the bottom of the cooker insert. Pour about 1 inch of hot water into the bottom of the cooker. Place the foil-covered pan on the rack, cover the cooker, and cook on Low until firm, 4 to 5 hours.

5. Remove the pan from the slow cooker, take off the foil, and set aside to cool. When it is completely cool, cover and refrigerate for at least 3 hours or overnight.

6. To serve, run a knife around the edge of the pan to loosen, then transfer the pâté to a serving plate. Garnish by sprinkling the top with paprika and mounding some basil in the center. Serve cool or at room temperature.

SOY-FREE SAUCE

This excellent gluten-free, soy-free alternative to soy sauce or tamari (or even Worcestershire sauce) is from *World Vegan Feast* by Bryanna Clark Grogan (© 2011, published by Vegan Heritage Press; used with permission).

2 tablespoons Marmite or other yeast extract

2 tablespoons salt

1½ cups hot water, vegetarian broth, or mushroom soaking water

2 tablespoons soy-free vegan gravy browner (such as Kitchen Bouquet)

MAKES 1¾ CUPS

Combine the Marmite and salt in 1 cup of the hot water, stirring until dissolved and well blended. Mix in the remaining ½ cup of water and the gravy browner. Store the mixture in an airtight container in the refrigerator, where it will keep for several weeks.

NOTE: To replace some of the complex qualities that a good fermented soy sauce or tamari supplies, try adding wine, broth, and/or mushroom broth or concentrate to your dish, in addition to using this soy-free sauce.

Artisanal Sweet and Spicy Wiener Balls

Remember the first time you tried one of those little smokies or mini hot dogs simmered in a "mystery" sweet and sour sauce, and then found out the sauce was made with grape jelly and chili sauce? This version improves upon the original with homemade ketchup and marmalade and tasty vegan wiener balls. For a shortcut version, use purchased marmalade and ketchup and your favorite vegan sausage links, cut into 1-inch pieces.

SERVES 4 TO 6

SLOW COOKER SIZE:
4-QUART

COOK TIME:
3 HOURS ON LOW

SOY-FREE

1 cup cooked white beans (page 104) or canned beans, rinsed and drained
¼ cup water or vegetable broth
¾ teaspoon liquid smoke
1 teaspoon smoked paprika
½ teaspoon onion powder
¼ teaspoon garlic powder
½ teaspoon salt
¼ teaspoon freshly ground black pepper
1 cup vital wheat gluten
3 tablespoons nutritional yeast
1 cup Handcrafted Ketchup (page 238)
1 cup Orange Marmalade with a Twist of Lemon (page 237)
1 tablespoon rice vinegar
1 chipotle chile in adobo, minced

1. Process the beans in a food processor until smooth. Add the water, liquid smoke, paprika, onion and garlic powders, salt, and pepper, and process until smooth. Add the vital wheat gluten and nutritional yeast and process to form a stiff dough. (If the dough is too dry, add up to 3 tablespoons additional water.) Transfer to a work surface and knead for 2 minutes.

2. In the slow cooker insert, stir together the ketchup, marmalade, vinegar, and chipotle chile. Turn the cooker on Low. Pinch off a small piece of the dough and roll it between your palms to make a ¾-inch sphere, then add it to the mixture in the slow cooker. Repeat until all the wiener mixture is used up. Stir gently to coat the wiener balls with the sauce, cover, and cook on Low for about 3 hours. Serve hot from the slow cooker.

Southern-Style Sugar and Spice Pecans

A popular treat in the South, a mixture of crunchy pecans coated with brown sugar, cinnamon, and other spices is wonderful, especially around the holidays. They make a great gift, too. When Terri Merritts tested this recipe for me she had to make it twice—it was such a huge hit with her family that they ate the entire first batch before she could photograph it. In her words, "The pecans turned out beautifully and taste divine. The recipe is perfect." Terri always lines the slow cooker crock with a Reynolds Slow Cooker Liner for easy cleanup. Use a soy-free vegan butter to make this soy-free.

⅓ cup vegan butter
1 pound unsalted pecan halves (about 4 cups)
½ cup light brown sugar
1½ teaspoons ground cinnamon
¼ teaspoon ground allspice
¼ teaspoon ground ginger
⅛ teaspoon ground nutmeg or cloves

MAKES ABOUT 4 CUPS

SLOW COOKER SIZE:
4-QUART

COOK TIME:
30 MINUTES ON HIGH
PLUS 2 HOURS ON LOW

GLUTEN-FREE

SOY-FREE OPTION

1. Melt the butter in the slow cooker on High for 15 minutes. Add the pecans, stirring to coat. In a small bowl, combine the sugar and spices, then sprinkle the mixture over the pecans, stirring to coat evenly. Cover and cook on High for 15 minutes.

2. Reduce the setting to Low, remove the lid, and cook, stirring occasionally, until the pecans are nicely glazed, about 2 hours.

3. Spread the nut mixture in a single layer on a baking sheet and set aside to cool. Serve warm or at room temperature. If not serving right away, cool the nuts completely, then transfer to an airtight container and store in the refrigerator for up to 4 weeks or in the freezer for up to 3 months.

Seven-Spice Cashews

Spiced nuts are delicious, but they can be expensive to purchase. So why not make your own? It's easy to do and, best of all, you can season them just the way you like. This recipe combines sweet and savory spices for cashews that can be used to top salads or stir-fries, or just eaten out of hand. This flavor combination is also good with almonds.

MAKES ABOUT 4 CUPS

SLOW COOKER SIZE:
4-QUART

COOK TIME:
15 MINUTES ON HIGH
PLUS 2 HOURS ON LOW

GLUTEN-FREE

SOY-FREE

¼ cup maple syrup
2 tablespoons light brown sugar
1¼ teaspoons ground cumin
1 teaspoon ground coriander
1 teaspoon ground cinnamon
½ teaspoon salt
¼ teaspoon sweet paprika
¼ teaspoon cayenne pepper
¼ teaspoon ground ginger
¼ teaspoon ground allspice
1 pound unsalted cashews (about 4 cups)

1. Lightly oil the slow cooker insert or spray it with cooking spray. Combine all of the ingredients except the cashews in a small bowl and mix well. Place the cashews in the slow cooker, then add the reserved mixture, stirring to coat. Cover and cook on High for 15 minutes.

2. Reduce the setting to Low, remove the lid, and cook, stirring occasionally, for 2 hours.

3. Spread the nut mixture in a single layer on a baking sheet and set aside to cool. Serve at room temperature. If not serving right away, cool the nuts completely, then transfer to an airtight container and store in the refrigerator for up to 4 weeks or in the freezer for up to 3 months.

Life of the Party Mix

Some things never get old, like the retro appeal of party mix. Use your slow cooker to make a batch of this favorite snack food without worrying about it burning on top of the stove. A larger, shallow slow cooker works best for this recipe, as it allow you to stir the ingredients together much more easily. If you don't want a spicy mix, leave out the Tabasco and cayenne.

¼ cup vegan butter
2 tablespoons vegan Worcestershire sauce
½ teaspoon Tabasco sauce
5 cups Rice Chex cereal (or similar cereal)
1½ cups small pretzel sticks or other small pretzels
1 cup unsalted roasted peanuts or almonds
1 cup unsalted roasted cashews
½ teaspoon seasoned salt
½ teaspoon onion powder
¼ teaspoon cayenne pepper (optional)

MAKES ABOUT 10 CUPS

SLOW COOKER SIZE:
5- TO 6-QUART

COOK TIME:
2 HOURS AND 15
MINUTES ON HIGH
PLUS 2 HOURS ON LOW

GLUTEN-FREE OPTION

SOY-FREE OPTION

1. Melt the butter in the slow cooker on High for 15 minutes. Stir in the Worcestershire and Tabasco, then add all of the remaining ingredients and mix gently to combine and coat.

2. Cook uncovered on High for 2 hours, stirring every 30 minutes. Reduce the heat to Low and cook for another 2 hours, stirring occasionally.

3. Spread the mixture in a single layer on a baking sheet and set aside to cool completely. Store in an airtight container until ready to use. The party mix will keep for several weeks.

NOTE: If using salted nuts, omit the seasoned salt. For gluten-free, use gluten-free pretzels. For soy-free, use a soy-free vegan butter, and omit the Worcestershire sauce and use a soy-free sauce (purchased or homemade, page 35) or add some soy-free vegetable broth base or additional salt.

Oregon Trail Mix

Who hasn't bought a bag of trail mix and wished there were more of one ingredient and less of another? Now you can blaze new trails by making your own customized mix. This recipe includes some of my favorite ingredients, but you can use it as a guideline to make a personalized trail mix, perhaps substituting your favorite dry cereal for some of the nuts, or using a different combination of dried fruit. For a gluten-free version, use gluten-free pretzels. For a soy-free version, use a soy-free vegan butter.

MAKES ABOUT 8 CUPS

SLOW COOKER SIZE:
4-QUART

COOK TIME:
2½ HOURS ON LOW

GLUTEN-FREE OPTION

SOY-FREE OPTION

2 cups unsalted almonds or cashews
1½ cups walnut halves
½ cup unsalted sunflower seeds
2½ cups pretzel sticks or other small pretzels
½ cup dried cranberries
½ cup dried blueberries
½ cup dried mangos or apricots, cut into ½-inch pieces
⅓ cup sugar
¼ cup vegan butter, melted
3 tablespoons water
1 teaspoon pure vanilla extract

1. Combine the almonds, walnuts, sunflower seeds, pretzels, cranberries, blueberries, and mangos in the slow cooker. Stir to mix.

2. In a small bowl, combine the sugar, melted butter, water, and vanilla and stir to mix. Pour the wet mixture over the dry mixture, stirring gently to coat evenly. Cook, uncovered, on High, stirring occasionally, for 2½ hours. (If your cooker runs hot, check the mixture at 2 hours to make sure it isn't sticking or burning.)

3. Spread the mixture in a single layer on a baking sheet and set aside to cool completely. Store in an airtight container until ready to use. The trail mix will keep for several weeks.

Soups That Satisfy

Of all the recipes one can make is a slow cooker, soups seem to be the most popular—and with good reason. Homemade soup is one of those soul-satisfying foods that everyone loves. A pot of soup is healthful, restorative, and delicious. When made in a slow cooker, it's also easy and convenient. Even those of us with busy schedules and hectic lifestyles can enjoy the simple pleasure of a bowl of hot, freshly made soup.

It's also fair to say that soups are the most flexible recipes that can be made in a slow cooker. You can add, increase, or eliminate various ingredients to suit your taste. You can even leave them cooking (or keeping warm) after they're done, and they'll still taste great.

Because soups usually contain more liquid than other recipes, I prefer to make them in a larger slow cooker; they need a few inches of space at the top so they can bubble up when cooking without spilling over.

Simple Slow-Simmered Vegetable Broth

Just toss some ingredients in the slow cooker, set it, and forget it. A few hours later, you'll have a pot full of flavorful and nutritious broth to use in soups, stews, and sauces. A large cooker is best so that you can make a big batch of broth. If you use a smaller cooker, just cut back proportionately on the amounts of the ingredients used. You can leave the peels on the vegetables as long as they're organic and well washed. The dried mushrooms add depth to the overall flavor in this medium-strength broth. The color is fairly dark, but the flavor is milder than you might assume. To make this broth soy-free, omit the soy sauce and use a soy-free sauce (purchased or homemade, page 35) or add some soy-free vegetable broth base or additional salt.

1 large yellow onion, thickly sliced
2 large carrots, cut into 1-inch chunks
1 large russet potato, peeled and cut into 1-inch chunks
1 celery rib, cut into 1-inch pieces
3 garlic cloves, crushed
⅓ cup coarsely chopped fresh flat-leaf parsley leaves
2 bay leaves
½ teaspoon black peppercorns
8 cups water
1 tablespoon soy sauce
½ teaspoon salt
3 dried shiitake or porcini mushrooms (optional)

MAKES ABOUT 8 CUPS

SLOW COOKER SIZE:
5- TO 6-QUART

COOK TIME:
8 HOURS ON LOW

GLUTEN-FREE

SOY-FREE OPTION

1. Combine the onion, carrots, potato, celery, garlic, parsley, bay leaves, and peppercorns in the slow cooker. Add the water, soy sauce, salt, and dried mushrooms, if using. Cover and cook on Low for 8 hours.

2. Let the soup cool slightly, then strain through a fine-mesh sieve into a pot or bowl, pressing the vegetables against the sieve to release their juices. Portion the cooled broth into airtight containers and store in the refrigerator for up to 5 days or in the freezer for up to 3 months.

Vegetable Broth Options

Vegetable broth is a foundational ingredient in many of the recipes in this book. If you want to make your own broth, the recipe on page 43 makes it quick and easy for you to put on a pot of broth to simmer all day unattended. I like to make a large quantity of this broth and then portion and freeze it to use in other recipes.

If you don't have homemade broth on hand, there are other options. You could purchase one of the many ready-made vegetable broths on the market. The various brands differ widely in flavor and sodium content, so be sure to do a taste test before using any purchased broth in recipes. Some are so strong that they need to be diluted by as much as half with water. This can also be an expensive option, and I have yet to find a brand that I like enough to recommend.

What I do recommend, however, is to use vegetable base (paste, cubes, or powder) combined with water. My favorite brand of vegetable base is Superior Touch "Better Than Bouillon," which comes in the form of a highly concentrated paste. It is available in three vegan-certified flavors: no-beef, no-chicken, and vegetable. (Note: Their mushroom base is not vegan, as it contains whey.) I also recommend Massel vegetable "Ultracubes," as well as their vegetable stock powder.

Because every vegetable broth and broth product has a different degree of inherent saltiness, most of the recipes in this book that call for vegetable broth will also call for salt "to taste" so that you can decide how much salt is needed.

Cuban Black Bean Soup

prefer to use beans that have already been cooked to aid in digestibility, although you could use dried beans that have been soaked overnight if you prefer—the soup will just take longer to cook. The beans and *sofrito* ingredients are combined in the cooker at the same time for an easy and delicious soup. I especially like the addition of sherry in this soup to balance the flavors.

1 large yellow onion, chopped

1 large green bell pepper, seeded and chopped

1 jalapeño pepper, seeded and minced

3 garlic cloves, minced

4 cups vegetable broth or water

2 bay leaves

1 tablespoon dried oregano

2 teaspoons ground cumin

1 teaspoon salt, or more to taste

1 teaspoon smoked paprika

¼ teaspoon chili powder

¼ teaspoon freshly ground black pepper

6 cups cooked black beans (page 104) or 4 (15-ounce) cans beans, rinsed and drained

3 tablespoons dry sherry (optional)

1 teaspoon sherry vinegar or cider vinegar

1 teaspoon liquid smoke

1 ripe Hass avocado, pitted, peeled, and diced, for garnish

1 large ripe tomato, chopped, for garnish

½ cup chopped fresh cilantro, for garnish

SERVES 4 TO 6

SLOW COOKER SIZE:
6-QUART

COOK TIME:
6 HOURS ON LOW

GLUTEN-FREE

SOY-FREE

1. Combine the onion, bell pepper, jalapeño pepper, and garlic in the slow cooker. Add the broth, bay leaves, oregano, cumin, salt, paprika, chili powder, and black pepper. Add the beans, stirring to mix well. Cover and cook on Low for 6 hours.

2. Remove and discard the bay leaves and stir in the sherry (if using), vinegar, and liquid smoke. Taste and adjust the seasonings, adding more salt if needed.

3. Ladle 2 cups (or as much as half of the soup) into a blender or food processor, puree, and stir it back into the rest of the soup in the cooker. Alternatively, use an immersion blender to puree some of the soup right in the cooker.

4. Serve hot, topped with the avocado, tomato, and cilantro.

Kale and Cannellini Bean Soup

This is one of those feel-good soups that make you feel energized when you eat it. Brothy and light but still filling, it's packed with nutrients and great flavors. Large, creamy cannellini beans are best in this soup, although other white beans may be substituted. Instead of kale, you can use any other sturdy dark leafy greens.

SERVES 4 TO 6

SLOW COOKER SIZE:
4- TO 6-QUART

COOK TIME:
6 HOURS ON LOW

GLUTEN-FREE

SOY-FREE

2 teaspoons olive oil (optional)

1 medium-size yellow onion, chopped

3 large garlic cloves, minced

1 large Yukon Gold potato, peeled and chopped

3 cups cooked cannellini or other white beans (page 104) or 2 (15-ounce) cans beans, rinsed and drained

6 cups vegetable broth

¼ teaspoon red pepper flakes

Salt and freshly ground black pepper

8 ounces kale, stemmed and coarsely chopped (about 6 cups)

1. For the best flavor, heat the oil in a medium-size skillet over medium-high heat. Add the onion and sauté until softened, about 5 minutes. Add the garlic and cook for 1 minute longer. Alternatively, omit the oil and sauté these ingredients in a few tablespoons of water or combine them in a microwave-safe bowl with a little water, cover, and microwave for 2 minutes.

2. Transfer the onion mixture to the slow cooker. Add the potato, beans, broth, red pepper flakes, and salt and black pepper to taste. The amount of salt needed will depend on the saltiness of your broth. Stir in the kale, cover, and cook on Low for 6 hours.

3. Taste and adjust the seasonings, if needed. Serve hot.

Lentil-Vegetable Soup

This soup is in regular rotation at our house, especially during the winter months when the choice of fresh vegetables is limited. The vegetables you add can be mixed and matched—I like the idea of adding a bit of thawed frozen vegetables to help round out the ingredients. To make this soup soy-free, omit the soy sauce and use a soy-free sauce (purchased or homemade, page 35) or add some soy-free vegetable broth base or additional salt.

1 large yellow onion, chopped
2 celery ribs, chopped
3 carrots, chopped
3 garlic cloves, minced
1 cup dried brown lentils, rinsed and picked over
1 cup thawed frozen edamame or baby lima beans
6 cups vegetable broth or water
1 (14-ounce) can fire-roasted diced tomatoes, with their juices
1 cup thawed frozen chopped spinach
1 tablespoon soy sauce
1 teaspoon dried basil
½ teaspoon dried thyme
Salt and freshly ground black pepper
½ teaspoon liquid smoke (optional)

1. Combine all of the ingredients (except for the optional liquid smoke) in the slow cooker. Cover and cook on Low until the lentils and vegetables are soft, 6 to 8 hours.

2. Add the liquid smoke, if using. Taste and adjust the seasonings, if needed. Serve hot.

SERVES 6

SLOW COOKER SIZE:
5- TO 6-QUART

COOK TIME:
6 TO 8 HOURS ON LOW

GLUTEN-FREE

SOY-FREE OPTION

North African Chickpea Soup

This fragrant soup assembles quickly and can be made with more or less heat, depending on how much cayenne you add. If you have *harissa* on hand, you can use it instead of cayenne to add heat as well as extra flavor. A recipe tester's Moroccan husband gave this soup a thumbs-up and suggests serving it with a nice crusty bread for dipping, as they would in Morocco.

SERVES 6

SLOW COOKER SIZE:
5- TO 6-QUART

COOK TIME:
6 TO 7 HOURS ON LOW

GLUTEN-FREE

SOY-FREE

2 teaspoons olive oil (optional)

1 large yellow onion, chopped

2 carrots, chopped

3 garlic cloves, chopped

1 teaspoon grated fresh ginger

1 teaspoon ground cumin

1 teaspoon ground coriander

½ teaspoon cayenne pepper

3 cups cooked chickpeas (page 104) or 2 (15-ounce) cans chickpeas, rinsed and drained

1 (14-ounce) can diced tomatoes, drained

6 cups vegetable broth

Salt and freshly ground black pepper

1 tablespoon fresh lemon juice

¼ cup chopped fresh flat-leaf parsley

1. For the best flavor, heat the oil in a large skillet over medium-high heat. Add the onion, carrots, garlic, and ginger and sauté until softened, about 5 minutes. Stir in the cumin, coriander, and cayenne. Alternatively, omit the oil and sauté these ingredients in a few tablespoons of water or combine them in a microwave-safe bowl with a little water, cover, and microwave for 2 minutes.

2. Transfer the onion mixture to the slow cooker. Add the chickpeas, tomatoes, broth, and salt and pepper to taste. The amount of salt needed will depend upon the saltiness of your broth. Cook on Low for 6 to 7 hours.

3. Stir in the lemon juice and parsley and cook for 10 minutes longer. Taste and adjust the seasonings, if needed. You can serve the soup as is, but it's even

better pureed. To do this, use an immersion blender and puree the soup right in the slow cooker. If you don't have an immersion blender, you can puree the soup in batches in a regular blender or food processor. Serve hot.

Red Bean Gumbo

Long, gentle cooking in a slow cooker is a great way to bring out the flavors in a gumbo, in which okra and filé powder are natural thickeners. For a heartier gumbo, add some sliced and sautéed vegan sausage just before serving. This recipe is both gluten-free (without the optional vegan sausage) and soy-free (if you use a soy-free vegan butter for the optional *beurre manié*).

2 teaspoons olive oil (optional)

1 large yellow onion, chopped

2 celery ribs, chopped

3 garlic cloves, minced

4 cups vegetable broth

1 (14-ounce) can diced fire-roasted tomatoes, with their juices

3 cups cooked dark red kidney beans or other red beans (page 104) or 2 (15-ounce) cans beans, rinsed and drained

1 small green bell pepper, seeded and chopped

1 cup sliced fresh or thawed frozen okra

1 teaspoon dried thyme

1 teaspoon filé powder (optional)

Salt and freshly ground black pepper

½ recipe Slow-Cooked Vegan Sausage Links (page 157) or 2 purchased vegan sausage links, such as Tofurky brand, sliced (optional)

1 teaspoon Tabasco sauce, or to taste

½ teaspoon liquid smoke

1 tablespoon *beurre manié* (page 28) or other thickener (optional)

3 cups cooked brown rice, for serving

SERVES 4

SLOW COOKER SIZE:
4- TO 6-QUART

COOK TIME:
6 TO 8 HOURS ON LOW

GLUTEN-FREE

SOY-FREE

1. For the best flavor, heat the oil in a large skillet over medium-high heat. Add the onion, celery, and garlic and sauté until softened, about 5 minutes.

Alternatively, omit the oil and sauté these ingredients in a few tablespoons of water or combine them in a microwave-safe bowl with a little water, cover, and microwave for 2 minutes.

2. Transfer the onion mixture to the slow cooker, add the broth, tomatoes and their juices, beans, bell pepper, okra, thyme, filé powder (if using), and salt and pepper to taste. Cover and cook on Low for 6 hours.

3. Meanwhile, sauté the sausage, if using, and set aside.

4. Taste the gumbo and adjust the seasonings. Just before serving, stir in the Tabasco and liquid smoke. If the gumbo isn't thick enough, turn the cooker to High and stir in the *beurre manié*, stirring until the broth thickens. Add the sautéed sausage slices, if using. To serve, spoon some cooked rice into soup bowls and ladle the hot gumbo on top.

Smoky Split Pea Soup

Split peas don't need to be soaked before going into the slow cooker. Just pick them over to remove any small stones and rinse them before using. The addition of liquid smoke and the optional vegan bacon provide that smoky flavor synonymous with split pea soup. This recipe is soy-free and gluten-free, depending on whether you use the optional vegan bacon and what it's made from.

SERVES 4 TO 6

SLOW COOKER SIZE:
4- TO 6-QUART

COOK TIME:
7 TO 8 HOURS ON LOW

GLUTEN-FREE

SOY-FREE

2 teaspoons olive oil (optional)
1 medium-size yellow onion, chopped
1 carrot, chopped
1 celery rib, chopped
1 medium-size Yukon Gold potato, peeled and diced
1 pound green split peas, rinsed and picked over
7 cups vegetable broth or water
1 bay leaf

1 teaspoon salt
1 teaspoon ground coriander
½ teaspoon ground cumin
¼ teaspoon freshly ground black pepper
1 teaspoon liquid smoke
4 slices vegan bacon, cooked and chopped (optional), for garnish
Minced fresh flat-leaf parsley, for garnish

1. For the best flavor, heat the oil in a large skillet over medium-high heat. Add the onion, carrot, and celery and sauté until softened, about 5 minutes. Alternatively, omit the oil and sauté these ingredients in a few tablespoons of water or combine them in a microwave-safe bowl with a little water, cover, and microwave for 2 minutes.

2. Transfer the vegetables to a large slow cooker. Add the potato, split peas, broth, bay leaf, salt, coriander, cumin, and pepper. Cover and cook on Low for 8 hours.

3. Just before serving, stir in the liquid smoke. Taste and adjust the seasonings. Serve hot, garnished with the vegan bacon (if using) and parsley.

Ribollita

This soup is a fine example of Italian peasant food—hearty, healthful, and inexpensive. I like it very thick. My mother made this when I was growing up, and I had the pleasure of enjoying it again in Tuscany a few years ago. Now I make it at home in my slow cooker. This soup is even better the next day. To make it gluten-free, use a gluten-free bread.

SERVES 6

SLOW COOKER SIZE:
5- TO 6-QUART

COOK TIME:
6 TO 8 HOURS ON LOW

GLUTEN-FREE OPTION

SOY-FREE

1 large yellow onion, chopped

3 carrots, chopped

2 celery ribs, chopped

4 or 5 garlic cloves, minced

6 cups chopped cabbage or kale

1 russet potato, peeled and chopped

3 cups cooked cannellini beans (page 104) or 2 (15-ounce) cans beans, rinsed and drained

1 (28-ounce) can Italian plum tomatoes, chopped, juices reserved

5 cups vegetable broth

½ teaspoon dried basil

½ teaspoon dried marjoram

¼ teaspoon red pepper flakes

Salt and freshly ground black pepper

2 cups Italian bread cubes, crusts removed

½ cup chopped fresh basil leaves

¼ cup grated vegan Parmesan cheese (optional)

1. Combine the onion, carrots, celery, and garlic in the slow cooker. Add the cabbage, potato, beans, tomatoes and their juices, broth, dried basil, marjoram, red pepper flakes, and salt and pepper to taste. Cover and cook on Low until the vegetables are tender, 6 to 8 hours.

2. If you prefer a smoother-textured soup, use an immersion blender to puree a portion of the soup right in the cooker, or transfer 2 to 3 cups of the soup to a food processor or blender, puree it, then stir it back into the soup. Stir in the bread cubes, cover, and cook for 10 minutes longer. Just before serving, stir in the fresh basil. Taste and adjust the seasonings, if needed. Serve hot, sprinkled with vegan Parmesan, if desired.

Summer Vegetable Soup

This vegetable-packed soup is inspired by the abundance of vegetables that seem to take over my kitchen and my menus every summer, especially after my weekly trip to the farmers' market. You can vary the vegetables according to personal preference and what's on hand or in season. Add some red pepper flakes if you like a little heat.

2 teaspoons olive oil (optional)
1 large yellow onion, chopped
2 garlic cloves, minced
2 carrots, chopped
1 celery rib, chopped
2 small red potatoes, scrubbed and diced
4 ounces green beans, ends trimmed and cut into 1-inch pieces
6 cups vegetable broth
Salt and freshly ground black pepper
1½ cups cooked cannellini or other white beans (page 104)
    or 1 (15-ounce) can beans, rinsed and drained
1 small zucchini or yellow squash, diced
1 large ripe tomato, diced
3 cups chopped chard, kale, or spinach
2 tablespoons chopped fresh flat-leaf parsley
2 tablespoons chopped fresh basil
1 tablespoon minced fresh dill or tarragon (optional)

SERVES 4 TO 6

SLOW COOKER SIZE:
5- TO 6-QUART

COOK TIME:
6 HOURS ON LOW

GLUTEN-FREE

SOY-FREE

1. For the best flavor, heat the oil in a medium-size skillet over medium-high heat. Add the onion and sauté until softened, about 5 minutes. Add the garlic and cook for 1 minute longer. Alternatively, omit the oil and sauté these ingredients in a few tablespoons of water or combine them in a microwave-safe bowl with a little water, cover, and microwave for 2 minutes.

2. Transfer the onion mixture to the slow cooker. Add the carrots, celery, potatoes, green beans, and broth. Season to taste with salt and pepper and cook on Low for 5 hours.

3. Add the cannellini beans, zucchini, tomato, and chard. Cover and continue to cook until the zucchini is tender, about 1 hour longer.

4. Just before serving, stir in the parsley, basil, and dill, if using. Taste and adjust the seasonings, if needed. Serve hot.

Grandmom Gennaro's Minestre

My grandmother always had a pot of minestrone soup—or *minestre*, as my family called it—on the stove. Like most of what my grandmother cooked, there was no recipe, just a little of this and some of that—and it was always delicious. I still make this long-cooking, full-flavored vegetable soup, only I use a slow cooker to get that rich flavor. Variations could include fresh or grilled corn during the summer, or perhaps a diced potato in fall and winter.

Note that the amount of vegetables listed here will fill a 4-quart cooker to within 2 inches of the top and will fill a 6-quart cooker a little over halfway. If using a 6-quart cooker, you can add extra vegetables and another cup of broth to make more servings. Use gluten-free pasta to make this gluten-free.

SERVES 4

SLOW COOKER SIZE:
4- TO 6-QUART

COOK TIME:
6 TO 7 HOURS ON LOW
PLUS 30 TO 45
MINUTES ON HIGH

GLUTEN-FREE OPTION

SOY-FREE

1 large yellow onion, minced

2 carrots, chopped

3 garlic cloves, minced

1 cup chopped celery

1½ cups cooked chickpeas (page 104) or 1 (15-ounce) can chickpeas, rinsed and drained

2 small zucchini, diced

1 (28-ounce) can diced tomatoes, with their juices

4 cups vegetable broth

½ teaspoon dried basil

½ teaspoon dried marjoram

1 bay leaf

Salt and freshly ground black pepper

⅓ cup uncooked stelline or other small soup pasta
¼ cup chopped fresh flat-leaf parsley
¼ cup chopped fresh basil

1. Combine the onion, carrots, and garlic in the slow cooker. Add the celery, chickpeas, zucchini, tomatoes and their juices, and broth. Stir in the dried basil, marjoram, bay leaf, and salt and pepper to taste. Cover and cook on Low for 6 to 7 hours.

2. Add the stelline to the slow cooker, cover, and cook on High until the pasta is tender, 30 to 45 minutes. Just before serving, stir in the parsley and fresh basil. Taste and adjust the seasonings, if needed. Serve hot.

Root Vegetable Bisque with Herbes de Provence

Traditional bisques are often thickened with rice, so I've added some to this recipe. The soup is pureed after cooking and then returned to the pot to serve. If you prefer a chunky rather than creamy soup, you can omit the pureeing step—just don't call it a bisque!

1 medium-size yellow onion, chopped
3 garlic cloves, chopped
2 carrots, coarsely chopped
2 medium-size parsnips, peeled and coarsely chopped
1 small turnip, peeled and diced
1 medium-size Yukon Gold potato, peeled and diced
⅓ cup uncooked brown rice
1 (14-ounce) can diced tomatoes, drained
4 cups vegetable broth
2 teaspoons dried *herbes de Provence*
Salt and freshly ground black pepper
2 tablespoons chopped fresh flat-leaf parsley, for garnish

SERVES 4 TO 6

SLOW COOKER SIZE:
4- TO 6-QUART

COOK TIME:
6 TO 8 HOURS ON LOW

GLUTEN-FREE

SOY-FREE

1. Combine the onion and garlic in the slow cooker. Add the carrots, parsnips, turnip, potato, and rice. Stir in the tomatoes, broth, *herbes de Provence*, and salt and pepper to taste. Cover and cook on Low until the vegetables are tender, 6 to 8 hours.

2. Use a stick blender to puree the soup right in the pot or transfer the soup, in batches, to a high-speed blender or food processor and puree until smooth, then return to the pot. Taste and adjust the seasonings, if needed. Serve hot, sprinkled with the parsley.

Baked Potato Soup

If you enjoy "loaded" baked potatoes, then you'll love this creamy soup, which has all of those same great flavors. As with its namesake, you can pile on as many toppings as you like: vegan bacon, sour cream, and cheddar cheese, plus minced chives or scallions. This recipe can be made gluten- or soy-free by choosing gluten- or soy-free toppings. Note that Daiya vegan cheese is both soy-free and gluten-free.

SERVES 4 TO 6

SLOW COOKER SIZE:
4- TO 6-QUART

COOK TIME:
6 TO 8 HOURS ON LOW

GLUTEN-FREE OPTION

SOY-FREE OPTION

2 teaspoons olive oil (optional)
1 medium-size yellow onion, chopped
3 garlic cloves, minced
4 or 5 large russet potatoes, peeled and cut into 1-inch dice (about 3 pounds)
4 cups vegetable broth, plus more if needed
1 to 2 teaspoons salt
½ teaspoon freshly ground black pepper
4 teaspoons vegan butter (optional)
1 cup plain unsweetened nondairy milk, plus more if needed
½ cup vegan sour cream, purchased or homemade (recipe follows), for garnish
½ cup shredded vegan cheddar cheese, for garnish (optional)
¼ cup chopped fresh chives or finely minced scallions, for garnish
4 slices vegan bacon, cooked and chopped, for garnish

1. For the best flavor, heat the oil in a medium-size skillet over medium-high heat. Add the onion and sauté until softened, about 5 minutes. Add the garlic and cook for 1 minute longer. Alternatively, omit the oil and sauté these ingredients in a few tablespoons of water or combine them in a microwave-safe bowl with a little water, cover, and microwave for 2 minutes.

2. Transfer the onion mixture to the slow cooker. Add the potatoes, broth, 1 teaspoon salt, and pepper. Cover and cook on Low until the potatoes are soft, 6 to 8 hours.

3. Use a potato masher to mash the potatoes right in the slow cooker, adding the vegan butter (if using) and the nondairy milk a little at a time. Taste to adjust the seasonings, adding up to 1 teaspoon of additional salt, if needed, depending on the saltiness of your broth. If the soup is too thick, add additional broth or nondairy milk.

4. Ladle the soup into bowls and top with as many of the garnishes as desired. Serve hot.

VEGAN SOUR CREAM

Use this soy-free vegan sour cream in any recipe calling for vegan sour cream.

1 cup raw cashews, soaked for 4 hours and well drained

⅓ cup water, plus more if needed

2 tablespoons fresh lemon juice

1 teaspoon apple cider vinegar

¼ teaspoon salt

MAKES ABOUT 1½ CUPS

Put the drained cashews in a food processor or high-speed blender. Add the water, lemon juice, vinegar, and salt. Process until completely smooth and creamy, 2 to 3 minutes. Taste and adjust the seasonings as desired. For a thinner consistency, add a little more water, 1 tablespoon at a time.

Chipotle Corn Chowder

Creamy and rich, this chowder can be made with either fresh or frozen corn kernels. For less heat, use only one chipotle chile instead of two. Pureeing a portion of the chowder helps thicken the broth and bring out the flavor of the corn.

SERVES 4

SLOW COOKER SIZE:
4- TO 6-QUART

COOK TIME:
6 HOURS ON LOW

GLUTEN-FREE

SOY-FREE

2 teaspoons olive oil (optional)
1 medium-size yellow onion, chopped
1 celery rib, chopped
1 large Yukon Gold potato, peeled and cut into ¼-inch dice
4 cups fresh or thawed frozen corn kernels
4 cups vegetable broth
1 or 2 chipotle chiles in adobo, minced
Salt and freshly ground black pepper
2 tablespoons minced fresh cilantro or flat-leaf parsley, for garnish

1. For the best flavor, heat the oil in a medium-size skillet over medium-high heat. Add the onion and celery and sauté until softened, about 5 minutes. Alternatively, omit the oil and sauté these ingredients in a few tablespoons of water or combine them in a microwave-safe bowl with a little water, cover, and microwave for 2 minutes.

2. Transfer the vegetables to the slow cooker. Add the potato, corn, broth, and chipotles. Season to taste with salt and pepper, cover, and cook on Low for 6 hours.

3. Use an immersion blender to blend a portion of the soup right in the pot, or ladle 2 cups of the soup solids into a food processor or blender and process until smooth, then stir the puree back into the chowder. Taste and adjust the seasonings, if needed. Ladle the soup into bowls and garnish with the cilantro.

Caramelized Onion Soup

Long, slow cooking is the secret to perfect caramelized onions, and a slow cooker is a great way to get the job done. Use the first part of the recipe to make just the caramelized onions to use in other recipes, or add the broth and other ingredients to make a rich-tasting onion soup. Use a gluten-free bread to make this recipe gluten-free. To make this recipe soy-free, omit the Worcestershire sauce and use a soy-free sauce (purchased or homemade, page 35) or add some soy-free vegetable broth base or additional salt, and use a soy-free vegan cheese.

2 tablespoons plus 1 teaspoon olive oil

4 or 5 medium-size yellow onions, thinly sliced

5 cups vegetable broth

⅓ cup brandy, dry red wine, or sherry (optional)

1 teaspoon vegan Worcestershire sauce

½ teaspoon dried thyme

Salt and freshly ground black pepper

4 slices French or Italian bread, cut into 1-inch cubes

Smoked paprika (optional)

Grated vegan Parmesan cheese or shredded vegan mozzarella cheese (optional)

SERVES 4 TO 6

SLOW COOKER SIZE:
5- TO 6-QUART

COOK TIME:
8½ HOURS ON LOW

GLUTEN-FREE OPTION

SOY-FREE OPTION

1. Spread 2 tablespoons of the oil in the slow cooker and add the onions, spreading evenly. Cover and cook on Low until the onions are very soft and well caramelized, about 8 hours.

2. Stir in the broth, brandy (if using), Worcestershire sauce, and thyme, and season to taste with salt and pepper. Cover and cook until hot, 30 to 45 minutes. Preheat the oven to 400°F.

3. In a bowl, combine the bread cubes, the remaining 1 teaspoon oil, and salt and pepper to taste, along with a few shakes of smoked paprika if you have some on hand. Spread in a single layer on a baking sheet and bake until toasted, turning occasionally, 15 to 20 minutes. Remove from the oven and sprinkle with the Parmesan, if using. If using mozzarella, sprinkle it on the toasted bread and run it under the broiler until melted. Ladle the soup into bowls and top with a few of the croutons. Serve immediately.

Crockpot Callaloo Soup

Because this recipe uses spinach instead of actual callaloo, it's more correct to say that it's a callaloo-inspired soup. The traditional Jamaican recipe uses callaloo leaves (aka taro leaves), which taste like a cross between spinach and cabbage, but they're not available to most people. If you can find actual callaloo leaves at an Asian market, then by all means use them instead of the spinach for a more authentic soup. You can also use chard, if you prefer. Either way, this is a delicious change from the usual vegetable soup, with its subtle heat and light coconut broth. If you use medium-size vegetables, the soup ingredients will fit in a 4-quart slow cooker. If you increase the vegetable sizes to large, you will need a 6-quart slow cooker.

SERVES 4

SLOW COOKER SIZE:
4- TO 6-QUART

COOK TIME:
6 HOURS ON LOW

GLUTEN-FREE

SOY-FREE

2 teaspoons olive oil (optional)
1 medium-size yellow onion, chopped
3 garlic cloves, chopped
2 medium-size sweet potatoes, peeled and diced (2 cups)
1 medium-size red bell pepper, seeded and chopped
1 to 2 jalapeños or other hot chiles, seeded and minced
1 (14.5-ounce) can diced tomatoes, drained
1½ cups cooked dark red kidney beans or other red beans (page 104) or 1 (15-ounce) can beans, rinsed and drained
4 cups vegetable broth
½ teaspoon fresh or dried thyme
¼ teaspoon ground allspice
Salt and freshly ground black pepper
8 ounces baby spinach
1 (13.5-ounce) can unsweetened coconut milk

1. For the best flavor, heat the oil in a medium-size skillet over medium-high heat. Add the onion and sauté until softened, about 5 minutes. Add the garlic and cook for 1 minute longer. Alternatively, omit the oil and sauté these ingredients in a few tablespoons of water or combine them in a microwave-safe bowl with a little water, cover, and microwave for 2 minutes.

2. Transfer the onion mixture to the slow cooker. Add the sweet potatoes, bell pepper, jalapeño, tomatoes, and beans. Stir in the broth, thyme, and allspice, and season to taste with salt and pepper. Cover and cook on Low for 5½ hours, or until the vegetables are tender.

3. Stir in the spinach and coconut milk. Taste and adjust the seasonings. Cover and cook until the spinach is wilted, about 30 minutes. Serve hot.

Cabbage and Yellow Beet Borscht

Yellow beets provide a new look to this satisfying borscht (although it can be made with red beets instead, if you prefer). To cut down on prep time, you can shred, rather than chop, the vegetables. This will change the texture of the soup, but some people prefer it this way.

Both the beets and the potato will begin to darken if not submerged in liquid right away. So, as soon as you cut or shred them, add them to the slow cooker along with the broth. This can be soy-free if you use a soy-free vegan sour cream.

SERVES 6

SLOW COOKER SIZE:
6-QUART

COOK TIME:
8 HOURS ON LOW

GLUTEN-FREE

SOY-FREE OPTION

5 cups vegetable broth

4 medium-size yellow beets, peeled and minced or shredded (3½ to 4 cups)

1 large yellow onion, minced

1 large carrot, minced or shredded

1 large russet potato, peeled and minced

3 cups shredded cabbage

1 teaspoon light brown sugar

1 teaspoon dried thyme

¼ cup minced fresh dill or 1 tablespoon dried dill weed

½ teaspoon caraway seeds

Salt and freshly ground black pepper

2 tablespoons fresh lemon juice

½ cup vegan sour cream, purchased or homemade (page 57), for garnish

1. Combine the broth, beets, onion, carrot, potato, and cabbage in the slow cooker. Add the sugar, thyme, half of the dill, and the caraway seeds. Cover and cook on Low for 8 hours.

2. Season to taste with salt and pepper. Stir in the lemon juice, then taste and adjust the seasonings, if needed.

3. Serve hot, or set aside to cool and then refrigerate until well chilled and serve cold. Garnish each serving with a spoonful of vegan sour cream and a sprinkling of the remaining dill.

Spicy Tortilla Soup

While you can certainly make your own strips of crispy tortillas for this soup, this recipe opts for the convenience of lightly crushed tortilla chips. This is one spicy and delicious soup. If you prefer less heat, cut back on the amount of chipotles used and be sure to remove the jalapeño ribs. If you use gluten-free tortilla chips and soy-free vegan sour cream, this recipe can be both gluten-free and soy-free.

2 teaspoons olive oil (optional)

1 medium-size yellow onion, minced

3 garlic cloves, minced

1 jalapeño chile, seeded and minced

2 tablespoons tomato paste

2 to 3 teaspoons chipotle chiles in adobo, minced

1 teaspoon ground cumin

1 (14-ounce) can diced tomatoes, with their juices

5 cups vegetable broth

Salt and freshly ground black pepper

½ cup chopped fresh cilantro leaves

3 cups lightly crushed tortilla chips

½ cup vegan sour cream, purchased or homemade (page 57), for garnish

1 ripe Hass avocado, pitted, peeled, and diced, for garnish

2 tablespoons toasted pepitas (green pumpkin seeds), for garnish

Lime wedges, for serving

SERVES 4

SLOW COOKER SIZE:
4- TO 5-QUART

COOK TIME:
4 TO 6 HOURS ON LOW

GLUTEN-FREE OPTION

SOY-FREE OPTION

1. For the best flavor, heat the oil in a medium-size skillet over medium-high heat. Add the onion and sauté until softened, about 5 minutes. Stir in the garlic, jalapeño, tomato paste, chipotles, and cumin and cook for 1 minute longer. Alternatively, omit the oil and sauté these ingredients in a few tablespoons of water or combine them in a microwave-safe bowl with a little water, cover, and microwave for 2 minutes.

2. Transfer the onion mixture to the slow cooker. Stir in the tomatoes and their juices and the broth, and season to taste with salt and pepper. Cover and cook on Low for 4 to 6 hours.

3. Shortly before serving time, stir in ¼ cup of the cilantro. Taste and adjust the seasonings. Divide the tortilla chips among 4 soup bowls. Ladle the soup over the tortilla chips and top each serving with a spoonful of sour cream, some avocado, a sprinkling of pepitas, and the remaining cilantro. Serve hot, with the lime wedges.

Four-Way Tomato Soup

This is nothing like the canned tomato soup you had as a child. Four kinds of tomatoes—fresh, sun-dried, crushed, and paste—contribute to the layers of flavor. Fresh yellow tomatoes are added at the end for contrast, but red tomatoes may be used if yellow are unavailable. For added flavor, substitute fire-roasted tomatoes for all or part of the diced plum tomatoes. Some roasted red pepper makes a good addition as well.

If adding the optional nondairy milk, choose one that is soy-free to make this a soy-free soup. Instead of adding the optional nondairy milk, you could stir in some soy creamer, or maybe a little vegan sour cream or even vegan cream cheese (blended in a bowl first with a bit of the hot broth).

SERVES 4 TO 6

SLOW COOKER SIZE:
4- TO 5-QUART

COOK TIME:
4 TO 6 HOURS ON LOW

GLUTEN-FREE

SOY-FREE

2 teaspoons olive oil (optional)
1 large yellow onion, chopped
2 garlic cloves, minced
2 tablespoons tomato paste
1 teaspoon brown sugar
1 teaspoon dried basil
1 teaspoon dried marjoram
1 cup vegetable broth
1 (28-ounce) can whole or diced Italian plum tomatoes, with their juices
1 (14-ounce) can crushed tomatoes
¼ cup oil-packed sun-dried tomatoes, chopped
Salt and freshly ground black pepper
½ cup plain unsweetened nondairy milk (optional)
2 tablespoons chopped fresh basil leaves, for garnish
1 cup yellow grape or cherry tomatoes, quartered, for garnish

1. For the best flavor, heat the oil in a medium-size skillet over medium-high heat. Add the onion and sauté until softened, about 5 minutes. Add the garlic and cook for 1 minute longer, then stir in the tomato paste, brown sugar, dried basil, and marjoram and cook for 1 minute longer. Alternatively, omit

the oil and sauté these ingredients in a few tablespoons of water or combine them in a microwave-safe bowl with a little water, cover, and microwave for 2 minutes.

2. Transfer the onion mixture to the slow cooker. Stir in the broth, plum tomatoes and their juices, crushed tomatoes, sun-dried tomatoes, and salt and pepper to taste. Cover and cook on Low for 4 to 6 hours.

3. Puree the soup in a food processor or blender, or use an immersion blender to puree it directly in the slow cooker. Taste and adjust the seasonings. For a creamier soup, stir in the nondairy milk. Ladle the hot soup into bowls and top each serving with fresh basil and yellow tomatoes.

Wild Mushroom Soup with Barley

The combination of barley and mushrooms is an Eastern European favorite, and this soup makes the best of both ingredients by layering the flavor with three kinds of mushrooms. Be sure to use pearl barley for the best results. For a soy-free version, omit the soy sauce and use a soy-free sauce (purchased or homemade, page 35) or add some soy-free vegetable broth base or additional salt.

½ ounce dried porcini mushrooms, rinsed
2 teaspoons olive oil (optional)
1 large yellow onion, chopped
1 large carrot, chopped
½ cup pearl barley
8 ounces cremini mushrooms, sliced
4 ounces shiitake mushrooms, stemmed and sliced
5 cups vegetable broth
1 (14-ounce) can crushed tomatoes
2 tablespoons soy sauce
1 teaspoon dried thyme
Salt and freshly ground black pepper
3 tablespoons minced fresh flat-leaf parsley or dill, for garnish

SERVES 4 TO 6

SLOW COOKER SIZE:
4- TO 6-QUART

COOK TIME:
6 HOURS ON LOW

SOY-FREE OPTION

1. Place the dried mushrooms in a heatproof bowl or cup and cover with hot water. Set aside to soften while you prep the remaining ingredients. When the dried mushrooms are soft, drain them, straining and reserving ½ cup of the soaking liquid. Slice the mushrooms and set aside.

2. For the best flavor, heat the oil in a medium-size skillet over medium-high heat. Add the onion and carrot and sauté until softened, about 5 minutes. Alternatively, omit the oil and sauté these ingredients in a few tablespoons of water or combine them in a microwave-safe bowl with a little water, cover, and microwave for 2 minutes.

3. Transfer the onion mixture to the slow cooker. Add the barley, cremini and shiitake mushrooms, broth, tomatoes, soy sauce, thyme, and salt and pepper to taste. Add the reserved mushroom liquid and porcini mushrooms, cover, and cook on Low for 6 hours.

4. Taste and adjust the seasonings. Serve hot, sprinkled with the parsley.

Yosenabe

A Japanese hot pot, or *nabe*, is a one-pot meal in which the ingredients are simmered together in a broth. While many kinds of *nabe* exist, this particular one is patterned after the popular *yosenabe,* where any ingredients you choose may be combined in one pot. After cooking, the pot (or slow cooker, in this case) is brought to the table for everyone to gather around and serve themselves. The remaining broth can be enjoyed with cooked rice or noodles. Offer soy sauce, toasted sesame seeds, and other condiments at the table for diners to use as desired. A shallow oval slow cooker is best for this recipe.

4 cups water

1 (3-inch) piece kombu sea vegetable

1 (1-inch) piece peeled fresh ginger

½ cup mirin

½ cup soy sauce

1 pound napa cabbage, thinly sliced

8 ounces seitan (purchased or homemade, page 136), cut into ¼-inch-thick strips

1 medium-size carrot, peeled and cut into sticks about ¼ inch thick by 2 inches long

4 ounces shiitake mushrooms, stemmed and thinly sliced

1 ounce enoki mushrooms, trimmed

1 bunch scallions, cut diagonally into 1-inch pieces

2 ounces cellophane noodles

8 ounces extra-firm tofu, cut into ½-inch dice

Salt

Soy sauce, sesame oil, toasted sesame seeds, and/or sea vegetable flakes, for garnish

SERVES 4

SLOW COOKER SIZE:
4- TO 6-QUART

COOK TIME:
2 TO 3 HOURS ON HIGH

1. Combine the water, kombu, ginger, mirin, and soy sauce in the slow cooker. Cover and cook on High for 15 minutes while you prepare the other ingredients.

2. Remove the kombu and ginger and discard. Arrange the cabbage in the bottom of the cooker. In separate groups on top of the cabbage, arrange the seitan, carrot, shiitake and enoki mushrooms, and scallions. Cover and cook on High until the ingredients are tender, 2 to 2½ hours.

3. Meanwhile, soak the noodles in water for about 15 minutes, then drain. Arrange the cellophane noodles in the cooker in between the other groups of ingredients, followed by the tofu, submerging them both in the broth. Taste the broth and add salt, if needed. Put the lid back on the cooker and cook for 30 minutes longer.

4. Bring the slow cooker to the dining table and serve immediately. Allow diners to serve themselves, taking some of the ingredients from the cooker into their own soup bowls and garnishing as desired with their choice of soy sauce, sesame oil, sesame seeds, and sea vegetable flakes.

Mulligatawny Soup

Chickpeas are used instead of chicken to make this flavorful soup, which was originally inspired by an Indian pepper sauce. The requisite apple adds a bit of sweetness to offset the spicy elements. If you prefer less heat, use a mild curry powder and cut back on the cayenne.

SERVES 4 TO 6

SLOW COOKER SIZE:
4- TO 6-QUART

COOK TIME:
6 HOURS ON LOW

GLUTEN-FREE

SOY-FREE

2 teaspoons olive oil (optional)
1 large yellow onion, chopped
3 garlic cloves, minced
2 teaspoons grated fresh ginger
1 tablespoon curry powder
1 teaspoon ground coriander
½ teaspoon cayenne pepper, or to taste
1 green bell pepper, seeded and chopped
1 red bell pepper, seeded and chopped
1 medium-size sweet potato, peeled and diced
1½ cups cooked chickpeas (page 104) or 1 (15-ounce) can chickpeas, rinsed and drained
1 Granny Smith apple, peeled, cored, and chopped
4 cups vegetable broth
Salt and freshly ground black pepper
1 (13-ounce) can unsweetened coconut milk
2 tablespoons fresh lemon juice
2 to 3 cups cooked brown basmati rice
Chopped fresh cilantro, for garnish

1. For the best flavor, heat the oil in a medium-size skillet over medium-high heat. Add the onion and sauté until softened, about 5 minutes. Add the garlic and ginger and cook for 1 minute longer. Stir in the curry powder, coriander, and cayenne. Alternatively, omit the oil and sauté these ingredients in a few tablespoons of water or combine them in a microwave-safe bowl with a little water, cover, and microwave for 2 minutes.

2. Transfer the onion mixture to the slow cooker. Add the bell peppers, sweet potato, chickpeas, apple, and broth. Season to taste with salt and pepper. Cover and cook on Low for 6 hours.

3. When ready to serve, stir in the coconut milk and lemon juice, then taste and adjust the seasonings, if needed. Spoon about ½ cup of rice into the bottom of each soup bowl, then ladle the soup onto the rice and garnish with cilantro.

Slow-Cooker Pho

Pho is an addictively delicious Vietnamese noodle soup. Trouble is, traditional pho is usually made with beef broth. When made in a slow cooker, however, this vegan version has the same great flavors of classic pho, without being heavy or greasy. The result is a light and flavorful soup filled with chewy noodles and seitan, bold seasonings, and a combination of raw and cooked vegetables. For a gluten-free version, omit the seitan and substitute strips of sautéed extra-firm tofu.

3 whole star anise
3 whole cloves
2 nickel-size slices fresh ginger
2 teaspoons vegetable oil (optional)
1 small yellow onion, minced
3 garlic cloves, minced
6 cups vegetable broth
3 tablespoons soy sauce
3 tablespoons hoisin sauce
2 tablespoons barley miso paste dissolved in ¼ cup hot water
6 ounces seitan (purchased or homemade, page 136), cut into strips
6 to 8 ounces dried rice noodles
1½ tablespoons fresh lime juice
1 cup fresh cilantro leaves, for garnish
½ cup fresh bean sprouts, for garnish
2 scallions, thinly sliced, for garnish
1 small green chile, seeded and thinly sliced, for garnish
Lime wedges, for serving

SERVES 4

SLOW COOKER SIZE:
4- TO 6-QUART

COOK TIME:
6 HOURS ON LOW

GLUTEN-FREE OPTION

1. Place the star anise, cloves, and ginger in the center of a small piece of cheesecloth. Gather the ends of the cheesecloth to enclose the spices and tie it closed with a piece of kitchen twine. Set aside.

2. For the best flavor, heat the oil in a medium-size skillet over medium-high heat. Add the onion and sauté until softened, about 5 minutes. Add the garlic and cook for 1 minute longer. Alternatively, omit the oil and sauté these ingredients in a few tablespoons of water or combine them in a microwave-safe bowl with a little water, cover, and microwave for 2 minutes.

3. Transfer the onion mixture to the slow cooker. Add the spice bag, broth, soy sauce, hoisin sauce, and miso mixture. Cover and cook on Low for 5½ hours.

4. Stir in the seitan and rice noodles. Cover and cook until the noodles are tender, about 30 minutes.

5. Add the lime juice and taste and adjust the seasonings, if needed. Ladle the soup into bowls and garnish with the cilantro, bean sprouts, scallions, and chile. Serve with the lime wedges.

Indonesian Noodle Soup

This luscious soup is inspired by the Indonesian soup known as *laksa*. It features rice noodles, tofu, and coconut milk, and is at once spicy hot and refreshing.

SERVES 4

SLOW COOKER SIZE:
4- TO 6-QUART

COOK TIME:
6½ HOURS ON LOW

GLUTEN-FREE

2 teaspoons vegetable oil (optional)
1 medium-size yellow onion, chopped
2 teaspoons grated fresh ginger
2 to 3 teaspoons curry powder
2 teaspoons ground coriander
½ teaspoon paprika
1 teaspoon sugar
1 teaspoon salt
¼ teaspoon ground turmeric
¼ teaspoon cayenne pepper

¼ teaspoon freshly ground black pepper
1 teaspoon Asian chili paste
4 cups vegetable broth
6 ounces dried rice noodles
8 ounces extra-firm tofu, cut into ½-inch dice
3 scallions, chopped
1 (14-ounce) can unsweetened coconut milk
1 tablespoon fresh lime juice
1 teaspoon sriracha sauce (optional)
½ English cucumber, peeled and chopped, for garnish
1 cup cherry tomatoes, quartered, for garnish
1 bunch fresh cilantro, chopped, for garnish
Lime wedges, for serving

1. For the best flavor, heat the oil in a medium-size skillet over medium-high heat. Add the onion, ginger, curry powder, coriander, paprika, and sugar and sauté for about 4 minutes to soften the onion and bloom the flavor of the spices. Sprinkle on a few drops of water, if needed, so the mixture doesn't burn. Alternatively, omit the oil and sauté the ingredients in a few tablespoons of water or combine them in a microwave-safe bowl with a little water, cover, and microwave for 1 to 2 minutes.

2. Transfer the onion mixture to the slow cooker. Add the salt, turmeric, cayenne, black pepper, and chili paste. Stir in the broth, cover, and cook on Low for 6 hours.

3. Stir in the noodles, tofu, scallions, and coconut milk. Cover and continue to cook until the noodles are tender, about 30 minutes.

4. Just before serving, stir in the lime juice. Taste and adjust the seasonings, adding the sriracha, if desired, for more heat. Ladle the soup into bowls and garnish with the cucumber, tomatoes, and cilantro. Serve with the lime wedges.

Miso Potato Soup

'd always enjoyed miso soup and potato soup as two separate entities until my neighbor Seung Hee Han served me a delicious soup that combines them both. Now I'm hooked.

SERVES 4

SLOW COOKER SIZE:
4- TO 6-QUART

COOK TIME:
6 HOURS ON LOW

GLUTEN-FREE

1 small yellow onion, minced

2 large russet potatoes, peeled and cut into ¼-inch dice

4 cups chopped napa cabbage

1 (2-inch) piece kombu sea vegetable (optional)

6 cups water

3 tablespoons soy sauce, plus more as needed

½ teaspoon salt

¼ teaspoon freshly ground black pepper

¼ cup white miso paste, or more as needed

¼ cup chopped scallions

1. Combine the onion, potatoes, cabbage, kombu (if using), water, and soy sauce in the slow cooker. Add the salt and pepper. Cover and cook on Low until the vegetables are tender, about 6 hours.

2. Spoon the miso paste into a bowl and add about 1 cup of the hot broth, stirring to blend and thin the miso. Scrape the miso mixture into the slow cooker and add the scallions. Taste and adjust the seasonings, adding more miso, soy sauce, or salt, if needed. Remove and discard the kombu, if using. Serve hot.

Stews and Chili

The slow cooker is a great way to cook a stew or chili. The long simmering brings out the flavors as it allows the various ingredients a chance to mingle. Once it's done cooking, you can serve it right from the cooker for a hearty meal that's ready when you are.

This chapter features several kinds of chili made with a variety of beans and vegetables. There's even a chili topped with cornbread that cooks right in the slow cooker. The selection of stew recipes runs the gamut from an all-American Farm Stand Stew to the international flavors of a Moroccan tagine, an Indian curry, and a Mexican posole.

For the best flavor and texture, onions and certain other ingredients should be sautéed in a skillet before adding them to the slow cooker, or at least cooked in the microwave for a few minutes, as directed in the recipes. This extra step will infuse your stew or chili with more flavor, and it will also help ensure that the vegetables become tender. If you skip this step, it may result in some of the ingredients being too hard or crunchy when the rest of the dish is ready to eat, and the overall flavor may not be as rich. That said, you may prefer to skip that step and simply "load the crock."

Two-Lentil Chili

Two kinds of lentils give this chili a great texture—the red lentils cook down and thicken while the brown lentils hold their shape. Make it as spicy as you want by adjusting the amounts of jalapeños and chili powder. I like to serve this chili over cooked brown rice or quinoa. For a soy-free chili, omit the soy sauce and use a soy-free sauce (purchased or homemade, page 35) or add some soy-free vegetable broth base or additional salt, and choose soy-free toppings.

2 teaspoons olive oil (optional)

1 medium-size yellow onion, chopped

4 garlic cloves, minced

1 or 2 jalapeño chiles, seeded and minced

1 bell pepper (any color), seeded and chopped

3 tablespoons chili powder

1 teaspoon dried oregano

1 teaspoon ground cumin

1 cup dried brown lentils, rinsed and picked over

1 cup dried red lentils, rinsed and picked over

1 (28-ounce) can crushed tomatoes

1 tablespoon soy sauce

1 teaspoon natural sugar

1 teaspoon unsweetened cocoa powder

Salt and freshly ground black pepper

4 cups water

Diced avocado, minced onion, vegan sour cream, shredded vegan cheese, and/or chopped cilantro, for garnish

SERVES 4 TO 6

SLOW COOKER SIZE:
4- TO 6-QUART

COOK TIME:
6 TO 8 HOURS ON LOW

GLUTEN-FREE

SOY-FREE OPTION

1. For the best flavor, heat the oil in a medium-size skillet over medium-high heat. Add the onion, garlic, chiles, and bell pepper and sauté until softened, about 4 minutes. Add the chili powder, oregano, and cumin and sauté for 30 seconds longer. Alternatively, omit the oil and sauté these ingredients in a few tablespoons of water or combine them in a microwave-safe bowl with a little water, cover, and microwave for 2 minutes.

2. Transfer the onion mixture to the slow cooker. Add both lentils, the tomatoes, soy sauce, sugar, cocoa, and salt and pepper to taste. (You may need to add up to 2 teaspoons of salt.) Stir in the water, cover, and cook on Low until the lentils and vegetables are tender, 6 to 8 hours.

3. Taste and adjust the seasonings, if needed. Serve hot, garnished with your favorite chili toppings.

Chipotle Black Bean Chili with Winter Squash

The sweetness of the butternut squash is a good foil for the smoky heat of the chipotle in this hearty black bean chili. Use more or less chipotles and/or chili powder, depending on your heat tolerance. You can always add some chipotles and chili powder early on and then add more later if desired, as slow cooking can dissipate the flavor of spices.

SERVES 6

SLOW COOKER SIZE:
5- TO 7-QUART

COOK TIME:
6 TO 8 HOURS ON LOW

GLUTEN-FREE

SOY-FREE

2 teaspoons olive oil (optional)

1 large yellow onion, chopped

4 garlic cloves, minced

1 tablespoon tomato paste

1 to 2 tablespoons minced chipotle chiles in adobo

3 tablespoons chili powder, or to taste

1 teaspoon ground cumin

1 teaspoon ground coriander

½ teaspoon dried oregano

1 small butternut squash, peeled, seeded, and cut into ½-inch dice (about 3 cups)

1 small red bell pepper, seeded and chopped

1 (14.5-ounce) can crushed tomatoes, with their juices

4 cups cooked black beans (page 104) or 3 (15-ounce) cans beans, rinsed and drained

1½ cups water

Salt and freshly ground black pepper

Diced avocado, minced onion, vegan sour cream, shredded vegan cheese, and/or chopped fresh cilantro, for garnish

1. For the best flavor, heat the oil in a medium-size skillet over medium-high heat. Add the onion and sauté until softened, about 5 minutes. Add the garlic and cook for 1 minute longer. Stir in the tomato paste, chipotles, chili powder, cumin, coriander, and oregano. Alternatively, omit the oil and sauté these ingredients in a few tablespoons of water or combine them in a microwave-safe bowl with a little water, cover, and microwave for 2 minutes.

2. Transfer the onion mixture to the slow cooker. Add the squash, bell pepper, tomatoes with their juices, beans, and water. Season to taste with salt and pepper, cover, and cook on Low for 6 to 8 hours.

3. Taste and adjust the seasonings, if needed. If the chili isn't thick enough, stir well, and cook uncovered for 30 minutes longer. Serve hot, garnished with your favorite chili toppings.

Indian-Spiced Chickpea-Potato Chili

The pairing of chickpeas and potatoes is popular in Indian cooking, and the combination is especially good in this chili-type dish seasoned with ginger, coriander, cumin, and other Indian spices. For a soy-free version, use a soy-free vegan yogurt.

SERVES 4 TO 6

SLOW COOKER SIZE:
4- TO 6-QUART

COOK TIME:
6 TO 8 HOURS
ON LOW

GLUTEN-FREE

SOY-FREE OPTION

2 teaspoons olive oil (optional)

1 large yellow onion, minced

3 garlic cloves, minced

1½ teaspoons grated fresh ginger

1 tablespoon curry powder

1 teaspoon ground coriander

1 teaspoon ground cumin

¼ teaspoon cayenne pepper

2 Yukon Gold potatoes, peeled and cut into ½-inch dice

1 (14.5-ounce) can crushed tomatoes

1 (4-ounce) can (hot or mild) minced green chiles, drained

4 cups cooked chickpeas (page 104) or 3 (15-ounce) cans chickpeas, rinsed and drained

1 cup water

Salt

¾ cup thawed frozen baby green peas

½ cup plain vegan yogurt

⅓ cup minced fresh cilantro leaves

1. For the best flavor, heat the oil in a medium-size skillet over medium-high heat. Add the onion and sauté until softened, about 5 minutes. Add the garlic and ginger and cook for 1 minute longer. Stir in the curry powder, coriander, cumin, and cayenne. Alternatively, omit the oil and sauté these ingredients in a few tablespoons of water or combine them in a microwave-safe bowl with a little water, cover, and microwave for 2 minutes.

2. Transfer the onion mixture to the slow cooker. Add the potatoes, tomatoes, chiles, chickpeas, and water. Season with salt, cover, and cook on Low for 6 to 8 hours. About 15 minutes before you're ready to serve, stir in the peas.

3. Stir the yogurt and the cilantro into the chili, then taste and adjust the seasonings, if needed. Serve hot.

The White Chili

No collection of chili recipes is complete without a white version. So here it is, made with white beans, potato, and hominy—and not a tomato in sight. Canned hominy is available in well-stocked supermarkets. Be sure to rinse it well before using. To make this chili soy-free, use a soy-free vegan sour cream.

2 teaspoons olive oil (optional)

1 large yellow onion, chopped

4 garlic cloves, minced

2 teaspoons ground cumin

2 teaspoons ground coriander

1 teaspoon dried marjoram

1 large russet potato, peeled and chopped

4 cups cooked cannellini or other white beans (page 104) or 3 (15-ounce) cans beans, rinsed and drained

1 (16-ounce) can hominy, rinsed and drained

1 (4-ounce) can (hot or mild) minced green chiles, drained

2 cups vegetable broth or water

1 teaspoon salt

¼ teaspoon freshly ground white pepper

Vegan sour cream (purchased or homemade, page 57), diced avocado, lime wedges, minced scallions, and/or chopped fresh cilantro, for garnish

SERVES 4 TO 6

SLOW COOKER SIZE:
4- TO 6-QUART

COOK TIME:
6 TO 8 HOURS ON LOW

GLUTEN-FREE

SOY-FREE

1. For the best flavor, heat the oil in a medium-size skillet over medium-high heat. Add the onion and sauté until softened, about 5 minutes. Add the garlic, cumin, coriander, and marjoram and cook for 1 minute longer. Alternatively, omit the oil and sauté these ingredients in a few tablespoons of water or combine them in a microwave-safe bowl with a little water, cover, and microwave for 2 minutes.

2. Transfer the onion mixture to the slow cooker. Add the potato, beans, hominy, chiles, broth, salt, and pepper. Cover and cook on Low for 6 to 8 hours.

3. Taste and adjust the seasonings, if needed. Serve hot, garnished with desired toppings.

Happy New Year Chili

Inspired by two Southern specialties, dirty rice and hoppin' John, this chili is a great way to begin the new year. It's ideal accompanied by the collards on page 201. To mellow the flavor of the tempeh, steam it for 15 minutes before using it in the recipe. Instead of tempeh, you may substitute 1 to 2 cups finely chopped seitan (which would make the chili soy-free, as long as you also use soy-free vegan sour cream for the topping), vegan sausage, or reconstituted TVP granules.

SERVES 4 TO 6

SLOW COOKER SIZE:
4- TO 6-QUART

COOK TIME:
4 TO 6 HOURS ON LOW

GLUTEN-FREE

SOY-FREE OPTION

2 teaspoons olive oil (optional)

1 large yellow onion, chopped

5 garlic cloves, minced

1 celery rib, chopped

1 fresh hot chile, seeded and minced (optional)

2 tablespoons tomato paste

1 small green bell pepper, seeded and chopped

8 ounces tempeh, chopped or crumbled

2 tablespoons chili powder

1 teaspoon ground cumin

1 teaspoon dried thyme

½ cup uncooked long-grain brown rice

3 cups cooked black-eyed peas (page 104) or 2 (15-ounce) cans black-eyed peas, rinsed and drained

1 (28-ounce) can diced tomatoes, with their juices

2 cups vegetable broth or water

Salt and freshly ground black pepper

Vegan sour cream, purchased or homemade (page 57), for serving

Tabasco sauce, for serving

1. For the best flavor, heat the oil in a medium-size skillet over medium-high heat. Add the onion, garlic, celery, and chile (if using) and sauté until softened, about 5 minutes. Stir in the tomato paste, bell pepper, tempeh, chili powder, cumin, and thyme and cook for 2 minutes longer. Alternatively, omit the oil and sauté these ingredients in a few tablespoons of water or combine them in a microwave-safe bowl with a little water, cover, and microwave for 2 minutes.

2. Transfer the onion mixture to the slow cooker. Add the rice, black-eyed peas, tomatoes and their juices, and broth. Season to taste with salt and pepper. Cover and cook on Low for 4 to 6 hours.

3. Taste and adjust the seasonings, if needed. Serve hot, offering vegan sour cream and Tabasco at the table.

Pantry Raid Chili

Even when you're too busy to cook, this easy-to-assemble chili requires very little prep, so you can literally toss it together with just a few items from your pantry. Hint: If you cook this recipe on High, it can be ready to eat in 2 to 3 hours. For a soy-free version, omit the soy sauce and use a soy-free sauce (purchased or homemade, page 35) or add some soy-free vegetable broth base or additional salt.

1 (24-ounce) jar fire-roasted chunky tomato salsa

2 tablespoons chili powder

1 teaspoon dried marjoram

½ teaspoon ground cumin

1 cup water

3 cups cooked pinto beans (page 104) or 2 (15-ounce) cans beans, rinsed and drained

1 tablespoon soy sauce

Salt and freshly ground black pepper

2 cups thawed frozen corn kernels

Diced avocado, minced onion, vegan sour cream, shredded vegan cheese, and/or chopped fresh cilantro, for garnish

SERVES 4

SLOW COOKER SIZE:
4-QUART

COOK TIME:
4 TO 6 HOURS ON LOW

GLUTEN-FREE

SOY-FREE OPTION

1. Combine the salsa, chili powder, marjoram, cumin, and water in the slow cooker, and stir to combine. Add the beans and soy sauce and season to taste with salt and pepper. Cover and cook on Low for 4 to 6 hours.

2. Stir in the corn kernels and cook, uncovered, for 10 minutes longer to let the corn get hot. Serve hot, garnished with your favorite chili toppings.

Holy Mole Red Bean Chili

The rich depth of flavor from the mole sauce elevates a humble chili to new heights. I especially like the addition of chopped seitan in this chili, but you may substitute reconstituted TVP granules or strips, Soy Curls (see page 17), or tempeh, if you prefer.

SERVES 4 TO 6

SLOW COOKER SIZE:
4- TO 6-QUART

COOK TIME:
6 TO 8 HOURS ON LOW

GLUTEN-FREE OPTION

SOY-FREE

2 teaspoons olive oil (optional)

1 large yellow onion, chopped

4 garlic cloves, minced

½ small green bell pepper, seeded and chopped

3 tablespoons tomato paste

2 tablespoons unsweetened cocoa powder

2 tablespoons almond butter

2 to 3 tablespoons chili powder

1 tablespoon minced chipotle chiles in adobo

½ teaspoon ground cinnamon

1 (14.5-ounce) can diced fire-roasted tomatoes, drained and juices reserved

1 (14-ounce) can crushed tomatoes

3 cups cooked dark red kidney beans (page 104) or 2 (15-ounce) cans beans, rinsed and drained

8 ounces seitan (purchased or homemade, page 136), chopped

2 cups water

1 teaspoon salt

¼ teaspoon freshly ground black pepper

Diced avocado, pepitas (green pumpkin seeds), chopped scallions, and/or chopped cilantro, for garnish

1. For the best flavor, heat the oil in a medium-size skillet over medium-high heat. Add the onion and sauté until softened, about 5 minutes. Stir in the garlic and bell pepper and cook for 3 minute longer. Stir in the tomato paste, cocoa, almond butter, chili powder, chipotles, cinnamon, and the juices from the diced tomatoes and cook for 2 minutes longer, stirring to blend. Alternatively, omit the oil and sauté these ingredients in a few tablespoons of water or combine them in a microwave-safe bowl with a little water, cover, and microwave for 2 minutes.

2. Transfer the onion mixture to the slow cooker. Stir in the diced tomatoes, crushed tomatoes, beans, seitan, water, salt, and pepper. Cover and cook on Low for 6 to 8 hours.

3. Taste and adjust the seasonings, if needed. Serve hot, garnished with desired toppings.

Cornbread-Topped Chili

The steamy heat of the slow cooker allows the cornbread to cook right on top of the simmering vegetables. Spooning the cornbread batter onto the vegetables gives it a rustic look. You can make this chili as mild or as spicy as you like, depending on the heat of the chili powder you use and the addition of your choice of mild or hot green chiles. For soy-free, omit the soy sauce and use a soy-free sauce (purchased or homemade, page 35) or add some soy-free vegetable broth base or additional salt, and omit the optional TVP.

2 teaspoons olive oil (optional)

1 large yellow onion, minced

3 garlic cloves, minced

3 tablespoons chili powder

1 teaspoon ground coriander

1 teaspoon ground cumin

1 small bell pepper (any color), seeded and chopped

4 cups cooked dark red kidney beans, black beans, or pinto beans, or a combination (page 104) or 3 (15-ounce) cans beans, rinsed and drained

½ cup TVP granules reconstituted with ½ cup boiling water *or* 1 cup thawed frozen vegan burger crumbles (optional)

1 cup fresh or thawed frozen corn kernels

1 (4-ounce) can (mild or hot) chopped green chiles, drained

1 (14-ounce) can crushed tomatoes

½ cup water

1 tablespoon soy sauce

SERVES 4

SLOW COOKER SIZE:
5- TO 6-QUART

COOK TIME:
5 TO 6 HOURS ON LOW
PLUS 1 HOUR ON HIGH

GLUTEN-FREE

SOY-FREE OPTION

1 tablespoon minced fresh cilantro leaves
Salt and freshly ground black pepper
1 cup medium-ground cornmeal
2 teaspoons baking powder
½ teaspoon baking soda
½ cup plain unsweetened nondairy milk
2 tablespoons olive oil

1. Lightly oil the insert of the slow cooker or spray it with nonstick cooking spray. For the best flavor, heat the oil in a medium-size skillet over medium-high heat. Add the onion and sauté until softened, about 5 minutes. Stir in the garlic, chili powder, coriander, and cumin and cook for 30 seconds longer. Alternatively, omit the oil and sauté these ingredients in a few tablespoons of water or combine them in a microwave-safe bowl with a little water, cover, and microwave for 2 minutes.

2. Transfer the onion mixture to the prepared slow cooker and add the bell pepper, beans, TVP (if using), corn, and chiles. Stir in the tomatoes, water, soy sauce, and cilantro. Season to taste with salt and pepper. Cover and cook on Low for 5 to 6 hours.

3. In a large bowl, combine the cornmeal, baking powder, baking soda, and ½ teaspoon salt. Add the nondairy milk and oil and stir to blend.

4. Drop the cornbread batter by the spoonful onto the simmering chili, then turn the heat setting to High. Cover and cook until the topping is cooked through, about 1 hour. For best results, serve within 15 minutes after the cornbread is finished cooking.

Brunswick Bean Stew

Like the classic Southern stew, this vegan version contains corn and limas and a rich smoky flavor, but it leaves out the wild game in favor of two kinds of beans. Seitan and vegan sausage are also good additions for an even heartier stew. For soy-free, omit the Worcestershire or soy sauce and use a soy-free sauce (purchased or homemade, page 35) or add some soy-free vegetable broth base or additional salt.

2 teaspoons olive oil (optional)

1 large yellow onion, minced

1 celery rib, chopped

2 carrots, thinly sliced

4 garlic cloves, minced

2 teaspoons grated fresh ginger

1 green bell pepper, seeded and chopped

1½ cups thawed frozen lima beans

1½ cups cooked dark red kidney beans (page 104) or 1 (15-ounce) can beans, rinsed and drained

1½ cups cooked pinto beans (page 104) or 1 (15-ounce) can beans, rinsed and drained

1 (14.5-ounce) can diced tomatoes, with their juices

1 tablespoon vegan Worcestershire sauce or soy sauce

2 teaspoons brown mustard

1 teaspoon brown sugar

3½ cups vegetable broth

Salt and freshly ground black pepper

1 cup fresh or thawed frozen corn kernels

1 teaspoon liquid smoke

2 tablespoons minced fresh flat-leaf parsley, for garnish

SERVES 6

SLOW COOKER SIZE:
5- TO 7-QUART

COOK TIME:
8 HOURS ON LOW

GLUTEN-FREE

SOY-FREE OPTION

1. For the best flavor, heat the oil in a large skillet over medium-high heat. Add the onion, celery, and carrots and sauté until just softened, about 5 minutes. Stir in the garlic and ginger and cook for 1 minute longer. Alternatively, omit the oil and sauté these ingredients in a few tablespoons of water or combine them in a microwave-safe bowl with a little water, cover, and microwave for 2 minutes.

2. Transfer the onion mixture to the slow cooker, and add the bell pepper, lima beans, kidney beans, pinto beans, and tomatoes and their juices. In a small bowl, combine the Worcestershire sauce, mustard, and brown sugar, stirring to blend. Stir in about ¼ cup of the broth, then add the mixture to the slow cooker, along with the remaining broth and salt and pepper to taste. Cover and cook on Low for 8 hours.

3. Stir in the corn and liquid smoke and cook, uncovered, for about 10 minutes to let the corn heat up. Taste and adjust the seasonings, if needed. For a thicker stew, puree a small amount of the stew right in the slow cooker using an immersion blender or scoop out 1 to 2 cups of stew and puree it in a blender or food processor, then stir the puree back into the rest of the stew in the cooker. Serve hot, sprinkled with the parsley.

Split Pea and Barley Stew

This savory stew can be assembled quickly and benefits from long, slow cooking, making it ideal for putting on before work to cook all day. Do the chopping and load the crock the night before, refrigerate overnight, and it will be ready to go the next morning. This golden stew was adapted from a recipe shared with me by Nancy and Jonathan Shanes. For a soy-free version, omit the soy sauce and use a soy-free sauce (purchased or homemade, page 35) or add some soy-free vegetable broth base or additional salt.

SERVES 6

SLOW COOKER SIZE:
5- TO 7-QUART

COOK TIME:
8 HOURS ON LOW

SOY-FREE OPTION

1 large yellow onion, chopped

1½ pounds sweet potatoes, peeled and cut into 1½-inch chunks

3 medium-size carrots, cut into ½-inch chunks

1 cup dried split peas, rinsed and picked over

⅔ cup pearl barley

1 (28-ounce) can diced tomatoes, with their juices

4 cups vegetable broth, plus more as needed

1 tablespoon soy sauce

1 teaspoon salt
¼ teaspoon freshly ground black pepper
1 teaspoon liquid smoke (optional)

1. Combine the onion, sweet potatoes, carrots, split peas, barley, tomatoes and their juices, broth, soy sauce, salt, and pepper in the slow cooker. Cover and cook on Low until the ingredients are tender, about 8 hours.

2. Just before serving, stir in the liquid smoke, if using. Taste and adjust the seasonings, if needed; depending on the saltiness of your broth, you may need to add up to 1 more teaspoon of salt. If the stew is too dry, stir in up to 1 more cup of broth.

Farm Stand Stew

Mix and match vegetables—for example, if you don't like fennel, leave it out and add more green beans, or include some bok choy or kale, or maybe some fresh corn kernels. If adding a more delicate vegetable, such as a leafy green or corn, add it about 1 hour before serving time so that it doesn't overcook. For soy-free, omit the soy sauce and use a soy-free sauce (purchased or homemade, page 35) or add some soy-free vegetable broth base or additional salt.

2 teaspoons olive oil (optional)
1 large red onion, chopped
3 garlic cloves, minced
1 small red or yellow bell pepper, seeded and chopped
1 medium-size carrot, thinly sliced
4 ounces green beans, cut into 1-inch pieces
8 ounces small red or white potatoes, scrubbed and left whole if about 1 inch in diameter, halved or quartered if larger
1 medium-size fennel bulb, trimmed and coarsely chopped
3 cups cooked cannellini or other white beans (page 104) or 2 (15-ounce) cans beans, rinsed and drained
2 small zucchini, cut into ½-inch pieces
3 cups vegetable broth

SERVES 4 TO 6

SLOW COOKER SIZE:
5- TO 6-QUART

COOK TIME:
6 TO 8 HOURS ON LOW

GLUTEN-FREE

SOY-FREE OPTION

¼ cup dry white wine
2 tablespoons soy sauce
1 teaspoon dried basil
1 teaspoon dried marjoram or thyme
1 bay leaf
Salt and freshly ground black pepper
1 large ripe tomato, cut into 1-inch dice
¼ cup chopped fresh flat-leaf parsley or basil

1. For the best flavor, heat the oil in a medium-size skillet over medium-high heat. Add the onion and sauté until softened, about 5 minutes. Add the garlic and cook for 1 minute longer. Alternatively, omit the oil and sauté these ingredients in a few tablespoons of water or combine them in a microwave-safe bowl with a little water, cover, and microwave for 2 minutes.

2. Transfer the onion mixture to the slow cooker. Add the bell pepper, carrot, green beans, potatoes, fennel, cannellini beans, zucchini, broth, wine, soy sauce, dried basil, marjoram, and bay leaf. Season to taste with salt and pepper. Cover and cook on Low for 6 hours.

3. Just before serving, taste and adjust the seasonings, if needed, then gently stir in the tomato and parsley. Remove the bay leaf and serve hot.

Chickpea and Mushroom Tagine

A tagine is a Moroccan stew cooked slowly in an earthenware pot that is also called a tagine. Happily, a tagine also cooks well in a slow cooker! Serve this fragrant stew over freshly cooked couscous or rice.

2 teaspoons olive oil (optional)
1 large yellow onion, chopped
3 garlic cloves, minced
1 teaspoon grated fresh ginger
2 teaspoons ground coriander
1 teaspoon sweet paprika
½ teaspoon ground cumin

½ teaspoon ground turmeric

¼ teaspoon cayenne pepper

1 large red bell pepper, seeded and chopped

3 cups cooked chickpeas (page 104) or two 15-ounce cans chickpeas, rinsed and drained

8 ounces portobello mushroom caps, gills scraped out and discarded, cut into 1-inch dice

1 (14.5-ounce) can diced tomatoes, drained

6 dried apricots, quartered

1½ cups vegetable broth

Salt and freshly ground black pepper

1 (9-ounce) can artichoke hearts, drained and quartered

½ cup thawed frozen peas

¼ cup golden raisins

1 tablespoon fresh lemon juice

2 tablespoons almond butter

¼ cup pitted green olives (preferably imported), halved

Freshly cooked couscous or rice, for serving

2 tablespoons minced fresh flat-leaf parsley or cilantro, for garnish

¼ cup toasted sliced almonds, for garnish

SERVES 4 TO 6

SLOW COOKER SIZE:
4- TO 6-QUART

COOK TIME:
6 TO 8 HOURS ON LOW

GLUTEN-FREE

SOY-FREE

1. For the best flavor, heat the oil in a medium-size skillet over medium-high heat. Add the onion and sauté until softened, about 5 minutes. Add the garlic, ginger, coriander, paprika, cumin, turmeric, and cayenne and cook for 1 minute longer. Alternatively, omit the oil and sauté these ingredients in a few tablespoons of water or combine them in a microwave-safe bowl with a little water, cover, and microwave for 2 minutes.

2. Transfer the onion mixture to the slow cooker. Add the bell pepper, chickpeas, mushrooms, tomatoes, apricots, and broth. Season to taste with salt and pepper. Cover and cook on Low for 6 to 7½ hours.

3. Add the artichoke hearts, peas, raisins, and lemon juice. Ladle about ½ cup of the broth into a cup and whisk in the almond butter until smooth, then stir the mixture back into the stew in the cooker. Cover and cook for 30 minutes longer.

4. When ready to serve, stir in the olives. Taste and adjust the seasonings, if needed. Serve over couscous, and sprinkle with the parsley and almonds.

Creole-Style Jambalaya

Just as different areas of the country have different ideas of barbecue sauce, there are regional variations on jambalaya. Tempeh and red beans are used here, although a good spicy vegan sausage (sliced, sautéed, and added at the end of the cooking time) would be a wonderful inclusion. Serve over your favorite freshly cooked rice, passing more hot sauce at the table.

SERVES 4 TO 6

SLOW COOKER SIZE:
4- TO 6-QUART

COOK TIME:
6 TO 8 HOURS ON LOW

GLUTEN-FREE

2 teaspoons olive oil

8 ounces tempeh, cut into 1-inch pieces

1 large yellow onion, chopped

1 medium-size green bell pepper, seeded and chopped

1 celery rib, chopped

4 garlic cloves, minced

3 cups cooked dark red kidney beans (page 104) or 2 (15-ounce) cans beans, rinsed and drained

1 (15-ounce) can crushed tomatoes

1 (14.5-ounce) can fire-roasted tomatoes, drained

1 cup vegetable broth

1 teaspoon filé powder (optional)

1 teaspoon dried thyme

½ teaspoon smoked paprika

¼ teaspoon cayenne pepper

2 large bay leaves

½ teaspoon Old Bay Seasoning

Salt and freshly ground black pepper

1 teaspoon Tabasco or Texas Pete hot sauce, plus more for serving

½ teaspoon liquid smoke

Freshly cooked rice, for serving

1. Heat the oil in a large skillet over medium-high heat. Add the tempeh and cook until browned, about 5 minutes. Transfer the tempeh to a plate and set aside. To the same skillet, add the onion, bell pepper, celery, and garlic; cover and cook until softened, about 5 minutes, adding a little water to sauté the vegetables so they don't stick. Alternatively, combine the vegetables and a few tablespoons of water in a microwave-safe bowl, cover, and microwave for 2 minutes.

2. Transfer the vegetable mixture to the slow cooker. Add the beans, both tomatoes, broth, filé powder, thyme, paprika, cayenne, bay leaves, and Old Bay, and season to taste with salt and pepper—you'll need to start with at least 1 teaspoon of salt. Add the tempeh, cover, and cook on Low until the vegetables are tender, about 6 hours.

3. Just before serving, add the Tabasco and liquid smoke, then taste and adjust the seasonings, if needed. Serve over rice.

Italian-Style Vegetable Stew

This recipe was inspired by a chicken dish my mother used to make. When I was a child, I remember enjoying everything about it—except for the chicken. Now I can have it my way, with delicious vegetables and herbs simmered in a luscious broth. I like to serve this over freshly cooked noodles, but it's also good with warm crusty bread for dunking.

2 teaspoons olive oil (optional)
1 large yellow onion, chopped
4 garlic cloves, minced
2 tablespoons tomato paste
1 teaspoon dried oregano
1 teaspoon dried basil
1 teaspoon fresh or dried rosemary
3 carrots, thinly sliced
1 celery rib, chopped
2 medium-size Yukon gold potatoes, peeled and diced
1 small red bell pepper, seeded and chopped
3 cups cooked chickpeas (page 104) or 2 (15-ounce) cans chickpeas, rinsed and drained
1 (14.5-ounce) can diced tomatoes, with their juices
½ cup dry white wine
1 cup vegetable broth
2 bay leaves
Salt and freshly ground black pepper

SERVES 4

SLOW COOKER SIZE:
5- TO 6-QUART

COOK TIME:
6 TO 8 HOURS ON LOW

GLUTEN-FREE

SOY-FREE

1. For the best flavor, heat the oil in a medium-size skillet over medium-high heat. Add the onion and sauté until softened, about 5 minutes. Add the garlic and cook for 1 minute longer, then stir in the tomato paste, oregano, basil, and rosemary. Alternatively, omit the oil and sauté these ingredients in a few tablespoons of water or combine them in a microwave-safe bowl with a little water, cover, and microwave for 2 minutes.

2. Transfer the onion mixture to the slow cooker. Add the carrots, celery, potatoes, bell pepper, chickpeas, tomatoes and their juices, and wine. Add the broth and bay leaves and season to taste with salt and pepper. Cover and cook on low until the vegetables are tender, 6 to 8 hours.

3. Taste and adjust the seasonings, if needed. Remove and discard the bay leaves before serving.

African-Inspired Peanut Stew

This colorful stew has a deep, rich flavor owing to the peanut butter and spices, and it's so easy to make. Crunchy peanut butter works especially well in this dish, adding an extra layer of texture. Serve over rice, couscous, or quinoa.

SERVES 6

SLOW COOKER SIZE:
5- TO 6-QUART

COOK TIME:
6 HOURS ON LOW

GLUTEN-FREE

SOY-FREE

2 teaspoons olive oil (optional)

1 medium-size yellow onion, minced

3 garlic cloves, minced

2 teaspoons grated fresh ginger (optional)

1 teaspoon ground coriander

1 teaspoon ground cumin

1 teaspoon curry powder

¼ teaspoon cayenne pepper

2 medium-size sweet potatoes, peeled and cut into ½-inch dice

1 green bell pepper, seeded and cut into ½-inch dice

3 cups cooked kidney beans (page 104) or 2 (15-ounce) cans beans, rinsed and drained

1 (14.5-ounce) can diced tomatoes, with their juices

⅓ cup peanut butter, preferably crunchy

1½ cups vegetable broth

Salt and freshly ground black pepper

6 cups coarsely chopped fresh spinach or Swiss chard

1. For the best flavor, heat the oil in a medium-size skillet over medium-high heat. Add the onion and sauté until softened, about 5 minutes. Add the garlic and cook for 1 minute longer, then stir in the ginger (if using), coriander, cumin, curry powder, and cayenne. Alternatively, omit the oil and sauté these ingredients in a few tablespoons of water or combine them in a microwave-safe bowl with a little water, cover, and microwave for 2 minutes.

2. Transfer the onion mixture to the slow cooker. Stir in the sweet potatoes, bell pepper, beans, and tomatoes and their juices.

3. Ladle about ½ cup of the broth into a small bowl and whisk in the peanut butter, then scrape the mixture into the slow cooker along with the remaining broth. Season to taste with salt and pepper. Cover and cook on low for 5 hours.

4. Stir in the chopped spinach, then cover and continue cooking for 1 hour. Alternatively, place the spinach in a microwave-safe bowl, cover, and microwave until wilted, 2 to 3 minutes, then add the spinach to the stew just before serving time.

Lentil and Chickpea Curry

Both chickpeas and lentils are popular in Indian cooking, as are cauliflower and potatoes. Put them all in the same pot and you have one delicious dish. The slow cooker is an ideal way to cook curries, because it allows the aromatic spices to permeate the other ingredients.

SERVES 4

SLOW COOKER SIZE:
4- TO 6-QUART

COOK TIME:
6 TO 8 HOURS
ON LOW

GLUTEN-FREE

SOY-FREE

2 teaspoons olive oil (optional)

1 large yellow onion, minced

3 garlic cloves, peeled

1 teaspoon grated fresh ginger

¼ cup tomato paste

1 tablespoon curry powder

1 teaspoon ground coriander

1 teaspoon dried thyme

½ teaspoon ground cumin

¼ teaspoon cayenne pepper

¼ teaspoon ground turmeric

½ cup dried brown lentils

1 large green bell pepper, seeded and chopped

3 cups small cauliflower florets

1 large russet potato, peeled and diced

3 cups cooked chickpeas (page 104) or 2 (15-ounce) cans chickpeas, rinsed and drained

1½ cups water

Salt and freshly ground black pepper

2 tablespoons lime marmalade or minced mango chutney

1 tablespoon white wine vinegar

½ cup thawed frozen green peas

1 cup unsweetened coconut milk (optional)

2 tablespoons minced fresh flat-leaf parsley or cilantro, for garnish

1. For the best flavor, heat the oil in a medium-size skillet over medium-high heat. Add the onion, garlic, ginger, and tomato paste and sauté for 5 minutes, adding a few drops of water if needed so that it doesn't burn. Stir in the curry powder, coriander, thyme, cumin, cayenne, and turmeric and cook for 1 minute longer. Alternatively, omit the oil and sauté these ingredients in a few tablespoons of water or combine them in a microwave-safe bowl with a little water, cover, and microwave for 2 minutes.

2. Transfer the onion mixture to the slow cooker and add the lentils, bell pepper, cauliflower, potato, chickpeas, and water. Season to taste with salt and pepper, cover, and cook on Low until the vegetables are tender, 6 to 7½ hours.

3. Blend the marmalade and vinegar in a small bowl and stir it into the curry, along with the peas. Cook for 30 minutes longer. For a thicker curry, puree 1 to 2 cups of the stew in a blender or food processor, then stir the puree back into the rest of the stew. Alternatively, use an immersion blender to puree some of the curry right in the cooker, then stir to mix. For a saucier stew, stir in 1 cup of coconut milk and let it heat up for a few minutes. Taste and adjust the seasonings, if needed. Serve hot, sprinkled with the parsley.

Portobello and White Bean Goulash

Because mushrooms, sauerkraut, and white beans have a natural affinity for one another, they seemed like a good flavor combination for this goulash, seasoned with caraway and dill. Serve over wide egg-free noodles or gluten-free noodles, if desired. For soy-free, use a soy-free vegan sour cream.

2 teaspoons olive oil (optional)

1 large yellow onion, minced

3 garlic cloves, minced

2 tablespoons tomato paste

2 tablespoons sweet Hungarian paprika

1 teaspoon caraway seeds

1½ cups vegetable broth

1 (14.5-ounce) can diced tomatoes, drained

1 cup sauerkraut, rinsed and drained

3 cups cooked white beans (page 104) or 2 (15-ounce) cans beans, rinsed and drained

¼ cup dry white wine

2 bay leaves

5 large portobello mushroom caps, gills scraped out and discarded, cut into 1-inch dice

Salt and freshly ground black pepper

½ cup vegan sour cream, purchased or homemade (page 57)

Cooked wide noodles, for serving

2 tablespoons minced fresh flat-leaf parsley or dill

SERVES 4

SLOW COOKER SIZE:
4- TO 6-QUART

COOK TIME:
4 TO 6 HOURS ON LOW

GLUTEN-FREE OPTION

SOY-FREE OPTION

1. For the best flavor, heat the oil in a large skillet over medium-high heat. Add the onion and sauté until softened, about 5 minutes. Add the garlic and cook for 1 minute longer. Stir in the tomato paste, paprika, caraway seeds, and ½ cup of the broth. Cook, stirring, for 1 minute longer. Alternatively, omit the oil and sauté these ingredients in a few tablespoons of water or combine them in a microwave-safe bowl with a little water, cover, and microwave for 2 minutes.

2. Transfer the onion mixture to the slow cooker. Stir in the tomatoes, sauerkraut, beans, wine, bay leaves, mushrooms, and the remaining 1 cup broth. Season to taste with salt and pepper and stir to combine. Cover and cook on Low for 4 to 6 hours.

3. Just before serving, ladle ½ cup of the broth into a small bowl and stir in the vegan sour cream. Stir this mixture back into the goulash, taste to adjust the seasonings, and serve at once over the noodles, garnished with the parsley.

Seitan Stroganoff

The seitan cooks right in the slow cooker, absorbing all of the delicious flavors of the surrounding ingredients as it cooks. For a gluten-free stroganoff, omit the seitan instructions and add more mushrooms along with some Soy Curls (see page 17) or tempeh, and use a gluten-free flour to help thicken the sauce. For soy-free, omit the soy sauce and use a soy-free sauce (purchased or homemade, page 35) and a soy-free vegan sour cream.

SEITAN:

1½ cups vital wheat gluten

2 tablespoons tapioca starch

2 tablespoons nutritional yeast

1 teaspoon garlic powder

1 teaspoon onion powder

¼ teaspoon salt

2 tablespoons soy sauce

1 tablespoon ketchup

1 tablespoon olive oil

½ teaspoon vegan gravy browner (such as Kitchen Bouquet; optional)

1 cup water

STROGANOFF:

2 teaspoons olive oil (optional)

2 large yellow onions, chopped

3 garlic cloves, minced

2 tablespoons tomato paste

1 tablespoon sweet Hungarian paprika

1 teaspoon dried thyme

1 teaspoon Dijon mustard

¼ cup soy sauce

⅓ cup dry red wine

2 tablespoons all-purpose flour

8 ounces mushrooms (any kind), sliced

2 cups vegetable broth

1 bay leaf

Salt and freshly ground black pepper

½ cup vegan sour cream, purchased or homemade (page 57)

1 tablespoon minced fresh dill, for the garnish

SERVES 4

SLOW COOKER SIZE:
4- TO 6-QUART

COOK TIME:
6 TO 8 HOURS ON LOW
PLUS 20 MINUTES
ON HIGH

GLUTEN-FREE OPTION

SOY-FREE OPTION

1. For the seitan: In a large bowl, combine the vital wheat gluten, tapioca starch, nutritional yeast, garlic and onion powders, and salt. In a separate bowl, combine the soy sauce, ketchup, oil, and gravy browner (if using). Stir in the water to blend, then pour the wet mixture into the dry mixture, stirring to form a stiff dough. Transfer the dough to a flat work surface and knead the

dough for about 2 minutes. Flatten the dough and cut it into 1-inch pieces. Set aside.

2. For the stroganoff: For the best flavor, heat the oil in a large skillet over medium-high heat. Add the onions and sauté until softened, about 5 minutes. Add the garlic and cook for 1 minute longer. Stir in the tomato paste, paprika, thyme, mustard, soy sauce, and wine, and blend until smooth. Alternatively, omit the oil and sauté these ingredients in a few tablespoons of water or combine them in a microwave-safe bowl with a little water, cover, and microwave for 2 minutes.

3. Transfer the onion mixture to the slow cooker. Sprinkle with the flour, stirring to coat. Stir in the mushrooms, broth, and bay leaf, and season to taste with salt and pepper. Place the seitan pieces in the cooker, submerging them as much as possible and arranging them so they don't touch. Cover and cook on Low for 6 to 8 hours.

4. Remove the lid and cook on High for 20 minutes. Remove the bay leaf. Ladle about 1 cup of the broth into a bowl and slowly stir in the vegan sour cream, then stir the mixture back into the stew. Serve at once, garnished with the dill.

Seitan Posole

This vegan version of a traditional Mexican stew is fragrant, fun, and delicious enough to serve company. I like to make it in a large slow cooker and set it out with warm tortillas and bowls of accompaniments for everyone to add according to their own taste. My favorite garnishes are avocado, cilantro, and pepitas, but you can also put out bowls of salsa, shredded lettuce, sliced radishes, and vegan sour cream. To make this gluten-free, instead of seitan, you may use Soy Curls (see page 17) or just add extra pinto beans. This recipe can be made soy-free by omitting the soy sauce and using a soy-free sauce (purchased or homemade, page 35) or adding some soy-free vegetable broth base or additional salt.

2 teaspoons olive oil (optional)

1 large yellow onion, chopped

1 carrot, thinly sliced

4 garlic cloves, minced

2 tablespoons tomato paste

2 teaspoons chili powder

1 teaspoon dried oregano

½ teaspoon ground coriander

½ teaspoon ground cumin

1 small red bell pepper, seeded and cut into ½-inch dice

1 (4-ounce) can chopped (hot or mild) green chiles, drained

1 (14.5-ounce) can diced tomatoes, drained

2 (15-ounce) cans hominy, rinsed and drained

3 cups cooked pinto beans (page 104) or 2 (15-ounce) cans beans, rinsed and drained

8 ounces seitan (purchased or homemade, page 136), chopped

2 tablespoons soy sauce

3 cups vegetable broth

Salt and freshly ground black pepper

Diced avocado, chopped fresh cilantro, and pepitas (green pumpkin seeds, optional), for garnish

Lime wedges, for serving

SERVES 6

SLOW COOKER SIZE:
4- TO 6-QUART

COOK TIME:
6 TO 8 HOURS ON LOW

GLUTEN-FREE OPTION

SOY-FREE OPTION

1. For the best flavor, heat the oil in a medium-size skillet over medium-high heat. Add the onion, carrot, and garlic and sauté until softened, about 5 minutes. Stir in the tomato paste, chili powder, oregano, coriander, and cumin and cook for 1 minute longer. Stir in a few tablespoons of water, if needed, so the mixture doesn't burn. Alternatively, omit the oil and sauté these ingredients in a few tablespoons of water or combine them in a microwave-safe bowl with a little water, cover, and microwave for 2 minutes.

2. Transfer the onion mixture to the slow cooker. Add the bell pepper, chiles, tomatoes, hominy, pinto beans, seitan, soy sauce, and broth. Season to taste with salt and pepper. Cover and cook on Low for 6 to 8 hours.

3. When ready to serve, taste and adjust the seasonings, if needed. If you desire a thicker stew, remove the lid and cook for 20 minutes longer on High. Ladle into bowls and garnish with the avocado, cilantro, and pepitas, if using. Serve with lime wedges on the side.

Three-Bean Cholent

Because cholent, a traditional Sabbath dish, requires long, slow cooking, it's ideal for the slow cooker. This is one of the few recipes in this book that begins with dried beans and takes longer than 8 hours to cook. Note that kidney beans need to be boiled for 10 minutes before adding them to the slow cooker as a precaution to destroy a potentially harmful toxin (see page 19). Because this recipe requires a long cooking time, if you are planning to cook and serve it on the same day, consider prepping the vegetables the night before and combining them with the canned tomatoes in a covered bowl in the refrigerator overnight—the tomatoes will keep the potatoes from browning. Combine the other ingredients in another refrigerated bowl. Then, in the morning, simply combine the drained soaked beans (after boiling for 10 minutes), vegetables, and other ingredients in the slow cooker and turn it on. This recipe can be made soy-free by omitting the soy sauce and Worcestershire sauce and using a soy-free sauce (purchased or homemade, page 35) or adding some soy-free vegetable broth base or additional salt.

SERVES 6

SLOW COOKER SIZE:
5- TO 7-QUART

COOK TIME:
8 TO 11 HOURS
ON LOW

SOY-FREE OPTION

½ cup dried red kidney beans, rinsed and picked over
½ cup dried lima beans, rinsed and picked over
½ cup dried white beans, rinsed and picked over
1 large yellow onion, chopped
2 celery ribs, chopped
4 garlic cloves, minced
1½ pounds small red-skinned potatoes, scrubbed and cut into 1-inch chunks
2 carrots, cut into ¼-inch slices
½ cup pearl barley
1 (14.5-ounce) can diced tomatoes, with their juices
2 tablespoons tomato paste
1 teaspoon Dijon mustard
1 teaspoon sugar
3 cups vegetable broth

1 tablespoon soy sauce

1 teaspoon vegan Worcestershire sauce

1 teaspoon smoked paprika

1 teaspoon salt

¼ teaspoon freshly ground black pepper

8 ounces seitan (purchased or homemade, page 136), cut into 1-inch pieces, *or* ½ cup TVP granules reconstituted with ½ cup boiling water (optional)

1. Combine the beans in a bowl and add enough water to cover the beans by 2 inches. Leave the beans to soak overnight.

2. Drain the beans and transfer to a saucepan with enough water to cover. Boil the beans for 10 minutes, then drain and transfer to the slow cooker. Add the onion, celery, garlic, potatoes, carrots, barley, and tomatoes and their juices.

3. In a small bowl, combine the tomato paste, mustard, and sugar. Add about ½ cup of the broth and blend until smooth, then add to the slow cooker. Add the remaining broth, soy sauce, Worcestershire, paprika, salt, and pepper. Cover and cook on Low until the beans and vegetables are tender, 8 to 11 hours.

4. Add the seitan or TVP (if using), cover, and cook for 30 minutes longer. Taste and adjust the seasonings, if needed, and serve.

chapter

5

Beans and Grains

Beans and slow cookers were made for each other, since beans take a notoriously long time to cook and in fact benefit from long, slow cooking. Because beans are rich in protein, fiber, and nutrients, they are key ingredients in many vegan recipes. While beans are used in recipes throughout this book, it's in this chapter that they play a starring role, with recipes such as Smoky Molasses-Maple Baked Beans, Burgundy Red Beans, and Crockery Cassoulet.

Because beans are often paired with grains, there are several grain-based recipes in this chapter as well. It's important to note that some grains can be difficult to prepare in a slow cooker. Of the various types of rice, it is converted rice that cooks the best in a slow cooker, when added during the last hour of cooking. Risotto, with its creamy texture, can be made well in a slow cooker. Most grains, however, are best when cooked separately on top of the stove or in a rice cooker and either added to the slow cooker just before serving or enjoyed alongside of (or under) what you've cooked in the slow cooker.

The first recipe in this chapter is called Basic Beans; it provides basic proportions and timing for cooking dried beans in a slow cooker. For additional information about beans, including cooking guidelines and soaking methods, see the section on Beans beginning on page 18.

Basic Beans

This is a basic recipe for slow-cooking dried beans such as pintos, kidneys, cannellinis, chickpeas, and black-eyed peas. To add some flavor to the beans, include the optional onion, garlic, and bay leaves. If you prefer them unseasoned, just cook them in water and you will have beans that are ready to use in any kind of recipe calling for cooked beans.

MAKES 6 TO 7 CUPS

SLOW COOKER SIZE:
4- TO 7-QUART

COOK TIME:
6 TO 8 HOURS ON HIGH

GLUTEN-FREE

SOY-FREE

1 pound dried beans, rinsed and picked over
1 large yellow onion, quartered (optional)
2 garlic cloves, crushed (optional)
2 bay leaves (optional)

1. Salt-soak the beans according to one of the methods described on page 20.

2. Place the beans in the slow cooker. (If cooking kidney beans or cannellini beans, boil them for 10 minutes on top of the stove before adding to the slow cooker.) Add the onion, garlic, and bay leaves (if using), and enough water to cover. Cover and cook on High until tender, 6 to 8 hours, depending on the type of bean.

Variations on a Bean

Jazz up plain cooked beans with a variety of global flavors in these variations on a (bean) theme! To make the beans more digestible, drain the Basic Beans after cooking, then proceed with the desired variation.

Bean Basics

It's important to note that most of the recipes using beans in this book call for cooked beans. This is done for four basic reasons:

Digestibility: Cooking the beans first, then draining off the cooking liquid, makes the beans easier to digest.

Timing: Starting with cooked beans helps ensure that everything in the slow cooker will be done at the same time, thus making your cooking time more reliable.

Flexibility: Calling for cooked beans allows you the option of using canned beans or beans that you've previously cooked and frozen.

Convenience: Using cooked beans encourages you to cook a large batch of dried beans in the slow cooker and then portion and freeze them for later use. For economy and flavor, portioning and freezing home-cooked beans gives you the same convenience as canned beans. If you use frozen beans, thaw them first. If you use canned beans, they should be rinsed and drained. Either way, the resulting bean dishes prepared in the slow cooker will be delicious and full of flavor.

SOUTHWEST BEANS

1 recipe Basic Beans (page 104)

1 (4-ounce) can chopped mild green chiles, drained

1 teaspoon ground cumin

1 teaspoon smoked paprika

½ teaspoon dried oregano

Salt and freshly ground black pepper

Water or vegetable broth, as needed (optional)

GLUTEN-FREE

SOY-FREE

Drain off any remaining cooking liquid from the beans, if desired, then stir in the chiles, cumin, paprika, and oregano, and season to taste with salt and pepper. Reduce the heat to Low, cover, and cook for 30 minutes to blend the flavors. For a more saucy consistency, add up to 1 cup water or broth.

ASIAN BEANS

GLUTEN-FREE

SOY-FREE OPTION

1 recipe Basic Beans (page 104)

2 tablespoons soy sauce or soy-free sauce (page 35)

1 teaspoon grated ginger (optional)

2 scallions, minced

2 teaspoons toasted sesame oil

Drain off any remaining cooking liquid from the beans, if desired, then stir in the soy sauce, ginger (if using), scallions, and sesame oil.

MEDITERRANEAN BEANS

GLUTEN-FREE

SOY-FREE

2 teaspoons olive oil (optional)

3 garlic cloves, minced

¼ cup oil-packed sun-dried tomatoes, chopped

1 teaspoon dried basil

½ teaspoon dried oregano

¼ to ½ teaspoon red pepper flakes

1 recipe Basic Beans (page 104)

Salt and freshly ground black pepper

For the best flavor, heat the oil in a small skillet over medium-high heat. Add the garlic and cook until fragrant, about 30 seconds. Stir in the tomatoes, basil, oregano, and red pepper flakes. Alternatively, omit the oil and sauté these ingredients in a few tablespoons of water or combine them in a microwave-safe bowl with a little water, cover, and microwave for 1 minute. Rewarm the beans if necessary, drain them, and then stir the seasoning mixture into the beans. Season to taste with salt and pepper.

Smoky Molasses-Maple Baked Beans

These baked beans have a rich depth of flavor thanks to two kinds of natural sweeteners, chipotle chiles, and long slow cooking.

2 teaspoons olive oil (optional)

1 medium-size yellow onion, minced

5 to 6 cups cooked navy beans (page 104) or 4 (15-ounce) cans beans, rinsed and drained

¼ cup maple syrup

¼ cup light molasses (not blackstrap)

3 tablespoons tomato paste

1 tablespoon minced chipotle chiles in adobo

2 teaspoons brown mustard

1 teaspoon rice vinegar

½ teaspoon salt

¼ teaspoon freshly ground black pepper

¼ cup water, plus more as needed

1 teaspoon liquid smoke

SERVES 4 TO 6

SLOW COOKER SIZE:
4-QUART

COOK TIME:
6 TO 7 HOURS ON LOW

GLUTEN-FREE

SOY-FREE

1. For the best flavor, heat the oil in a small skillet over medium-high heat. Add the onion and sauté until softened, about 5 minutes. Alternatively, omit the oil and sauté the onion in a few tablespoons of water or combine the onion in a microwave-safe bowl with a little water, cover, and microwave for 2 minutes.

2. Transfer the onions to the slow cooker. Add the beans and set the heat to Low.

3. In a medium-size bowl, combine the maple syrup, molasses, tomato paste, chipotles, mustard, vinegar, salt, and pepper. Add the ¼ cup water, stirring until blended, then add the mixture to the slow cooker.

4. Cover and cook on Low for 6 hours. Just before serving, stir in the liquid smoke. If the sauce is too thick, add a little more water. If the sauce is too thin, remove the lid, turn the slow cooker to High, and cook for 30 minutes longer, or until any extra liquid evaporates. Taste and adjust the seasonings, if needed.

Barbecue Beans with Coffee and Bourbon

Let the slow cooker be the star of your next cookout instead of the grill with these flavorful beans that are slow-simmered in a zesty barbecue sauce made with coffee, bourbon, and maple syrup. Whoever coined the phrase "lip-smackin' good" surely had these beans in mind. For soy-free, omit the soy sauce and use a soy-free sauce (purchased or homemade, page 35) or add some soy-free vegetable broth base or additional salt.

SERVES 4 TO 6

SLOW COOKER SIZE:
4- TO 6-QUART

COOK TIME:
6 HOURS ON LOW

GLUTEN-FREE

SOY-FREE OPTION

2 teaspoons olive oil (optional)
1 large yellow onion, minced
3 garlic cloves, minced
⅓ cup ketchup or barbecue sauce
⅓ cup strong brewed coffee
¼ cup bourbon
¼ cup dark brown sugar or granulated natural sugar
2 tablespoons maple syrup or molasses (not blackstrap)
1 tablespoon brown mustard
1 tablespoon soy sauce
½ cup water
5 to 6 cups cooked navy beans (page 104) or 4 (15-ounce) cans beans, rinsed and drained

1. For the best flavor, heat the oil in a medium-size skillet over medium-high heat. Add the onion and sauté until softened, about 5 minutes. Add the garlic and cook for 1 minute longer. Alternatively, omit the oil and sauté these ingredients in a few tablespoons of water or combine them in a microwave-safe bowl with a little water, cover, and microwave for 2 minutes.

2. Transfer the onion mixture to the slow cooker. Stir in the ketchup, coffee, and bourbon, and set the heat to Low.

3. In a bowl, combine the sugar, maple syrup, mustard, soy sauce, and water. Stir until well blended, then add to the slow cooker. Stir in the beans. Cover and cook on Low for 6 hours.

Burgundy Red Beans

The Burgundy wine region of France is the inspiration for this hearty bean dish. Cremini mushrooms add to the texture and flavor, although seitan makes a good addition as well. Serve over mashed potatoes or cooked noodles (gluten-free, if desired), with a green vegetable alongside. If this turns out more brothy than you'd like, just stir 1 tablespoon of *beurre manié* (page 28)—or a cornstarch slurry—into the liquid just before serving time (with the slow cooker turned to High). Or use an immersion blender to puree a small amount of the mixture right in the cooker, then stir to thicken.

2 teaspoons olive oil (optional)

1 large yellow onion, minced

2 large carrots, thinly sliced

4 garlic cloves, minced

2 tablespoons tomato paste

1 teaspoon dried thyme

½ teaspoon dried marjoram

2 bay leaves

8 ounces cremini mushrooms, quartered or sliced

6 cups cooked dark red kidney beans (page 104) or 4 (15-ounce) cans beans, rinsed and drained

1 cup vegetable broth

2 tablespoons tapioca starch or cornstarch

½ cup dry red wine

Salt and freshly ground black pepper

1 teaspoon vegan gravy browner (such as Kitchen Bouquet; optional)

Mashed potatoes or cooked noodles, for serving

2 tablespoons minced fresh flat-leaf parsley, for garnish

SERVES 4

SLOW COOKER SIZE:
5- TO 6-QUART

COOK TIME:
5 TO 6 HOURS ON LOW

GLUTEN-FREE

SOY-FREE

1. For the best flavor, heat the oil in a large skillet over medium-high heat. Add the onion and carrots and sauté until softened, about 5 minutes. Stir in the garlic, tomato paste, thyme, and marjoram and cook for 1 minute longer. Alternatively, omit the oil and sauté these ingredients in a few tablespoons of

water or combine them in a microwave-safe bowl with a little water, cover, and microwave for 2 minutes.

2. Transfer the onion mixture to the slow cooker. Add the bay leaves, mushrooms, beans, and broth. Place the tapioca starch in a small bowl and stir in the wine until smooth, then add to the pot, season to taste with salt and pepper, and stir gently to combine. Cover and cook on Low until the vegetables are tender, 4 to 6 hours.

3. Just before serving, remove the bay leaves and stir in the gravy browner, if using. Taste and adjust the seasonings, if needed. Serve hot over noodles or mashed potatoes, sprinkled with the parsley.

Greek-Style Beans with Tomatoes and Spinach

Greek gigante beans or large butter beans work best for this wholesome dish and are easiest to find in a dried state. As with most bean dishes in this book, this recipe starts with beans that have already been cooked, so be sure to plan ahead so that you can get your beans cooked before making this recipe.

SERVES 4 TO 6

SLOW COOKER SIZE:
4- TO 5-QUART

COOK TIME:
6 HOURS ON LOW

GLUTEN-FREE

SOY-FREE

2 teaspoons olive oil (optional)

1 large yellow onion, minced

5 garlic cloves, minced

4 cups cooked gigante beans or large butter beans (page 104) or 3 (15-ounce) cans beans, rinsed and drained

1 (28-ounce) can diced tomatoes, with their juices

1 teaspoon dried marjoram

1 teaspoon dried basil

Salt and freshly ground black pepper

5 cups chopped baby spinach

1 teaspoon lemon zest (optional)

1. For the best flavor, heat the oil in a medium-size skillet over medium-high heat. Add the onion and sauté until softened, about 5 minutes. Add the garlic and cook for 1 minute longer. Alternatively, omit the oil and sauté these ingredients in a few tablespoons of water or combine them in a microwave-safe bowl with a little water, cover, and microwave for 2 minutes.

2. Transfer the onion mixture to the slow cooker and add the beans, tomatoes and their juices, marjoram, basil, and salt and pepper to taste. Stir to combine.

3. Cover and cook on Low for 6 hours. About 10 minutes before serving, stir in the spinach and lemon zest, if using. Cover and continue to cook for 10 minutes to wilt the spinach. Taste and adjust the seasonings, if needed. Serve hot.

Crockery Cassoulet

White beans are an essential part of any classic French cassoulet, and here they take center stage as they slowly simmer with vegetables and herbs. The addition of vegan sausage at the end of the cooking time provides added texture and flavor. Serve with crusty French bread.

2 teaspoons olive oil (1 teaspoon optional)

1 large yellow onion, minced

2 large carrots, thinly sliced

5 garlic cloves, minced

1½ tablespoons tomato paste

4½ cups cooked Great Northern, cannellini, or other white beans (page 104) or 3 (15-ounce) cans beans, rinsed and drained

1 (14-ounce) can diced tomatoes, drained

½ cup vegetable broth

⅓ cup white wine

1 teaspoon dried thyme

¼ teaspoon dried marjoram

2 bay leaves

Salt and freshly ground black pepper

SERVES 4 TO 6

SLOW COOKER SIZE:
4- TO 6-QUART

COOK TIME:
6 TO 8 HOURS ON LOW

⅓ cup panko or plain dry bread crumbs

½ recipe Slow-Cooked Vegan Sausage Links (page 157) or 2 purchased vegan sausage links or Tofurky vegan kielbasa links, sliced

½ to 1 teaspoon liquid smoke

2 tablespoons minced fresh flat-leaf parsley, for garnish

1. For the best flavor, heat 1 teaspoon of the oil in a large skillet over medium-high heat. Add the onion and sauté until softened, about 5 minutes, adding a sprinkling of water, if needed, to keep it from burning. Add the carrots, garlic, and tomato paste and cook for 2 minutes longer. Alternatively, omit the oil and sauté these ingredients in a few tablespoons of water or combine them in a microwave-safe bowl with a little water, cover, and microwave for 2 minutes.

2. Transfer the onion mixture to the slow cooker. Add the beans, tomatoes, broth, wine, thyme, marjoram, and bay leaves. Season to taste with salt and pepper, cover, and cook on Low for 6 to 8 hours.

3. While the cassoulet is cooking, lightly toast the panko in a small dry skillet until lightly browned. Set aside.

4. Heat the remaining 1 teaspoon oil in a medium-size skillet over medium-high heat. Add the sausage and cook until browned on both sides.

5. When the cassoulet is ready to serve, remove and discard the bay leaves, and stir in the sausage and liquid smoke. Taste and adjust the seasonings, if needed. Top with the reserved bread crumbs and the parsley. Serve hot.

Two-Lentil Dal

Aromatic spices turn everyday beans and lentils into an exotic dish with the flavors of India. If a smoother texture is desired, use an immersion blender to puree a portion of the dal right in the slow cooker, or transfer about 2 cups of the cooked dal to a blender or food processor and puree it, then stir the puree back into the pot. Serve over freshly cooked basmati rice.

2 teaspoons olive oil (optional)
1 large yellow onion, minced
1½ teaspoons grated fresh ginger
1 teaspoon ground cumin
1 teaspoon ground coriander
½ teaspoon ground turmeric
½ teaspoon dry mustard
¼ teaspoon ground cardamom
¼ teaspoon cayenne pepper
1 cup dried red lentils, rinsed and picked over
1 cup dried brown lentils, rinsed and picked over
4 cups water
Salt and freshly ground black pepper
Freshly cooked basmati rice, for serving
3 tablespoons minced fresh cilantro or flat-leaf parsley, for garnish

SERVES 4 TO 6

SLOW COOKER SIZE:
4-QUART

COOK TIME:
8 HOURS ON LOW

GLUTEN-FREE

SOY-FREE

1. For the best flavor, heat the oil in a medium-size skillet over medium-high heat. Add the onion and sauté until softened, about 5 minutes. Stir in the ginger, cumin, coriander, turmeric, mustard, cardamom, and cayenne and cook, stirring, for 30 seconds. Alternatively, omit the oil and sauté these ingredients in a few tablespoons of water or combine them in a microwave-safe bowl with a little water, cover, and microwave for 1 minute.

2. Transfer the onion and spice mixture to the slow cooker and add the red and brown lentils, water, and salt and black pepper to taste. Cover and cook on Low for 8 hours. Taste and adjust the seasonings, if needed. Serve over rice, with a sprinkling of cilantro.

Slow and Spicy Sloppy Joes

Sloppy Joes are a favorite in my house, so I like to make a big pot and then portion and freeze it for quick meals. In this recipe, the "meatiness" comes from a combination of lentils, seitan, and mushrooms. If you're not a fan of any one of them, just leave it out and add an extra amount of the others. Serve in split burger rolls with slaw on the side. For gluten-free, use tempeh or TVP instead of seitan and use gluten-free rolls. For soy-free, use seitan instead of tempeh or TVP, and omit the soy sauce and use a soy-free sauce (purchased or homemade, page 35) or add some soy-free vegetable broth base or additional salt.

SERVES 6 TO 8

SLOW COOKER SIZE:
4- TO 6-QUART

COOK TIME:
6 HOURS ON LOW

GLUTEN-FREE OPTION

SOY-FREE OPTION

2 teaspoons olive oil (optional)

1 large yellow onion, minced

3 garlic cloves, minced

1 small red or green bell pepper, seeded and minced

2 teaspoons chili powder

1 cup dried brown lentils, rinsed and picked over

1 cup canned crushed tomatoes

½ cup ketchup

8 ounces finely chopped seitan (purchased or homemade, page 136) or tempeh, or ½ cup TVP granules reconstituted with ½ cup boiling water

8 ounces finely chopped mushrooms of your choice

2 cups water

2 tablespoons soy sauce

1 tablespoon minced chipotle chiles in adobo

1 tablespoon yellow or brown mustard

1 tablespoon light brown sugar or natural sweetener

1 teaspoon salt

Freshly ground black pepper

1 teaspoon liquid smoke

Toasted rolls, for serving

1. For the best flavor, heat the oil in a medium-size skillet over medium-high heat. Add the onion and sauté until softened, about 5 minutes. Add the garlic, bell pepper, and chili powder, stirring to coat. Cook for 30 seconds longer.

Alternatively, omit the oil and sauté these ingredients in a few tablespoons of water or combine them in a microwave-safe bowl with a little water, cover, and microwave for 2 minutes.

2. Transfer the onion mixture to the slow cooker and add the lentils, tomatoes, ketchup, seitan, mushrooms, and water.

3. In a bowl, combine the soy sauce, chipotle chile, mustard, brown sugar, salt, and pepper to taste and stir to combine. Add to the slow cooker, cover, and cook on Low for 6 hours. Stir in the liquid smoke, then taste and adjust the seasonings, if needed, adding a bit more water if the mixture is too dry. Serve hot, spooned into the toasted rolls.

N'awlins Red Beans and Rice

Red beans and rice is a Louisiana Creole dish traditionally made and served on Mondays. You can spoon the red beans over the cooked rice, but I prefer to add my rice to the cooking red beans to give the rice extra flavor. Most types of rice tend to get mushy when cooked directly in a slow cooker, so I add cooked brown rice to this recipe near the end of the cooking time. If you prefer to cook your rice right in the slow cooker, you will get the best results by adding ¾ cup converted white rice about an hour before the end of cooking time and increasing the water by ¾ cup. For gluten-free, omit the optional chorizo or use gluten-free. For soy-free, omit the soy sauce and use a soy-free sauce (purchased or homemade, page 35) or add some soy-free vegetable broth base or additional salt, and omit the optional chorizo or use soy-free.

SERVES 4

SLOW COOKER SIZE:
5- TO 7-QUART

COOK TIME:
6 HOURS ON LOW

GLUTEN-FREE OPTION

SOY-FREE OPTION

2 teaspoons olive oil (optional)

1 large yellow onion, minced

1 celery rib, minced

4 garlic cloves, minced

1 teaspoon smoked paprika

½ teaspoon dried thyme

¼ teaspoon cayenne pepper

1 green bell pepper, seeded and chopped

3 cups cooked dark red kidney beans (page 104) or 2 (15-ounce) cans beans, rinsed and drained

1 (14.5-ounce) can diced tomatoes, drained

1 large bay leaf

1½ cups water or vegetable broth

1 tablespoon soy sauce

Salt and freshly ground black pepper

3 cups cooked brown rice

2 scallions, minced

1 cup crumbled and cooked vegan chorizo (optional)

½ teaspoon liquid smoke (optional)

1. For the best flavor, heat the oil in a medium-size skillet over medium-high heat. Add the onion and sauté until softened, about 5 minutes. Add the garlic, paprika, thyme, and cayenne and cook, stirring, for 1 minute longer. Alternatively, omit the oil and sauté these ingredients in a few tablespoons of water or combine them in a microwave-safe bowl with a little water, cover, and microwave for 2 minutes.

2. Transfer the onion mixture to the slow cooker. Add the bell pepper, beans, tomatoes, bay leaf, water, and soy sauce. Season to taste with salt and pepper, cover, and cook on Low for 5½ hours. Stir in the rice and scallions, cover, and cook for 30 minutes longer.

3. Just before serving, stir in the sausage and/or liquid smoke, if using. Taste and adjust the seasonings, if needed. Remove the bay leaf and serve hot.

"Dirty John" Quinoa

In this recipe, quinoa replaces rice and combines with black-eyed peas to create a new spin on two Southern classics, dirty rice and hoppin' John, with the same great taste and stick-to-your-ribs goodness of both dishes. If you prefer to use rice instead of quinoa, you have two options: (1) use uncooked brown basmati rice and cook for 3½ to 4 hours on High, or (2) cook your brown rice separately and add it to the slow cooker just before serving time. If you like, you may substitute another variety of cooked beans for the black-eyed peas. For an even heartier dish, add some cooked crumbled or chopped vegan sausage just before serving time. To make this dish soy-free, omit the Worcestershire sauce and use a soy-free sauce (purchased or homemade, page 35) or add some soy-free vegetable broth base or additional salt.

2 teaspoons olive oil (optional)
1 small yellow onion, minced
2 garlic cloves, minced
1 teaspoon dried thyme
1 cup quinoa, rinsed and drained
1 cup chopped mushrooms of your choice
3 cups cooked black-eyed peas (page 104) or 2 (15-ounce) cans black-eyed peas, rinsed and drained
1 (14.5-ounce) can diced tomatoes, drained and finely chopped
1 (4-ounce) can diced mild green chiles, drained and finely chopped
1 teaspoon vegan Worcestershire sauce
1 teaspoon smoked paprika
1½ cups vegetable broth
Salt and freshly ground black pepper
Hot sauce, for serving

SERVES 4 TO 6

SLOW COOKER SIZE:
4-QUART

COOK TIME:
2 HOURS ON HIGH

GLUTEN-FREE

SOY-FREE

1. For the best flavor, heat the oil in a medium-size skillet over medium-high heat. Add the onion and sauté until softened, about 5 minutes. Add the garlic and thyme and cook for 30 seconds longer. Alternatively, omit the oil and sauté these ingredients in a few tablespoons of water or combine them in a microwave-safe bowl with a little water, cover, and microwave for 2 minutes.

2. Transfer the onion mixture to the slow cooker. Add the quinoa, mushrooms, black-eyed peas, tomatoes, chiles, Worcestershire sauce, paprika, and broth. Season to taste with salt and pepper. Cover and cook on High until the quinoa is tender, about 2 hours. If your slow cooker runs "hot," check it after 1½ hours.

3. Taste and adjust the seasonings, if needed. Serve hot, passing the hot sauce at the table.

Artichoke Risotto

In order to achieve the right texture and flavor, this risotto requires a few minutes of skillet time before combining in the slow cooker. It's not a bad trade-off when compared to all of the hands-on stirring involved in making conventional risotto. Using nutritional yeast makes this soy-free, although you can substitute a soy-free vegan Parmesan instead.

SERVES 4

SLOW COOKER SIZE:
4-QUART

COOK TIME:
2 HOURS ON HIGH

GLUTEN-FREE

SOY-FREE

2 teaspoons olive oil (optional)
1 small yellow onion or 2 shallots, minced
¼ cup dry white wine
1¼ cups Arborio rice
3½ cups vegetable broth, plus more if needed
2 teaspoons chopped fresh thyme leaves or 1 teaspoon dried thyme
½ teaspoon salt
2 cups canned or thawed frozen artichoke hearts, chopped
2 tablespoons nutritional yeast or ¼ cup grated vegan Parmesan cheese
2 teaspoons fresh lemon juice
Freshly ground black pepper
¼ cup chopped toasted walnuts, for garnish
2 tablespoons snipped fresh chives, for garnish

1. For the best flavor, heat the oil in a medium-size skillet over medium-high heat. Add the onion and sauté until softened, about 5 minutes. Stir in the wine and cook for 30 seconds, then add the rice and cook, stirring, for 2 minutes. Alternatively, omit the oil and sauté these ingredients in a few tablespoons of water or combine them in a microwave-safe bowl with a little water, cover, and microwave for 2 minutes.

2. Transfer the rice mixture to the slow cooker. Add the broth, thyme, and salt, cover, and cook on High until all of the liquid is absorbed and the rice is just tender, about 2 hours.

3. Stir in the artichokes, nutritional yeast, lemon juice, and pepper to taste. Taste and adjust the seasonings, if needed. If the mixture is too dry, stir in a little more hot broth as needed.

4. Serve hot, spooned into shallow bowls. Sprinkle each serving with the toasted walnuts and chives.

Creamy Polenta with Mushroom Ragu

Making polenta in the slow cooker is easy because it doesn't require all of the stirring and close watching that is necessary in the stovetop method. If you use water instead of broth, you will need about ½ teaspoon additional salt. You could also use half broth and half water, if you prefer.

Instead of topping with the mushroom ragu, the polenta may be enjoyed as is with a pat of vegan butter or a drizzle of olive oil and freshly cracked pepper, or with any of the following topping variations: fresh chopped basil or sage, grated vegan Parmesan, shredded vegan mozzarella, sautéed sliced vegan sausage, sautéed broccoli rabe, and garlic. Alternatively, you may cool the polenta, refrigerate it to firm up, and then slice it and fry it. Fried polenta may be topped with any of the same toppings as well. Use a soy-free vegan butter to make this soy-free.

SERVES 4 TO 6

SLOW COOKER SIZE:
4- TO 6-QUART

COOK TIME:
4 TO 6 HOURS ON LOW

GLUTEN-FREE

SOY-FREE OPTION

7 cups boiling vegetable broth or water

1 teaspoon salt

1½ cups coarse-ground polenta

2 teaspoons olive oil

3 garlic cloves, minced

1 pound cremini mushrooms, sliced

Salt and freshly ground black pepper

2 tablespoons dry red wine (optional)

3 cups marinara sauce or your favorite tomato sauce for pasta

1 tablespoon vegan butter or olive oil (optional)

1. Generously oil the slow cooker insert or coat it with nonstick cooking spray and set the cooker on High. Carefully pour in the boiling broth, add the salt, then slowly whisk in the cornmeal, stirring until blended. Cover and cook on Low, stirring occasionally if possible, until the polenta has thickened, 4 to 6 hours. If the polenta is too thin, remove the lid and cook for 30 minutes longer.

2. Heat the oil in a large skillet over medium heat. Add the garlic and cook until fragrant and slightly softened, about 1 minute. Add the mushrooms and cook until softened. Season to taste with salt and pepper. Add the wine, if using, then stir in the marinara sauce and heat until hot.

3. Taste the polenta and adjust the seasonings, if needed. Top with bits of vegan butter, if using, and several grinds of black pepper. Spoon the polenta into shallow bowls and top with a spoonful of the mushroom ragu. Serve hot.

Barley Orzotto with White Beans and Vegetables

Similar to risotto, orzotto is made with pearl barley and is prepared in regions of northern Italy. Like risotto, it cooks up thick and creamy. The addition of white beans and a variety of vegetables makes this a satisfying one-dish meal.

2 teaspoons olive oil (optional)
1 medium-size yellow onion, minced
1 large carrot, minced
1 small celery rib, minced
3 garlic cloves, minced
1 teaspoon minced fresh thyme or ½ teaspoon dried thyme
¼ cup dry white wine
1 cup pearl barley
½ small red bell pepper, seeded and minced
6 ounces mushrooms of your choice, chopped
1½ cups cooked cannellini beans (page 104) or 1 (15-ounce) can beans, rinsed and drained
3 cups vegetable broth
Salt and freshly ground black pepper
¾ cup fresh or thawed frozen peas

SERVES 4

SLOW COOKER SIZE:
4- TO 6-QUART

COOK TIME:
2 TO 2½ HOURS
ON HIGH

SOY-FREE

1. For the best flavor, heat the oil in a medium-size skillet over medium-high heat. Add the onion, carrot, and celery and sauté until softened, about 5 minutes. Stir in the garlic, thyme, and wine and cook for 1 minute longer. Alternatively, omit the oil and sauté these ingredients in a few tablespoons of water or combine them in a microwave-safe bowl with a little water, cover, and microwave for 2 minutes.

2. Transfer the onion mixture to the slow cooker. Stir in the barley, then add the bell pepper, mushrooms, beans, and broth. Season to taste with salt and pepper. Cover and cook on High for 2 hours. Taste and adjust the seasonings, if needed. If the barley is not quite tender, cook for another 30 minutes, with the lid off if the barley is too saucy. If it's too dry, stir in a small amount of hot water or broth. When the barley is tender, stir in the peas. Serve hot in shallow bowls.

Cheesy Chile Grits and Sweet Taters

love the contrasting flavor the sweet potatoes provide in this dish. If you're not a fan of sweet potatoes, substitute white potatoes, or try pinto or black beans for a different flavor experience. Your choice of mild or hot chiles will dictate whether this is a mild or spicy dish.

Having been raised on polenta, I immediately took a liking to grits when I moved to the South. After all, they are both made from ground, dried corn kernels. Look for stone-ground grits for the best flavor.

Like polenta, grits can also be enjoyed fried. Simply transfer the cooked grits to a loaf pan or baking dish, smooth the top, cover, and refrigerate until chilled. Then cut the grits into ½-inch-thick slices and fry in olive oil or vegan butter until browned.

For a more classic way to serve this dish, omit the chiles and sweet potatoes and serve with collard greens and black-eyed peas. Use a soy-free vegan cheese, such as Daiya, to make this recipe soy-free—or try the Creamy Cheesy Sauce (page 123) instead.

SERVES 4 TO 6

SLOW COOKER SIZE:
4- TO 6-QUART

COOK TIME:
6 TO 8 HOURS ON LOW

GLUTEN-FREE

SOY-FREE OPTION

4½ cups vegetable broth or water

1½ cups stone-ground grits

1 large or 2 medium-size sweet potatoes, peeled and cut into ½-inch dice (about 2 cups)

4 scallions, minced

1 (4-ounce) can chopped mild or hot green chiles, drained

Salt and freshly ground black pepper

1 cup Creamy Cheesy Sauce (recipe follows) or shredded vegan cheddar or pepper Jack cheese

1. Combine the broth and grits in the slow cooker, add the sweet potatoes, scallions, and chiles, and season to taste with salt and pepper. Cover and cook on Low until the sweet potatoes are tender, 6 to 8 hours.

2. Just before serving, stir in the cheese sauce. Serve hot in shallow bowls.

CREAMY CHEESY SAUCE

This rich and creamy sauce made with cashews adds a nice "cheesy" flavor to recipes.

1 cup cashews, soaked for 4 hours and drained
½ cup nutritional yeast
1 teaspoon Dijon mustard
½ teaspoon garlic powder
½ teaspoon onion powder
½ teaspoon paprika
½ teaspoon vegetable broth powder
½ teaspoon salt
1 cup water or unsweetened almond milk
2 tablespoons fresh lemon juice

Combine all of the ingredients in a food processor or high-speed blender and process until smooth.

MAKES ABOUT
2 CUPS

The Importance of Checking Labels

If you're following a vegan diet, you already know how critical it is to scrutinize the labels of packaged goods for hidden animal products. Similarly, if you're living gluten- or soy-free, be sure to remain vigilant for hidden gluten or soy in products such as gluten in oats or hydrolized soy protein in vegan sauces.

Hearty Main Dishes

Many of the recipes in this chapter are vegan versions of classic global dishes that lend themselves to slow cooking, such as a French *pot-au-feu*, a Moroccan tagine, and an Indian curry. There are some all-American classics as well, including one of my own favorites, Mom-Style Vegan Meatloaf. Many of these recipes traditionally call for meat, which the slow-cooking process helps to make tender. Since these meatless recipes don't require tenderizing, the slow cooker is used for the sheer convenience and enriched flavor that long, gentle cooking can bring to the ingredients.

This chapter also includes uniquely vegan recipes for braising tofu and making seitan from scratch. In addition, there are recipes for lasagna, mac and cheese, potpies, and other casseroles—dishes usually associated with oven baking, all of which further illustrate the versatility of the slow cooker.

Seitan Pot Roast

For this pot roast, the seitan cooks along with the vegetables for a delicious and satisfying meal that will fill your house with its wonderful aroma. To serve, you can simply spoon the cooking liquid over the seitan and vegetables or, if you prefer, you can thicken it into a sauce (see the note on page 14 for ways to thicken liquids). Or, instead, try serving it with the Fat-Free Mushroom Gravy (page 183). To make this soy-free, omit the soy sauce and use a soy-free sauce (purchased or homemade, page 35) or add some soy-free vegetable broth base or additional salt.

SERVES 4 TO 6

SLOW COOKER SIZE:
6- TO 7-QUART

COOK TIME:
6 TO 8 HOURS ON LOW

SOY-FREE OPTION

SEITAN:

1½ cups vital wheat gluten

½ cup chickpea flour

¼ cup nutritional yeast

1 teaspoon onion powder

½ teaspoon dried thyme

½ teaspoon salt

¼ teaspoon freshly ground black pepper

2 tablespoons soy sauce

1 tablespoon ketchup

3 teaspoons olive oil

1¼ cups water

¼ teaspoon paprika

1 large yellow onion, thinly sliced

3 carrots, cut into ½-inch slices

2 parsnips, cut into ½-inch slices

1 pound Yukon Gold potatoes, peeled and cut into 1 ½-inch chunks

2 garlic cloves, crushed

½ teaspoon dried thyme

Salt and freshly ground black pepper

1 cup vegetable broth

¼ cup dry white wine

1 tablespoon soy sauce

Fat-Free Mushroom Gravy (page 183; optional)

1. For the seitan: In a large bowl, combine the vital wheat gluten, chickpea flour, nutritional yeast, onion powder, thyme, salt, and pepper. Add the soy sauce, ketchup, 2 teaspoons of the oil, and the water. Mix well to form a stiff dough. Knead until smooth, about 3 minutes. Drizzle the remaining 1 teaspoon oil onto the seitan and spread it with your fingers to coat. Sprinkle on the paprika and rub it in to coat the seitan. Leave the seitan dough in one piece or cut it into large chunks, depending on if you prefer to slice it from one large piece, or would rather have separate chunks to divide for different uses.

2. Lightly oil the sides and bottom of the slow cooker insert or spray it with nonstick cooking spray. Add the onion, carrots, parsnips, potatoes, and garlic to the cooker. Sprinkle the vegetables with the thyme and season to taste with salt and pepper. Pour in the broth, wine, and soy sauce. If the seitan is in chunks, arrange them among the vegetables. If the seitan is in one piece, place a small square of oiled parchment paper or aluminum foil (about the size of the seitan) on top of the vegetables and place the seitan on top. Cover and cook on Low until the seitan is cooked and the vegetables are tender, 6 to 8 hours.

3. Remove the seitan from the slow cooker and discard the parchment, if using. If the seitan is in one piece, cut it into thin slices. Arrange the seitan on a large serving platter. Surround with the cooked vegetables. Spoon the cooking liquid over the seitan and vegetables and serve hot with the gravy, if using.

Hoisin- and Miso-Braised Tofu

The key to cooking tofu successfully in a slow cooker is braising. A wide, shallow slow cooker (such as a large oval) is needed for this recipe in order to arrange the tofu in a single layer. The beauty of this dish is in its simplicity. Serve with stir-fried Asian vegetables and rice.

SERVES 4

SLOW COOKER SIZE:
5- TO 7-QUART

COOK TIME:
4 HOURS ON LOW

GLUTEN-FREE

4 scallions, finely minced
1 pound extra-firm tofu, drained, pressed, and cut into ½-inch-thick slices
¼ cup hoisin sauce
2 tablespoons miso paste
1 teaspoon agave nectar
1 teaspoon rice vinegar
½ teaspoon grated ginger
½ teaspoon Asian chili paste
2 tablespoons water

1. Lightly oil the insert of the slow cooker or spray it with nonstick cooking spray. Spread the scallions evenly in the bottom of the cooker. Arrange the tofu slices on top of the scallions, with as many slices in a single layer as possible and the rest on top.

2. In a small bowl, whisk together the hoisin, miso, agave, vinegar, ginger, chili paste, and water. Spread the mixture evenly over the tofu. Cover and cook on Low for 4 hours, carefully turning over the tofu slices about halfway through the cooking time, if possible.

3. Carefully remove the tofu from the slow cooker and top with any remaining hoisin mixture.

Seitan Pot-au-Feu

This version of the rustic French "pot on fire" classic combines a variety of vegetables slow-simmered in broth with chunks of seitan cooked alongside and broth for extra flavor. A large slow cooker is best for this recipe. To make it in a smaller slow cooker, cut the ingredient volume by about half. Serve with cornichons and horseradish or mustard on the side and crusty French bread. To make this soy-free, omit the soy sauce and use a soy-free sauce (purchased or homemade, page 35) or add some soy-free vegetable broth base or additional salt.

SEITAN:

1¼ cups vital wheat gluten, plus more if needed

¼ cup chickpea flour

3 tablespoons nutritional yeast

½ teaspoon onion powder

¼ teaspoon salt

Freshly ground black pepper

1 teaspoon olive oil

2 tablespoons soy sauce

1¼ cups water, plus more if needed

2 medium-size carrots, peeled and cut into sticks about ¼ inch thick by 2 inches long

1 or 2 medium-size parsnips, peeled and cut into sticks about ¼ inch thick by 2 inches long

3 or 4 small white potatoes, scrubbed and halved or quartered

2 leeks, white parts only, trimmed and cut into 2-inch pieces, or 1 medium-size yellow onion, diced

1 small savoy cabbage, cut into wedges (about 1 pound)

1 celery rib, halved lengthwise and cut into 2-inch pieces

4 garlic cloves, crushed

1 *bouquet garni* (see Note)

½ cup dry white wine

1 teaspoon dried thyme

2 tablespoons chopped fresh flat-leaf parsley

SERVES 4

SLOW COOKER SIZE:
6- TO 7-QUART

COOK TIME:
6 TO 8 HOURS ON LOW

SOY-FREE OPTION

1 teaspoon salt
¼ teaspoon pepper
4 cups vegetable broth
Coarse-ground brown mustard, horseradish, and cornichons, for serving

1. For the seitan: In a large bowl, combine the vital wheat gluten, chickpea flour, nutritional yeast, onion powder, salt, and a few grinds of black pepper. Mix well, then stir in the oil, soy sauce, and water until well mixed. Use your hands to knead the mixture for about 5 minutes. If the mixture is dry, add a very small amount of extra water. If it is too wet, sprinkle on some additional vital wheat gluten. Divide the seitan into 4 to 6 smaller pieces and set aside.

2. Arrange the carrots, parsnips, potatoes, leeks, cabbage, celery, and garlic in the slow cooker. Add the *bouquet garni* and the seitan chunks. Add the wine, thyme, parsley, salt, and pepper, then pour in the broth. Cover and cook on Low until the seitan is cooked and the vegetables are tender, 6 to 8 hours.

3. Remove the *bouquet garni* and discard. Taste and adjust the seasonings, if needed. Transfer the seitan and vegetables to a large serving platter. Ladle the broth into small individual cups to serve with the *pot-au-feu*. Set out small serving bowls containing the cornichons, mustard, and horseradish.

Note: To make a *bouquet garni*, in a 5-inch square of cheesecloth (or in a coffee filter or tea ball, if you don't have cheesecloth), place 1 teaspoon black peppercorns, 1 teaspoon whole cloves, 2 crumbled bay leaves, 1 teaspoon celery seeds, and 1 teaspoon dried thyme. Gather up the edges of the cheesecloth and tie with kitchen twine.

Vegetable Curry

Let the luscious fragrance of curry fill your house all day as it simmers in your slow cooker. Serve over hot cooked basmati rice with chutney on the side. For a creamier curry, stir in about ½ cup of unsweetened coconut milk or vegan yogurt just before serving.

2 teaspoons vegetable oil (optional)

1 large yellow onion, minced

3 garlic cloves, minced

2 tablespoons tomato paste

2 tablespoons curry powder

1 teaspoon ground coriander

¼ teaspoon cayenne pepper

1 bell pepper (any color), seeded and chopped

3 red-skinned potatoes, scrubbed and diced

3 cups small cauliflower florets

1½ cups green beans, cut into 1-inch pieces

1 (14.5-ounce) can diced tomatoes, drained

1½ cups cooked dark red kidney beans (page 104) or 1 (15-ounce) can beans, rinsed and drained

2 bay leaves

½ cup vegetable broth

Salt and freshly ground black pepper

½ cup thawed frozen green peas

SERVES 4

SLOW COOKER SIZE:
4- TO 6-QUART

COOK TIME:
6 TO 8 HOURS ON LOW

GLUTEN-FREE

SOY-FREE

1. For the best flavor, heat the oil in a medium-size skillet over medium-high heat. Add the onion and sauté until softened, about 5 minutes. Add the garlic, tomato paste, curry powder, coriander, and cayenne and cook for 1 minute longer. Alternatively, omit the oil and sauté these ingredients in a few tablespoons of water or combine them in a microwave-safe bowl with a little water, cover, and microwave for 2 minutes.

2. Transfer the onion mixture to the slow cooker. Add the bell pepper, potatoes, cauliflower, green beans, tomatoes, kidney beans, bay leaves, and broth. Season to taste with salt and pepper. Cover and cook on Low until the vegetables are tender, 6 to 8 hours.

3. A few minutes before serving, stir in the peas. Taste and adjust the seasonings, if needed. Remove the bay leaves. For a thicker curry, use an immersion blender to puree a portion of the mixture or scoop out about 2 cups of the mixture and puree it in a blender or food processor, then stir the puree back into the slow cooker. Serve hot.

Seitan Ropa Vieja

There are many variations of this flavorful Latin American dish. This vegan version, made with a combination of seitan, black beans, and mushrooms, is my favorite! Served over rice, it makes a delicious dinner when accompanied by a green vegetable. It's also terrific spooned into warm tortillas and topped with diced avocado or vegan sour cream.

SERVES 4

SLOW COOKER SIZE:
4- TO 6-QUART

COOK TIME:
4 TO 6 HOURS ON LOW

SOY-FREE

2 teaspoons olive oil (optional)

1 small yellow onion, sliced paper-thin

3 garlic cloves, minced

1 green bell pepper, seeded and sliced paper-thin

⅓ cup tomato paste

1 teaspoon ground cumin

1 cup crushed tomatoes

½ teaspoon dried oregano

½ teaspoon natural sugar

1 pound seitan (purchased or homemade, page 136), shredded or very thinly sliced

2 portobello mushrooms caps, gills scraped and discarded, shredded or thinly sliced

1½ cups cooked black beans (page 104) or 1 (15-ounce) can beans, rinsed and drained

1 cup vegetable broth

1 teaspoon chopped fresh cilantro

Salt and freshly ground black pepper

1 tablespoon fresh lime juice

Flour tortillas or hot cooked rice, for serving

1. For the best flavor, heat the oil in a medium-size skillet over medium-high heat. Add the onion and sauté until softened, about 5 minutes. Add the garlic and bell pepper and continue cooking for 1 minute. Stir in the tomato paste and cumin and cook for 1 minute longer. Alternatively, omit the oil and sauté these ingredients in a few tablespoons of water or combine them in a microwave-safe bowl with a little water, cover, and microwave for 2 minutes.

2. Transfer the onion mixture to the slow cooker. Add the crushed tomatoes, oregano, sugar, seitan, mushrooms, beans, broth, cilantro, and salt and pepper to taste. Stir until well combined. Cover and cook on Low until the vegetables are tender, 4 to 6 hours.

3. Just before serving, add the lime juice, then taste and adjust the seasonings, if needed. Serve hot, spooned into tortillas or over rice.

Rustic Potpie Topped with Chive Biscuits

This rustic potpie features a top crust of tender drop biscuits that cook right in the slow cooker. The steam heat produces a soft and tender biscuit topping. If you prefer a drier texture to the biscuits, let the cooked potpie sit uncovered for about 10 minutes before serving. To make this gluten-free, use diced tempeh or extra-firm tofu instead of seitan and use a gluten-free flour blend. For soy-free, omit the soy sauce and use a soy-free sauce (purchased or homemade, page 35) or add some soy-free vegetable broth base or additional salt, and a soy-free nondairy milk.

2 tablespoons plus 2 teaspoons olive oil
1 medium-size yellow onion, minced
2 large carrots, peeled and minced
2 tablespoons tomato paste
1 teaspoon dried thyme
½ teaspoon dried marjoram
1 cup plus 3 tablespoons all-purpose flour
3 tablespoons dry red wine
1 tablespoon soy sauce
1 cup vegetable broth
2 medium-size Yukon Gold potatoes, peeled and cut into ½-inch dice
8 ounces cremini mushrooms, coarsely chopped

SERVES 4

SLOW COOKER SIZE:
4- TO 6-QUART

COOK TIME:
4 TO 6 HOURS ON LOW
PLUS 1 HOUR ON HIGH

GLUTEN-FREE OPTION

SOY-FREE OPTION

8 ounces seitan (purchased or homemade, page 136), cut into ½-inch dice
Salt and freshly ground black pepper
¾ cup thawed frozen green peas
1½ teaspoons baking powder
1 tablespoon dried or snipped fresh chives
½ cup plain unsweetened nondairy milk

1. Lightly oil the slow cooker insert or spray it with nonstick cooking spray. Heat 2 teaspoons of the oil in a large skillet over medium-high heat. Add the onion and carrots and sauté for 5 minutes. Stir in the tomato paste, thyme, and marjoram and cook for 1 minute longer. Sprinkle on 3 tablespoons of the flour and cook for 30 seconds. Add the wine, soy sauce, and broth, stirring after each addition.

2. Transfer the onion mixture to the slow cooker. Add the potato, mushrooms, seitan, ½ teaspoon salt, and ¼ teaspoon pepper. Cover and cook on Low until the vegetables are tender, 4 to 6 hours. Taste and adjust the seasonings, if needed, then stir in the peas.

3. In a large bowl, combine the remaining 1 cup flour, the baking powder, chives, and ½ teaspoon salt. Quickly stir in the nondairy milk and the remaining 2 tablespoons oil until just blended. Drop the biscuit mixture by large spoonfuls onto the surface of the simmering stew. Turn the heat setting to High, cover, and cook until the dough is cooked through, about 1 hour longer.

4. Serve within 15 minutes after the biscuit dough has finished cooking.

VARIATIONS

Instead of the seitan, you may use cooked chickpeas or chopped tempeh. You could also use sweet potatoes instead of the white potatoes, or add turnips in addition to the carrots, and so on. Different herbs could be used in the biscuits—instead of chives, try dill and a little dried savory, if you have some.

Chipotle-Polenta Bake

This yummy casserole couldn't be easier to make. Just combine all of the ingredients in the cooker, turn it on, and walk away—that is, until the wonderful fragrance draws you back to enjoy your meal. This soft and spicy polenta is spooned into bowls and topped with your garnishes of choice. If you prefer a milder flavor, cut back on the amount of chili powder and chipotle.

If you prefer fried polenta slices, transfer the cooked soft polenta to a greased loaf pan and refrigerate to chill and firm up. Then cut the polenta into slices and pan-fry them in a small amount of olive oil. Serve topped with a little hot sauce or a dab of vegan sour cream and some salsa.

1¼ cups medium-ground cornmeal

1¼ teaspoons salt

3 tablespoons chili powder

2 teaspoons olive oil

5 cups boiling vegetable broth

5 scallions, minced

1½ cups cooked pinto beans (page 104) or 1 (15-ounce) can beans, rinsed and drained

1½ cups fresh or thawed frozen corn kernels

2 tablespoons minced chipotle chiles in adobo

Louisiana hot sauce

Your favorite salsa, for serving

2 tablespoons minced fresh cilantro, for garnish

Sliced jalapeño chiles, sliced black olives, and/or vegan sour cream, for garnish (optional)

SERVES 4

SLOW COOKER SIZE:
5-QUART

COOK TIME:
6 HOURS ON LOW

GLUTEN-FREE

SOY-FREE

1. Generously oil the insert of the slow cooker or spray it with nonstick cooking spray. Add the cornmeal, salt, chili powder, and oil. Stir in the boiling broth until well blended, then stir in the scallions, beans, corn, chipotle chiles, and hot sauce to taste. Cover and cook on Low for 6 hours.

2. Serve hot, topped with salsa and sprinkled with cilantro and any of the optional garnishes.

Seitan in the Slow Cooker

It's easy to make your own homemade seitan (wheat meat). It tastes best when left to gently simmer for several hours—and, once again, the slow cooker comes to the rescue. For a firmer texture, add an additional ¼ cup vital wheat gluten to the mix. The cooking liquid may be strained and used as a stock in sauces, soups, and other recipes.

MAKES ABOUT 1½ POUNDS
SLOW COOKER SIZE: 4- TO 6-QUART
COOK TIME: SETTING: 5 TO 6 HOURS ON LOW

1¾ cups vital wheat gluten
¼ cup chickpea flour
¼ cup nutritional yeast
1 teaspoon onion powder
½ teaspoon garlic powder
½ teaspoon salt
¼ teaspoon freshly ground black pepper
6 tablespoons soy sauce
1 tablespoon olive oil
1¾ cups water or vegetable broth
1 medium-size yellow onion, quartered

1. In a large bowl, combine the vital wheat gluten, chickpea flour, nutritional yeast, onion and garlic powders, salt, and pepper. Stir in 3 tablespoons of the soy sauce, the olive oil, and the water, and continue stirring until well mixed. Knead for about 3 minutes.

2. Pour about 2 quarts of water into the slow cooker. Depending on your preference, leave the seitan dough whole or divide into 4 to 6 pieces and add to the water along with the onion and remaining 3 tablespoons of soy sauce. Cover and cook on Low until firm, 4 to 6 hours.

3. Transfer the cooked seitan to a baking sheet to cool. If you are not using the seitan right away, it can be stored submerged in its cooking liquid in an airtight container for up to 5 days in the refrigerator or for up to 3 weeks in the freezer.

Wine-Braised Seitan and Cremini Mushrooms

In this recipe, bite-size pieces of seitan and vegetables are braised in a fragrant red wine sauce redolent of thyme. The browning liquid deepens the color of the sauce to a rich brown. Serve this braise over freshly cooked noodles or rice or, if you prefer, add 1-inch chunks of potatoes to the cooker when you add the carrots and mushrooms. For soy-free, omit the soy sauce and use a soy-free sauce (purchased or homemade, page 35) or add some soy-free vegetable broth base or additional salt.

SEITAN:

1¾ cups vital wheat gluten

¼ cup tapioca starch

1 tablespoon nutritional yeast

½ teaspoon garlic powder

½ teaspoon onion powder

¼ teaspoon salt

¼ teaspoon freshly ground black pepper

1 tablespoon soy sauce

1 tablespoon olive oil

1 cup water

2 teaspoons olive oil (optional)

4 to 6 shallots, quartered

2 garlic cloves, minced

⅔ cup dry red wine

2 tablespoons tomato paste

2 teaspoons minced fresh thyme or 1 teaspoon dried thyme

2 carrots, peeled and thinly sliced

8 ounces cremini mushrooms, quartered

3 tablespoons tapioca starch

1½ cups vegetable broth

Salt and freshly ground black pepper

1 teaspoon vegan gravy browner (such as Kitchen Bouquet)

SERVES 4

SLOW COOKER SIZE:
4- TO 6-QUART

COOK TIME:
6 TO 8 HOURS ON LOW

SOY-FREE OPTION

1. For the seitan: In a large bowl, combine the vital wheat gluten, ¼ cup of the tapioca starch, nutritional yeast, garlic and onion powders, ¼ teaspoon salt, and ¼ teaspoon pepper. Stir in the soy sauce, 1 tablespoon of the oil, and the water to make a stiff dough. Use your hands to knead for about 3 minutes, then pat the dough out flat on a work surface and cut it into ½-inch dice. Set aside.

2. For the best flavor, heat oil in a small skillet over medium-high heat. Add the shallots and sauté until softened, about 3 minutes, then add the garlic and cook for 1 minute longer. Stir in the wine, tomato paste, and thyme and cook for 30 seconds longer. Alternatively, omit the oil and sauté these ingredients in a few tablespoons of water or combine them in a microwave-safe bowl with a little water, cover, and microwave for 2 minutes.

3. Transfer the shallot mixture to the slow cooker. Add the carrots and mushrooms and sprinkle with the tapioca starch. Pour in the broth and season to taste with salt and pepper. Add the cubes of seitan dough, nestling them among the vegetables and submerging them as much as possible. Try not to let the seitan cubes touch each other, if possible. Cover and cook on Low for 6 to 8 hours.

4. Gently stir in the browning liquid, then taste and adjust the seasonings, if needed. Serve hot.

    NOTE: If a thicker sauce is desired, remove the solids from the cooker, turn the heat up to High, and add 1 teaspoon of *beurre manié* (page 28), stirring to thicken.

Pasta with Sunday Gravy

Don't let the word *gravy* scare you off—it's just what many Italian-American families call tomato sauce. As in many Italian families, pasta with "Sunday gravy" was a fixture in my home when I was growing up. My mother would put on a big pot of rich sauce early in the morning and let it simmer slowly until dinnertime. The slow cooker is an ideal way to cook this sauce, which makes more than enough for one meal. Just use what you need and allow the remaining sauce to cool. Then portion it into airtight containers and store for future use—it will keep for several days in the refrigerator or for several weeks in the freezer. If you like, add cooked vegan meatballs, sausage, or burger crumbles to the sauce about 30 minutes before serving. Be sure to choose a gluten-free pasta to make this gluten-free.

2 teaspoons olive oil (optional)
1 small yellow onion, minced
5 garlic cloves, minced
2 teaspoons dried oregano
2 teaspoons dried basil
¼ to ½ teaspoon red pepper flakes (optional)
1 (6-ounce) can tomato paste
½ cup dry red wine
2 (28-ounce) cans crushed tomatoes
1 teaspoon natural sugar
1 teaspoon salt
¼ teaspoon freshly ground black pepper
1 pound pasta of your choice

SERVES 4 TO 6
(WITH LEFTOVERS)

SLOW COOKER SIZE:
4-QUART

COOK TIME:
6 HOURS ON LOW

GLUTEN-FREE OPTION

SOY-FREE

1. For the best flavor, heat the oil in a medium-size skillet over medium-high heat. Add the onion and sauté until softened, about 5 minutes. Add the garlic, oregano, basil, red pepper flakes (if using), and tomato paste and cook for 1 minute longer. Alternatively, omit the oil and sauté these ingredients in a few tablespoons of water or combine them in a microwave-safe bowl with a little water, cover, and microwave for 2 minutes.

2. Transfer the onion mixture to the slow cooker. Stir in the wine, tomatoes, sugar, salt, and pepper. Cover and cook on Low for 6 hours.

3. Close to serving time, cook the pasta according to the package directions. Drain well and transfer to a serving bowl or individual shallow pasta bowls or plates. Top with the sauce. Serve hot.

Topless Shepherd's Pie

Shepherd's pie is known for its topping of mashed potatoes, but try as I might I couldn't figure out how to both cook the shepherd's pie in the slow cooker and also mash the potatoes in it. So this recipe keeps it "topless" and lets the bottom layer of sliced potatoes stand in for the mashers. If you're a stickler for tradition, then simply make the mashed on the stovetop and spread them on top of the shepherd's pie for the last 30 minutes of cooking. For gluten-free, use a gluten-free flour blend. For soy-free, omit the soy sauce and use a soy-free sauce (purchased or homemade, page 35) or add some soy-free vegetable broth base or additional salt.

SERVES 6

SLOW COOKER SIZE:
6- TO 7-QUART

COOK TIME:
6 TO 8 HOURS ON LOW

GLUTEN-FREE OPTION

SOY-FREE OPTION

2 teaspoons olive oil
1 medium-size yellow onion, minced
2 garlic cloves, minced
1 teaspoon dried thyme
2 tablespoons all-purpose flour
1½ cups vegetable broth
2 russet potatoes, peeled and thinly sliced
Salt and freshly ground black pepper
2 carrots, peeled and finely chopped
8 ounces mushrooms, coarsely chopped
½ cup dried brown lentils, rinsed and picked over
⅔ cup thawed frozen baby lima beans
1 (14.5-ounce) can diced tomatoes, drained
½ cup thawed frozen peas
1 tablespoon soy sauce
½ teaspoon vegan gravy browner (such as Kitchen Bouquet)
1 tablespoon minced fresh flat-leaf parsley, for garnish

1. Heat the oil in a medium-size skillet over medium-high heat. Add the onion and sauté until softened, about 5 minutes. Stir in the garlic, thyme, and flour and cook for 1 minute longer. Stir in ½ cup of the broth and cook, stirring, for 1 minute. Remove from the heat and set aside.

2. Generously oil the bottom and sides of the slow cooker insert or spray it with nonstick cooking spray. Arrange the potato slices evenly in layers in the bottom of the cooker, seasoning each layer with salt and pepper. Top with the carrots, mushrooms, lentils, limas, tomatoes, peas, soy sauce, gravy browner, and the reserved onion mixture. Add the remaining 1 cup broth, cover, and cook on Low for 6 to 8 hours. Sprinkle with the parsley and serve hot.

Pasta and Beans with Three Herbs

Variations on the classic Italian pasta and bean dish *pasta e fagioli* are legion. Some versions are more soup-like than others, with a thin tomato broth, while others are heartier and less saucy—more like a pasta dish, which is how my mother always made it. This version is thick with vegetables and a rich sauce and seasoned with rosemary, basil, and sage. Use a gluten-free pasta to make this gluten-free.

2 teaspoons olive oil (optional)

1 large yellow onion, chopped

3 garlic cloves, minced

1 teaspoon dried basil

1 teaspoon dried rosemary

1 teaspoon dried crumbled sage

¼ teaspoon red pepper flakes

2 tablespoons tomato paste

2½ cups vegetable broth

2 large carrots, peeled and chopped

2 celery ribs, chopped

1 Yukon Gold potato, peeled and cut into ½-inch dice

1 (28-ounce) can diced tomatoes, with their juices

3 cups cooked cannellini or borlotti beans (page 104) or 2 (15-ounce) cans beans, rinsed and drained

Salt and freshly ground black pepper

8 ounces ditalini, tubetti, or other tiny pasta

1 tablespoon chopped fresh basil

SERVES 4

SLOW COOKER SIZE:
5- TO 6-QUART

COOK TIME:
4 TO 6 HOURS ON LOW
PLUS 30 MINUTES
ON HIGH

GLUTEN-FREE OPTION

SOY-FREE

1. For the best flavor, heat the oil in a medium-size skillet over medium-high heat. Add the onion and sauté until softened, about 5 minutes. Add the garlic, dried basil, rosemary, sage, and red pepper flakes, then stir in the tomato paste and cook for 1 minute longer. Stir in ½ cup of the broth. Alternatively, omit the oil and sauté these ingredients in a few tablespoons of water or combine them in a microwave-safe bowl with a little water, cover, and microwave for 2 minutes.

2. Transfer the onion mixture to the slow cooker. Add the carrots, celery, potato, tomatoes and their juices, beans, and remaining 2 cups broth. Season to taste with salt and pepper. Cover and cook on Low until the vegetables are tender, 4 to 6 hours.

3. Turn the heat to High, stir in the pasta, cover, and cook until the pasta is done, about 30 minutes. Alternatively, you can cook the pasta separately on the stovetop and add it to the slow cooker when ready to serve. Stir in the fresh basil and serve hot.

Ziti with Mushroom and Bell Pepper Ragu

Hard durum pasta (such as Barilla brand) works best in this recipe. If using a pasta other than a hard durum semolina, such as whole wheat or rice pasta, the pasta may become too soft when cooked directly in the slow cooker, so you may want to opt for stovetop cooking. In addition, this recipe needs to cook on High in order to properly cook the pasta. Alternatively, you may cook the sauce on Low for 6 to 8 hours, and then add stovetop-cooked pasta 20 minutes before serving. For gluten-free, use gluten-free pasta (and add it after the sauce has cooked); for soy-free, use a soy-free vegan Parmesan.

2 teaspoons olive oil (optional)

1 large yellow onion, minced

4 garlic cloves, minced

1 teaspoon dried basil or 1 tablespoon chopped fresh basil

2 teaspoons minced fresh oregano or 1 teaspoon dried oregano

2 tablespoons tomato paste

1 teaspoon natural sugar

½ cup dry red wine

1 large green or red bell pepper, seeded and minced

8 ounces white mushrooms, coarsely chopped

8 ounces uncooked ziti

1 (28-ounce) can plus 1 (14-ounce) can crushed tomatoes

1 cup hot water

Salt and freshly ground black pepper

2 tablespoons chopped fresh flat-leaf parsley

Vegan Parmesan cheese, for garnish (optional)

SERVES 4

SLOW COOKER SIZE:
4- TO 5-QUART

COOK TIME:
3 TO 4 HOURS ON HIGH

GLUTEN-FREE OPTION

SOY-FREE OPTION

1. For the best flavor, heat the oil in a large skillet over medium-high heat. Add the onion and sauté for 4 minutes. Add the garlic, dried basil (if using), oregano, tomato paste, and sugar. Stir in the wine and cook for 1 minute longer. Add the bell pepper and mushrooms and cook for 2 minutes longer. Alternatively, omit the oil and sauté these ingredients in a few tablespoons of water or combine them in a microwave-safe bowl with a little water, cover, and microwave for 2 minutes.

2. Transfer the onion mixture to the slow cooker. Add the ziti, tomatoes, hot water, and salt and pepper to taste. Stir to combine, making sure all of the pasta is submerged. Cover and cook on High until the pasta is tender, about 3 hours.

3. Stir in the fresh basil (if using) and the parsley. Serve hot, sprinkled with the vegan Parmesan, if desired.

Lasagna Primavera

Slow-cooked lasagna may sound unconventional, but it tastes great and is convenient to make. You will need to break the noodles to conform them to the shape of the slow cooker. For best results, use a large oval slow cooker. And be sure to use regular lasagna noodles in this recipe, not the no-boil kind. To make gluten-free, use gluten-free lasagna noodles.

SERVES 6

SLOW COOKER SIZE:
5- TO 6-QUART

COOK TIME:
4 HOURS ON LOW

GLUTEN-FREE OPTION

8 ounces uncooked lasagna noodles (about 8 noodles)
2 teaspoons olive oil (optional)
1 small yellow onion, minced
3 garlic cloves, minced
1 cup chopped broccoli florets or zucchini
1 medium-size carrot, shredded
8 ounces white mushrooms, chopped
1 (10-ounce) package frozen chopped spinach, thawed and squeezed dry
Salt and freshly ground black pepper
1 pound soft or medium tofu, drained
1 pound firm tofu, drained
⅓ cup nutritional yeast
¼ cup minced fresh flat-leaf parsley
2 teaspoons dried basil
1 teaspoon dried oregano
½ cup vegan Parmesan cheese, plus more for sprinkling
1 (24-ounce) jar marinara sauce or your favorite tomato sauce for pasta
1 cup shredded vegan mozzarella cheese (optional)

1. Break the noodles in half and place them in a large baking dish. Pour on enough boiling water to cover and set aside while you prepare the remaining ingredients.

2. For the best flavor, heat the oil in a large skillet over medium-high heat. Add the onion and sauté until softened, about 5 minutes. Add the garlic, broccoli, carrot, and mushrooms and cook for 1 minute longer. Alternatively, omit the oil and sauté these ingredients in a few tablespoons of water or combine

them in a microwave-safe bowl with a little water, cover, and microwave for 2 minutes. Drain off any excess liquid. Stir in the spinach and season to taste with salt and pepper. Set aside.

3. Crumble all of the tofu into a large bowl. Add the nutritional yeast, parsley, basil, oregano, vegan Parmesan, and salt and pepper to taste. Mix well, then taste to make sure the mixture has enough salt and plenty of pepper.

4. Lightly oil the insert of the slow cooker or spray it with nonstick cooking spray. Drain the noodles. Spread a thin layer of marinara sauce into the bottom of the slow cooker. Arrange a layer of the noodle pieces over the sauce, overlapping slightly as needed. Top the noodles with about one-third of the tofu mixture, followed by one-third of the vegetable mixture, and another layer of noodles. Spread a thin layer of marinara sauce over the noodles and sprinkle with vegan Parmesan. Repeat the layering two more times, ending with a layer of marinara sauce. Sprinkle with vegan Parmesan. Cover and cook on Low for 3½ hours.

5. Scatter the vegan mozzarella (if using) all over the top of the lasagna. Cover and cook for 30 minutes longer (whether or not you add the mozzarella).

6. Remove the lid, turn off the cooker, and let the lasagna stand for about 15 minutes before serving.

Mac and Cheesy

I like to add about 2 cups of chopped cooked kale, chard, or spinach before serving this comforting mac-and-cheese casserole. The greens provide a lovely color contrast and added nutrients and flavor. Other good additions would be steamed broccoli florets or asparagus or thawed frozen green peas, stirred in about 20 minutes before serving time.

SERVES 4

SLOW COOKER SIZE:
4-QUART

COOK TIME:
2 TO 2½ HOURS
ON HIGH

1 large russet potato, peeled and cut into ½-inch dice

1 large yellow onion, chopped

4 garlic cloves, minced

2 cups vegetable broth

1 cup unsalted raw cashews, soaked overnight and drained

¼ cup jarred pimientos or chopped roasted red bell pepper, well drained

2 tablespoons fresh lemon juice

1 tablespoon light miso paste

1 teaspoon yellow mustard

½ cup nutritional yeast

1 teaspoon onion powder

1 teaspoon salt

½ teaspoon ground turmeric

8 ounces uncooked elbow macaroni

Hot water or plain unsweetened nondairy milk, as needed

⅓ cup shredded vegan mozzarella cheese (optional)

⅓ cup toasted dry bread crumbs (optional)

1. In a large saucepan, combine the potato, onion, garlic, and broth and bring to a boil. Lower the heat to medium and cook until the potato is tender, about 10 minutes. Alternatively, combine these ingredients in a microwave-safe bowl, cover, and microwave until the potatoes are tender, about 5 minutes.

2. Grind the cashews to a paste in a blender or food processor. Add the cooked vegetables and broth, along with the pimientos, lemon juice, miso, mustard, nutritional yeast, onion powder, salt, and turmeric. Blend until smooth and creamy.

3. Generously oil the insert of the slow cooker or spray it with nonstick cooking spray. Scrape the sauce mixture into the slow cooker, then add the macaroni and stir to combine. Cover and cook on High for 2 hours.

4. Uncover and stir, adding hot water if the mixture is too thick and/or the pasta is not yet tender. Taste and adjust the seasonings, if needed. Stir in half of the vegan cheese, if using, then sprinkle the remaining cheese on top. Cover and cook up to 30 minutes longer if needed to melt the cheese.

5. Just before serving, sprinkle on the toasted bread crumbs, if using.

Chili Mac

This shortcut recipe can have chili mac cooking in no time. Instead of TVP or burger crumbles, you may substitute 8 ounces chopped, cooked tempeh or seitan or an additional 1½ cups of pinto beans. And be sure to use regular hard durum semolina pasta (such as Barilla brand). Other types of pasta (such as whole wheat or rice) may produce a too-soft pasta in the slow cooker. If you want to use one of those types, cook it separately on the stovetop and add it to the slow cooker shortly before serving time.

½ cup TVP granules reconstituted with ½ cup boiling water *or* 1 (12-ounce) package thawed frozen vegan burger crumbles

1 (24-ounce) jar tomato salsa of your choice

3 tablespoons chili powder

1 teaspoon ground cumin

3 cups cooked pinto or red kidney beans (page 104) or 2 (15-ounce) cans beans, rinsed and drained

1 (8-ounce) can tomato sauce

8 ounces uncooked elbow macaroni

1¾ cups hot water, plus more if needed

1 teaspoon salt

½ teaspoon freshly ground black pepper

1½ cups shredded vegan chedar cheese or Creamy Cheesy Sauce (page 123)

SERVES 6

SLOW COOKER SIZE:
5- TO 6-QUART

COOK TIME:
2 HOURS ON HIGH

1. Lightly oil the insert of the slow cooker or spray it with nonstick cooking spray. In the slow cooker, combine the TVP with the salsa, chili powder, cumin, beans, tomato sauce, macaroni, hot water, salt, and pepper. Stir to combine. Stir in half of the cheese, then sprinkle the top with the remaining cheese. Cover and cook on High for 1 hour and 45 minutes.

2. Uncover and check to see whether the pasta is tender. If the mixture is too dry, stir in a little hot water. Taste and adjust the seasonings, if necessary. If the pasta is undercooked, cover and cook about 15 minutes longer; otherwise serve immediately.

Mom-Style Vegan Meatloaf

An old-fashioned comfort food favorite made vegan—and in a slow cooker. This delicious loaf "bakes" in the slow cooker, right along with carrots and potatoes. Add a cooked green vegetable and dinner is served. The flavorful glaze makes a sauce unnecessary, but you can serve it with one if you like—or just pass the ketchup!

SERVES 4 TO 6

SLOW COOKER SIZE:
5- TO 7-QUART

COOK TIME:
4 HOURS ON LOW

2 teaspoons olive oil (optional), plus more for drizzling

1 small yellow onion, minced

2 garlic cloves, minced

1 tablespoon dried thyme

1½ cups cooked pinto beans (page 104) or 1 (15-ounce) can beans, rinsed and drained

12 ounces extra-firm tofu, drained, squeezed, and crumbled

¾ cup ketchup

2 tablespoons vegan Worcestershire sauce or soy sauce

1 tablespoon Dijon mustard

½ cup ground walnuts

½ cup old-fashioned rolled oats

¼ cup dried bread crumbs

½ cup vital wheat gluten

2 tablespoons tapioca starch

2 tablespoons minced fresh flat-leaf parsley

Salt and freshly ground black pepper

2 large carrots, peeled and cut into ¼-inch slices

2 or 3 Yukon Gold potatoes, peeled and cut into ½-inch slices

2 or 3 shallots, quartered lengthwise

2 tablespoons yellow or brown mustard

1 tablespoon light brown sugar

1 tablespoon cider vinegar

1. For the best flavor, heat the 2 teaspoons oil in a small skillet over medium-high heat. Add the onion and sauté until softened, about 5 minutes. Add the garlic and thyme and cook 1 minute longer. Alternatively, omit the oil and sauté these ingredients in a few tablespoons of water or combine them in a microwave-safe bowl with a little water, cover, and microwave for 2 minutes. Set aside.

2. In a food processor, combine the beans, tofu, ½ cup of the ketchup, Worcestershire, mustard, and reserved onion mixture and process to mix well. In a large bowl, combine the walnuts, oats, bread crumbs, vital wheat gluten, tapioca starch, and parsley. Season with 1 teaspoon salt and ¼ teaspoon pepper. Add the bean mixture and stir well to mix thoroughly. Turn out the mixture onto a work surface and shape into a round or oval to fit inside your slow cooker, pressing to make sure the loaf holds together.

3. Generously oil the insert of the slow cooker or spray it with nonstick cooking spray. Arrange the carrot slices evenly in the bottom of the cooker. Season with a little salt and pepper, then arrange the potato slices on top of the carrots. Drizzle with a little olive oil. Set the reserved loaf on top of the potatoes and surround with the shallots.

4. In a small bowl, combine the remaining ¼ cup ketchup with the mustard, brown sugar, and vinegar and mix well. Spread the mixture on top of the loaf. Cover and cook on Low for 4 hours.

5. Remove the lid, turn off the cooker, and allow the loaf to rest for 10 minutes. Transfer the loaf carefully with a large spatula to a large serving platter and surround it with the carrots, potatoes, and shallots. Slice the loaf carefully with a serrated knife.

Chili-Potato Gratin

I first discovered how good chili and potatoes taste together years ago when I topped a baked potato with some chili. This gratin reunites those flavors by layering sliced potatoes and chili in a slow cooker for a tasty weeknight meal. The thinner you slice the potatoes, the more quickly they will become tender. To make the recipe gluten-free, omit the optional bread crumbs or use gluten-free crumbs. To make it soy-free, use about 1½ cups of finely chopped seitan or cooked lentils instead of TVP, and choose a soy-free vegan cheese (such as Daiya).

SERVES 4 TO 6

SLOW COOKER SIZE:
5- TO 7-QUART

COOK TIME:
4 TO 6 HOURS ON LOW

GLUTEN-FREE OPTION

SOY-FREE OPTION

2 teaspoons olive oil (optional)
1 small yellow onion, minced
3 garlic cloves, minced
3 tablespoons tomato paste
¼ cup vegetable broth or water
1 to 2 tablespoons chili powder
1 teaspoon dried oregano
½ teaspoon ground cumin
½ teaspoon smoked paprika
¼ teaspoon cayenne pepper
1 (14.5-ounce) can petite diced tomatoes, drained and juices reserved
1 cup TVP granules reconstituted with 1 cup boiling water
2 or 3 large russet potatoes, peeled and sliced about ⅛ inch thick
Salt and freshly ground black pepper
1 cup shredded vegan mozzarella cheese or Creamy Cheesy Sauce (page 123)
¼ cup toasted panko or other dried bread crumbs (optional)

1. For the best flavor, heat the oil in a medium-size skillet over medium-high heat. Add the onion and sauté until softened, about 5 minutes. Add the garlic and cook for 1 minute longer, then stir in the tomato paste, broth, chili powder, oregano, cumin, paprika, and cayenne. Stir in the juice from the tomatoes so the mixture doesn't burn. Alternatively, omit the oil and sauté these ingredients in a few tablespoons of water or combine them in a microwave-safe bowl with a little water, cover, and microwave for 2 minutes. Stir in the tomatoes and reconstituted TVP.

2. Lightly oil the insert of the slow cooker or spray it with nonstick cooking spray. Spoon a thin layer of the chili mixture in the bottom of the cooker. Arrange a layer of potato slices on top, overlapping slightly. Season to taste with salt and pepper, then top with a thin layer of the chili mixture, followed by a sprinkling of the vegan cheese, another layer of potatoes, salt and pepper, and so on, until all of the potatoes, chili, and cheese are used up, ending with a final sprinkling of cheese on top. Cover and cook on Low until the potatoes are tender, 4 to 6 hours.

3. Remove the lid and let the gratin sit for 10 minutes before serving. Just before serving, sprinkle the panko on top, if using. Serve hot.

Jerk Tempeh with Sweet Potatoes and Onions

Tempeh stands up well to jerk seasonings, as the flavorful sauce mingles nicely with the tempeh chunks as it all cooks. Sweet potatoes and onions provide complementary flavors. To save time, you can use a bottled jerk sauce instead of making your own.

JERK SAUCE:

½ large or 1 small Vidalia or other sweet onion, cut into ½-inch dice

2 scallions, coarsely chopped

1 hot green chile, seeded and coarsely chopped

1 garlic clove, crushed

1 tablespoon grated fresh ginger

2 tablespoons lime or orange marmalade

1 tablespoon rice vinegar

2 teaspoons soy sauce

1 teaspoon dark brown sugar or natural sugar

1 teaspoon dried thyme

½ teaspoon ground allspice

SERVES 4 TO 6

SLOW COOKER SIZE:
5- TO 7-QUART

COOK TIME:
4 TO 6 HOURS ON LOW

GLUTEN-FREE

¼ teaspoon ground cinnamon

¼ teaspoon paprika

¼ teaspoon cayenne pepper

½ teaspoon salt

¼ teaspoon freshly ground black pepper

⅓ cup water

1 pound tempeh, steamed (if desired) and cut into 1-inch dice

2 large sweet potatoes, peeled and cut into 1-inch dice

½ large or 1 small Vidalia or other sweet onion, cut into ½-inch dice

1. For the jerk sauce: In a food processor, combine the onion, scallions, chile, garlic, and ginger and process until finely minced. Add the marmalade, vinegar, soy sauce, brown sugar, thyme, allspice, cinnamon, paprika, cayenne, salt, and pepper. Process to a paste. Add the water and process until well blended.

2. Lightly oil the insert of the slow cooker or spray it with nonstick cooking spray. Combine the tempeh, sweet potatoes, and onion in the cooker. Add the jerk mixture and stir to coat. Cover and cook on Low until the potatoes and onions are tender, 4 to 6 hours. Serve hot.

Layered Tamale Pie

This great weeknight meal is loaded with flavor and is also quick and easy to assemble ahead of time. For extra flavor, lightly toast the tortillas before using. Depending on your preference and the shape of your slow cooker, use 1 or 2 tortillas for each layer. For gluten-free, use tempeh or extra pinto beans instead of seitan. For soy-free, use seitan instead of tempeh, and use a soy-free vegan cheese (such as Daiya) and a soy-free vegan sour cream.

2 teaspoons olive oil (optional)

1 medium-size yellow onion, minced

4 garlic cloves, minced

2 canned chipotle chiles in adobo, minced

1 tablespoon tomato paste

1 tablespoon grated unsweetened dark chocolate

2 tablespoons chili powder

1 teaspoon ground cumin

1 teaspoon smoked paprika

1 teaspoon dried oregano

1 teaspoon dark brown sugar

½ teaspoon salt

¼ teaspoon freshly ground black pepper

1 (14.5-ounce) can crushed tomatoes

1½ cups cooked pinto beans (page 104) or 1 (15-ounce) can beans, rinsed and drained

1 (15-ounce) can vegan refried beans, stirred

8 ounces steamed diced tempeh, chopped seitan (purchased or homemade, page 136), or crumbled vegan chorizo

1½ cups fresh or thawed frozen corn kernels

6 to 12 soft corn tortillas

1½ cups shredded vegan cheddar cheese or Creamy Cheesy Sauce (page 123)

Vegan sour cream, purchased or homemade (page 57; optional)

Salsa (optional)

SERVES 6

SLOW COOKER SIZE:
5- TO 7-QUART

COOK TIME:
4 HOURS ON LOW

GLUTEN-FREE OPTION

SOY-FREE OPTION

1. For the best flavor, heat the oil in a large skillet over medium-high heat. Add the onion and sauté until softened, about 5 minutes. Add the garlic and cook for 1 minute longer, then stir in the chipotle chiles, tomato paste, chocolate, chili powder, cumin, paprika, oregano, brown sugar, salt, and pepper. Sprinkle with a little water so the mixture doesn't burn. Alternatively, omit the oil and sauté these ingredients in a few tablespoons of water or combine them in a microwave-safe bowl with a little water, cover, and microwave for 2 minutes. Stir in the tomatoes and set aside.

2. In a separate bowl, combine the pinto beans, refried beans, tempeh, and corn. Season to taste with salt and pepper. Add ½ cup of the sauce mixture, and mix well.

3. Generously oil the insert of the slow cooker or spray it with nonstick cooking spray. Spoon a thin layer of the sauce in the bottom of the cooker, then place 1 or 2 tortillas on top. Top with a thin layer of the bean mixture, followed by another tortilla, more sauce, and a sprinkling of vegan cheese. Repeat the layering until all of the ingredients are used, ending with the sauce topped with a little cheese. Cover and cook on Low for 4 hours. Serve hot, topped with sour cream and salsa, if desired.

Pasta and Vegetable Frittata

This frittata makes a satisfying one-dish meal and doesn't take too long to cook. It works best when made in a wide, shallow slow cooker. Depending on how shallow your slow cooker is, it can be a little tricky to remove the first wedge of the frittata, but after that, they should come out easily. Feel free to change up the type of vegetables used in this—cooked chopped asparagus, broccoli, and spinach are all good choices. Use gluten-free pasta for a gluten-free version of the recipe.

SERVES 4 OR 5

SLOW COOKER SIZE:
5-QUART

COOK TIME:
2 TO 3 HOURS ON LOW

GLUTEN-FREE OPTION

1 pound firm tofu, well drained
1 cup vegetable broth
3 tablespoons nutritional yeast
1 tablespoon cornstarch
½ teaspoon onion powder
¼ teaspoon ground turmeric
Salt and freshly ground black pepper
1 jarred roasted red bell pepper, chopped
2 teaspoons olive oil (optional)
4 scallions, minced
1 cup chopped white mushrooms
½ teaspoon dried basil
3 cups cooked spaghetti or other pasta
¾ cup thawed frozen peas
½ cup shredded vegan cheese of your choice (optional)

1. In a food processor or blender, combine the tofu, broth, nutritional yeast, cornstarch, onion powder, turmeric, and salt and pepper to taste. Add 1 tablespoon of the chopped roasted bell pepper and process until smooth and well blended. Set aside.

2. For the best flavor, heat the oil in a medium-size skillet over medium-high heat. Add the scallions, mushrooms, basil, and salt and pepper to taste and cook for 3 to 4 minutes. Alternatively, omit the oil and sauté these ingredients in a few tablespoons of water or combine them in a microwave-safe bowl with a little water, cover, and microwave for 2 minutes. Drain off any liquid exuded from the mushrooms.

3. Generously oil the insert of the slow cooker or spray it with nonstick cooking spray. Spread the cooked vegetables evenly in the bottom of the cooker. Add the spaghetti, peas, and remaining chopped roasted bell pepper. Add the reserved tofu mixture, stirring to combine all of the ingredients, then spread the mixture evenly. Sprinkle the cheese on top, if using. Cover and cook on Low until the frittata is firm, 2 to 3 hours.

4. Cut into wedges and serve hot.

Sunday Supper Strata

A ham strata is a casserole made with layers of bread and other ingredients, including a custard that is traditionally made with eggs and dairy. This version uses tofu and vegan mozzarella and lots of flavorful vegetables. Stratas are especially popular for brunch, but I like to serve mine for Sunday supper. You can dry the bread cubes for this recipe either by leaving them spread out on baking sheets all day or overnight or by placing them in a very low oven (about 225°F) for about 30 minutes. To make this gluten-free, use a gluten-free bread.

SERVES 4

SLOW COOKER SIZE:
4- TO 6-QUART

COOK TIME:
4 HOURS ON LOW

GLUTEN-FREE OPTION

2 cups crumbled firm tofu

1 cup vegetable broth

2 tablespoons nutritional yeast

½ teaspoon onion powder

½ teaspoon dried basil

¼ teaspoon ground turmeric

Salt and freshly ground black pepper

3 plum tomatoes, chopped, or 1 (14-ounce) can diced tomatoes, drained

½ cup chopped jarred roasted red bell pepper

½ cup chopped fresh basil

2 teaspoons olive oil (optional)

1 large yellow onion, minced

3 garlic cloves, minced

8 ounces cremini mushrooms, chopped

2 medium-size zucchini, thinly sliced

½ cup shredded vegan mozzarella cheese (optional)

8 ounces Italian bread, cut into ½-inch dice and dried (see headnote), 8 to 10 cups

1. In a food processor or blender, combine the tofu, broth, nutritional yeast, onion powder, dried basil, turmeric, and salt and pepper to taste and process until smooth and well blended. Set aside. In a bowl, combine the tomatoes, roasted bell pepper, and fresh basil, stirring to mix. Set aside.

2. For the best flavor, heat the oil in a large skillet over medium-high heat. Add the onion and sauté until softened, about 5 minutes. Add the garlic, mushrooms, and zucchini and cook for 2 minutes longer. Alternatively, omit the oil and sauté these ingredients in a few tablespoons of water or combine them in a microwave-safe bowl with a little water, cover, and microwave for 2 minutes.

3. Lightly oil the insert of the slow cooker or spray it with nonstick cooking spray. Spread half of the dried bread in the bottom of the slow cooker. Top with half of the tomato mixture, followed by half of the mushroom-zucchini mixture, then sprinkle on half of the vegan cheese, if using, the remaining bread, the remaining tomato mixture, and the remaining mushroom-zucchini mixture. Scrape the tofu mixture evenly over the top of the strata, pressing down on the bread with the back of a large spoon to moisten all the bread. Sprinkle the remaining vegan cheese on top, if using. Cover and cook on Low until the strata is firm, about 4 hours. Serve hot.

Slow-Cooked Vegan Sausage Links

Homemade vegan sausage links are delicious, economical, and a cinch to make at home in the slow cooker. For spicier sausage, add up to 1 teaspoon red pepper flakes. Instead of the reconstituted TVP, you may substitute ⅔ cup cooked (or canned) and mashed dark red kidney beans. Use these sausage links in any of the recipes calling for vegan sausage, such as the Red Bean Gumbo (page 49) or the Crockery Cassoulet (page 111). They're also great sautéed with sliced onion and bell pepper and served in a roll, or sliced and added to your favorite pasta dish.

1 cup vital wheat gluten
¼ cup nutritional yeast
¼ cup tapioca flour or chickpea flour
2 teaspoons paprika
1 teaspoon ground fennel seeds
½ teaspoon garlic powder
½ teaspoon onion powder
¼ teaspoon cayenne pepper
½ teaspoon salt
¼ teaspoon freshly ground black pepper
⅓ cup TVP granules reconstituted with ⅓ cup boiling water
2 tablespoons soy sauce
1 tablespoon olive oil
1 tablespoon ketchup
½ teaspoon liquid smoke
½ cup water, as needed

MAKES 6 LINKS

SLOW COOKER SIZE:
5- TO 7-QUART

COOK TIME:
4 HOURS ON LOW

1. In a food processor, combine the vital wheat gluten, nutritional yeast, tapioca flour, paprika, fennel, garlic and onion powders, cayenne, salt, and pepper. Pulse to mix. Add the reconstituted TVP, soy sauce, oil, ketchup, liquid smoke, and ¼ cup of the water and process until well mixed. If the mixture is too dry, add more of the water, a little at a time, until you have a medium-soft (but not wet) dough.

2. Turn out the dough onto a work surface and knead for 3 minutes, then divide the dough into 6 equal pieces. Roll and shape each piece into a link. Wrap each link separately in aluminum foil, twisting the ends to seal.

3. Place a rack, trivet, or a ring of crumpled aluminum foil in the bottom of the slow cooker insert and set a small heatproof plate on top for the links to rest on. Place the foil-wrapped links on the plate and pour in enough hot water to come up to the bottom of the plate. Cover and cook on Low for 4 hours.

4. Remove the links from the cooker, unwrap, and set aside to cool, then refrigerate them, loosely covered, for 1 to 2 hours to allow them to firm up before using. The sausage links may then be sautéed in a little oil until browned.

Spicy-Sweet Seitan Ribs

You can make a batch of these ribs up to 3 days in advance of when you want to serve them and refrigerate until needed. Then place them on the grill to reheat and give them some nice grill marks, brushing them with the barbecue sauce as they cook. I like to serve these with coleslaw and corn on the cob for a delicious (if messy) meal, or for the epitome of comfort food, serve them with the Scalloped Potatoes on page 216 and sautéed greens. For soy-free, omit the soy sauce and Worcestershire sauce and use a soy-free sauce (purchased or homemade, page 35) or add some soy-free vegetable broth base or additional salt.

1 chipotle chile in adobo

1 tablespoon soy sauce

1 tablespoon vegan Worcestershire sauce

1 tablespoon olive oil

1 teaspoon liquid smoke

2 cups Better Barbecue Sauce (page 239) or purchased barbecue sauce

1 cup water

2 tablespoons nutritional yeast

2 teaspoons onion powder

1½ teaspoons garlic powder

1 teaspoon smoked paprika

½ teaspoon salt

2 cups vital wheat gluten

½ cup chickpea flour

SERVES 4

SLOW COOKER SIZE:
5- TO 7-QUART

COOK TIME:
4 HOURS ON LOW

SOY-FREE OPTION

1. In a food processor, combine the chipotle chile, soy sauce, Worcestershire sauce, olive oil, liquid smoke, ¼ cup of the barbecue sauce, and the water and process until smooth. Add the nutritional yeast, onion and garlic powders, paprika, and salt and process to blend. Add the vital wheat gluten and chickpea flour and process until a well-mixed dough forms.

2. Lightly oil a 7 x 9-inch shallow baking dish. Turn out the dough onto a work surface and use your hands to flatten it into a 6 x 9-inch rectangle. Cut the seitan crosswise into 1-inch-thick slices. Spread ½ cup of the barbecue sauce in the bottom of the baking dish and arrange the seitan strips in a single row on top of the sauce (they will fit snugly next to each other and the sides will touch). Pour 1 cup of the barbecue sauce over the seitan. Cover the baking dish tightly with aluminum foil and place inside a large slow cooker. Carefully pour about ½ inch of hot water into the slow cooker. Cover and cook on Low for 4 to 6 hours, or until firm.

3. Remove the baking dish from the slow cooker, then transfer the seitan to a work surface and re-cut the ribs. Brush with the remaining ¼ cup barbecue sauce and serve hot.

Moroccan Tempeh and Chickpeas with Prunes and Apricots

The flavors of Morocco are a good match for the assertiveness of tempeh. I like to serve this with freshly cooked couscous or rice and steamed broccoli. The optional almond butter adds richness and depth to this dish, but it's also delicious without it. To make this soy-free, omit the tempeh entirely or substitute seitan (but remember that then it won't be gluten-free).

SERVES 4

SLOW COOKER SIZE:
5- TO 7-QUART

COOK TIME:
6 HOURS ON LOW

GLUTEN-FREE

SOY-FREE OPTION

2 teaspoons olive oil

1 large yellow onion, minced

3 garlic cloves, minced

1 tablespoon tomato paste

1 tablespoon almond butter (optional)

1½ teaspoons ground coriander

½ teaspoon ground cumin

¼ teaspoon paprika

¼ teaspoon ground cinnamon

¼ teaspoon cayenne pepper

1½ cups vegetable broth

3 cups cooked chickpeas (page 104) or 2 (15-ounce) cans chickpeas, rinsed and drained

8 ounces tempeh, steamed (if desired) and cut into 1-inch dice

1 (14.5-ounce) can diced tomatoes, drained

⅓ cup dried apricots, chopped

Salt and freshly ground black pepper

⅓ cup prunes, halved and pitted

1 cup thawed frozen green peas

2 tablespoons chopped fresh cilantro

1 tablespoon fresh lemon juice

1. Heat the oil in a large skillet over medium-high heat. Add the onion and sauté for 5 minutes. Stir in the garlic, tomato paste, and almond butter, if using. Add the coriander, cumin, paprika, cinnamon, and cayenne and cook,

stirring, for 1 minute. Stir in ½ cup of the broth, then transfer the mixture to the slow cooker. Add the chickpeas, tempeh, tomatoes, apricots, and the remaining 1 cup broth. Season to taste with salt and pepper. Cover and cook on Low for 6 hours.

2. Stir in the prunes, peas, cilantro, and lemon juice. Taste and adjust the seasonings, if needed. Serve hot.

Ethiopian-Style Tempeh and Lentils

Although it would be traditionally served with *injera*, a spongy crepe-like flatbread made with teff, this stew is also delicious served over couscous or rice. If you have berbere spice blend on hand, use 1 to 2 tablespoons in place of the spices listed in the recipe. To make this soy-free, substitute seitan for the tempeh (but remember that then it won't be gluten-free).

2 teaspoons olive oil (optional)
1 medium-size yellow onion, minced
2 garlic cloves, minced
2 tablespoons tomato paste
1 teaspoon ground cumin
1 teaspoon ground coriander
1 teaspoon ground fenugreek
1 teaspoon sweet paprika
½ teaspoon cayenne pepper
¼ teaspoon ground cardamom or allspice
¼ teaspoon ground ginger or nutmeg
1 (28-ounce) can crushed tomatoes
8 ounces tempeh, steamed (if desired) and cut into ½-inch dice
1 cup dried red lentils
3 cups vegetable broth
Salt and freshly ground black pepper

SERVES 4 TO 6

SLOW COOKER SIZE:
5- TO 7-QUART

COOK TIME:
6 TO 8 HOURS ON LOW

GLUTEN-FREE

SOY-FREE OPTION

1. For the best flavor, heat the oil in a medium-size skillet over medium-high heat. Add the onion and sauté until softened, about 5 minutes. Add the garlic and cook for 1 minute longer, then stir in the tomato paste and all of the spices. Alternatively, omit the oil and sauté these ingredients in a few tablespoons of water or combine them in a microwave-safe bowl with a little water, cover, and microwave for 2 minutes.

2. Transfer the onion mixture to the slow cooker. Stir in the tomatoes, then add the tempeh and lentils. Add the broth and season to taste with salt and pepper. Cook on low until the lentils and vegetables are soft, 6 to 8 hours.

3. Taste and adjust the seasonings, if needed. Serve hot.

Puttanesca Pizza

This will make a thick and chewy pizza similar to a deep-dish personal pan pizza you'd get in a restaurant. It will serve 2 as a main dish or 4 as a side dish. Why make pizza in a slow cooker? you might ask. See page 164 for 10 great reasons provided by my blog readers when I posed the question to them. For soy-free, omit the optional cheese or use a soy-free cheese (such as Daiya).

MAKES 1 PIZZA

SLOW COOKER SIZE:
5- TO 7-QUART

COOK TIME:
1 HOUR AND
45 MINUTES ON HIGH

SOY-FREE OPTION

DOUGH:
1½ cups unbleached all-purpose flour
1½ teaspoons instant yeast
½ teaspoon salt
½ teaspoon Italian seasoning
1 tablespoon olive oil
½ cup warm water, or as needed

SAUCE:
½ cup crushed tomatoes
¼ cup pitted kalamata olives, sliced
¼ cup pitted green olives, sliced

1 tablespoon capers, rinsed and drained

1 tablespoon chopped fresh flat-leaf parsley

¼ teaspoon dried basil

¼ teaspoon dried oregano

¼ teaspoon garlic powder

¼ teaspoon sugar

¼ teaspoon hot red pepper flakes

Salt and freshly ground black pepper

½ cup shredded vegan mozzarella cheese (optional)

1. For the dough: Lightly oil the inside of a large bowl. In a food processor, combine the flour, yeast, salt, and Italian seasoning. With the machine running, add the oil through the feed tube, then slowly add as much water as needed to form a slightly sticky dough ball. Transfer the dough to a floured surface and knead for 1 to 2 minutes, until it is smooth and elastic. Shape the dough into a ball and transfer to the prepared bowl, turning the dough to coat it with oil. Cover the bowl with plastic wrap and set aside to rise at warm room temperature until doubled in size, about 1 hour.

2. While the dough is rising, make the sauce. In a bowl, combine the tomatoes, both kinds of olives, capers, parsley, basil, oregano, garlic powder, sugar, red pepper flakes, and salt and black pepper to taste.

3. Generously oil the insert of a large slow cooker or spray it with nonstick cooking spray. Punch down the dough and transfer it to a lightly floured surface. Flatten the dough, then shape it to just fit inside your slow cooker. Place the dough in the cooker and spread the sauce over the dough. To prevent condensation from dripping onto the pizza, drape a clean kitchen towel over the cooker, then put on the lid. Cook on High for 1 hour and 45 minutes. If using the vegan mozzarella, sprinkle it on the pizza after 1 hour and 15 minutes, then cook for 30 minutes longer to allow it to melt.

10 Great Reasons to Make Pizza in a Slow Cooker

Once I excitedly discovered that I could make pizza in a slow cooker, I realized that "because I can" might not be enough reason to include the recipe in this cookbook, so I put the question out to my blog readers. The overwhelming majority encouraged me to include the pizza recipe. Here is just a sampling of the many responses I received:

1. "I like that you can put the pizza in the slow cooker, then go shopping, or go outside and do gardening, or shovel snow. . . and then when you come back home, it's ready!"

2. "You don't have to worry if it's going to burn in the oven."

3. "I live in Phoenix, where it is often over 100° during the day. I try not to use the oven and am using my slow cookers as much as possible."

4. "If you don't have an oven, like some students, it's good to know you can still 'bake.'"

5. "I think slow-cooker pizza would be awesome. I could get it ready before I picked up my son, and we could rush around to activities and get homework done and then sit down to a leisurely dinner."

6. "I would make pizza in a slow cooker if I were taking it to a party and didn't know if the oven would be available, or if I were having a party and needed the oven for other dishes, if I were remodeling the kitchen, or if I just needed to start dinner early and then be able to leave it alone."

7. "This would be great for people whose ovens don't heat very evenly, like the small ovens they often have in apartments."

8. "We're always struggling to find things to eat quickly enough with our weird soccer practice time and getting the kids off to bed—I often resort to PB&J in the car and then some fruit when we get home. This would be a nice alternative!"

9. "It is much more green to use the slow cooker than to heat an oven—especially to a high heat and then only use about 12 minutes' worth."

10. "Some nights anything other than plonking leftovers in the microwave is too much, so a slow-cooker pizza could be just the thing for a nice unwind with a DVD after a hectic day. Everyone loves pizza."

Black Bean Chili and Sweet Potato Casserole

The combination of black beans and sweet potatoes is a favorite that tastes great in this easy weeknight meal. Instead of black beans, you could substitute 1½ cups of crumbled vegan chorizo or finely chopped seitan (but remember that then it won't be gluten-free). For soy-free, choose a soy-free vegan cheese, such as Daiya.

2 teaspoons olive oil (optional)
1 small yellow onion, minced
3 garlic cloves, minced
3 tablespoons tomato paste
3 tablespoons chili powder
1 teaspoon dried oregano
1 teaspoon ground cumin
½ teaspoon smoked paprika
1 (16-ounce) jar tomato salsa
3 cups cooked black beans (page 104) or 2 (15-ounce) cans beans, rinsed and drained
1½ pounds sweet potatoes, peeled and thinly sliced
Salt and freshly ground black pepper
1 cup shredded vegan cheddar cheese (such as Daiya) or Creamy Cheesy Sauce (page 123)
2 tablespoons minced scallions, for garnish

SERVES 4 TO 6

SLOW COOKER SIZE:
4- TO 5-QUART

COOK TIME:
4 HOURS ON LOW

GLUTEN-FREE

SOY-FREE OPTION

1. For the best flavor, heat the oil in a medium-size skillet over medium-high heat. Add the onion and sauté until softened, about 5 minutes. Add the garlic and cook for 1 minute longer, then stir in the tomato paste, chili powder, oregano, cumin, and paprika. Stir in a small amount of water, if needed, so the mixture doesn't burn. Alternatively, omit the oil and sauté these ingredients in a few tablespoons of water or combine them in a microwave-safe bowl with a little water, cover, and microwave for 2 minutes. Stir in the salsa and black beans, then taste and adjust the seasonings, if needed.

2. Generously oil the insert of the slow cooker or spray it with nonstick cooking spray. Spoon a thin layer of the chili mixture on the bottom of the cooker. Arrange a layer of sweet potato slices on top, overlapping slightly. Season to taste with salt and pepper, then top with a thin layer of the chili mixture, followed by a sprinkling of the vegan cheddar, more sweet potatoes, chili, vegan cheddar, salt and pepper, and so on, until all of the sweet potatoes and chili are used up, ending with the remaining vegan cheddar on top. Cover and cook on Low until the potatoes are tender, about 4 hours.

3. When ready to serve, sprinkle with the scallions. Serve hot.

Slow-Cooked Seitan Fajitas

Once the flavorful fajita filling is cooked, you can simply spoon it into tortillas and enjoy. Or, instead of using it in fajitas, try serving the filling over rice or quinoa for a tasty main dish. This recipe can be made soy-free by omitting the soy sauce and using a soy-free sauce (purchased or homemade, page 35) or adding some soy-free vegetable broth base or additional salt.

SERVES 4 TO 6

SLOW COOKER SIZE:
4- TO 5-QUART

COOK TIME:
6 HOURS ON LOW

SOY-FREE OPTION

SEITAN:
1½ cups vital wheat gluten
¼ cup chickpea flour
2 tablespoons nutritional yeast
½ teaspoon garlic powder
½ teaspoon onion powder
¼ teaspoon salt
¼ teaspoon freshly ground black pepper
2 tablespoons soy sauce
2 teaspoons olive oil (optional)
1 cup water, plus more if needed

2 tablespoons tomato paste
1½ cups tomato salsa
1 tablespoon chili powder
1 tablespoon soy sauce
2 large bell peppers (any color), seeded and cut into ¼-inch-thick strips
1 large yellow onion, thinly sliced
1 garlic clove, minced
Salt and freshly ground black pepper
2 tablespoons freshly squeezed lime juice
6 (7-inch) flour tortillas, warmed
1 ripe Hass avocado, peeled, pitted, and diced, for garnish
1 large ripe tomato, diced, for garnish

1. For the seitan: In a bowl, combine the vital wheat gluten, chickpea flour, nutritional yeast, garlic and onion powders, salt, and pepper. Stir in the soy sauce, oil, and as much water as needed to make a stiff dough. Use your hands to knead for about 3 minutes, then pat the dough out flat on a work surface and cut it into ¼ x 4-inch strips.

2. In a bowl, combine the tomato paste, salsa, chili powder, and soy sauce and stir to combine.

3. Combine the bell peppers, onion, and garlic in the slow cooker. Place the seitan strips on top of and in between the vegetables, arranging the seitan pieces so that they don't touch each other, if possible. Pour the salsa mixture on top of the seitan and vegetables. Season to taste with salt and pepper. Cover and cook on Low for 6 hours.

4. Stir in the lime juice, then taste and adjust the seasonings, if needed. To serve, spoon the mixture into warm tortillas, topped with avocado and tomato.

Simply Stuffed

Stuffed vegetables and slow cookers were made for each other. You can cook your stuffed summertime favorites like bell peppers, zucchini, and eggplant without heating up the kitchen with the oven. In the fall and winter, the slow cooker provides gentle heat to cook great stuffed winter squashes and stuffed cabbage rolls until tender and delicious, all without worrying about the burning or drying out that can happen in the oven.

A large oval slow cooker works best for the recipes in this chapter. If you have only a smaller cooker, then you may need to halve the recipe, or just make as much as will fit inside your cooker. In some cases, as with eggplant halves, you can even stack the stuffed vegetables on top of each other.

The slow cooker can also be used to cook just the stuffing, using the eponymous recipe in this chapter. There is also a recipe for a holiday-worthy stuffed and rolled seitan roast called Seitan Roulade.

Among the stuffed vegetables here are Stuffed Zucchini Puttanesca, Quinoa-Stuffed Bell Peppers, and Stuffed Collard Rolls. Best of all, you can mix and match the various stuffings with the vegetables of your choice. For example, you can use the red bean and bulgur stuffing to stuff bell peppers instead of eggplant.

Just the Stuffing

This is my go-to bread stuffing, based on my mom's recipe, but cooked in a slow cooker instead of a bird. In this recipe I use white Italian bread, just as my mother did, but you can use any type of bread you prefer, including gluten-free.

SERVES 6 TO 8

SLOW COOKER SIZE:
4- TO 5-QUART

COOK TIME:
3 TO 4 HOURS ON LOW

GLUTEN-FREE OPTION

SOY-FREE

2 teaspoons olive oil (optional)
1 large yellow onion, minced
2 celery ribs, minced
1½ teaspoons dried thyme
1 teaspoon dried marjoram
1 teaspoon ground sage
1 loaf Italian bread, cut into ½-inch dice (about 10 cups)
¼ cup minced fresh flat-leaf parsley
1 teaspoon salt
½ teaspoon freshly ground black pepper
1½ cups vegetable broth, or as needed

1. For the best flavor, heat the oil in a large skillet over medium-high heat. Add the onion and celery and sauté until softened, about 5 minutes. Stir in the thyme, marjoram, and sage. Alternatively, omit the oil and sauté these ingredients in a few tablespoons of water or combine them in a microwave-safe bowl with a little water, cover, and microwave for 2 minutes.

2. Generously oil the slow cooker insert or spray it with nonstick cooking spray. Add the bread cubes, onion mixture, parsley, salt, and pepper. Stir in enough of the broth to just moisten. Taste and adjust the seasonings, adding more salt depending on the saltiness of your broth, and extra herbs, if desired. Cover and cook on Low until firm, 3 to 4 hours. Serve hot.

VARIATIONS

Mushroom Stuffing: Add up to 8 ounces chopped mushrooms of your choice to the onion and celery mixture and cook for 1 minute before adding to the stuffing mixture.

Cranberry-Walnut Stuffing: Add up to 1 cup toasted chopped walnuts and ⅓ cup sweetened dried cranberries to the stuffing mixture.

Tips for Cooking Stuffing in a Slow Cooker

When stuffing is cooked for too long or at too high a temperature in a slow cooker, it can sometimes harden at the edges. You can avoid this by taking the following precautions:

- Generously oil the bottom and sides of the crock or spray it with nonstick cooking spray.
- Pack the stuffing loosely in the slow cooker.
- Cook on Low for no longer than 4 hours.
- Stir around the edges occasionally while cooking.
- Line the sides of your slow cooker with a lightly oiled "band" of aluminum foil.
- Place the stuffing in a covered casserole dish to cook inside the slow cooker.

Sausage Stuffing: Add up to 2 cups cooked crumbled or chopped vegan sausage to the stuffing mixture.

Chestnut Stuffing: Add 1½ cups cooked chestnuts to the stuffing mixture.

Southwestern Stuffed Bell Peppers

These zesty stuffed peppers are especially fun to make with "stoplight" peppers—a packaged combination of red, green, and yellow bell peppers. Make the stuffing as spicy as you like by increasing or decreasing the amount of chipotles.

SERVES 4

SLOW COOKER SIZE:
5½- TO 6-QUART

COOK TIME:
4 HOURS ON LOW

GLUTEN-FREE

SOY-FREE

2 teaspoons olive oil (optional)

4 garlic cloves, minced

4 scallions, chopped

1 tablespoon chili powder

1½ teaspoon ground cumin

1¼ teaspoon dried oregano

2 cups cooked brown or white rice

1½ cups cooked pinto beans or black beans (page 104) or 1 (15-ounce) can beans, rinsed and drained

1 cup fresh or thawed frozen corn kernels

1 cup diced fresh tomatoes or 1 (14-ounce) can diced tomatoes, drained

2 teaspoons minced chipotle chiles in adobo

Salt and freshly ground black pepper

4 large bell peppers (any color or a combination)

1 (14-ounce) can tomato sauce

½ teaspoon sugar

1. For the best flavor, heat the oil in a small skillet over medium heat. Add the garlic and scallions and sauté for 3 minutes. Stir in the chili powder, 1 teaspoon of the cumin, and 1 teaspoon of the oregano. Alternatively, omit the oil and sauté these ingredients in a few tablespoons of water or combine them in a microwave-safe bowl with a little water, cover, and microwave for 2 minutes.

2. Transfer the garlic and scallion mixture to a large bowl. Add the rice, beans, corn, tomatoes, and chipotles chiles, and season to taste with salt and pepper. Mix well.

3. Slice off the tops off the bell peppers and remove and discard the seeds and membranes. Fill the peppers evenly with the rice mixture, packing lightly. Arrange the peppers upright in the slow cooker.

4. In a bowl, combine the tomato sauce, remaining ½ teaspoon cumin, remaining ¼ teaspoon oregano, sugar, and salt and pepper to taste. Pour the sauce over and around the peppers in the slow cooker. Cover and cook on Low until the peppers are fork-tender but still hold their shape, about 4 hours. Serve hot.

Tunisian-Inspired Stuffed Bell Peppers

The flavors of North Africa infuse these peppers with an exotic flavor and aroma. *Harissa*, a North African chili paste, lends an authentic flavor, but another type of chili paste, such as *sambal oelek*, can be used in a pinch.

4 large bell peppers (assorted colors look great)
2 teaspoons olive oil
1 medium-size yellow onion, minced
2 carrots, peeled and minced
1 large zucchini, minced
3 garlic cloves, minced
3 tablespoons tomato paste
2 teaspoons harissa or hot chili paste
2 teaspoons ground coriander
1 teaspoon paprika
1 teaspoon ground cinnamon
½ tablespoon ground cumin
1 teaspoon salt
¼ teaspoon freshly ground black pepper
2 cups boiling water or vegetable broth
2 cups couscous
1 cup cooked chickpeas (page 104) or 1 (15-ounce) can chickpeas
1 tablespoon minced fresh flat-leaf parsley leaves, for garnish

SERVES 4

SLOW COOKER SIZE:
5- TO 7-QUART

COOK TIME:
4 HOURS ON LOW

SOY-FREE

1. Slice off the tops of the peppers and remove and discard the seeds and membranes. Remove the stems and chop the pepper tops; set aside.

2. Heat the oil in a saucepan over medium-high heat. Add the onion and sauté for 4 minutes. Add the carrots, chopped pepper tops, zucchini, and garlic and cook, stirring, for 2 minutes. Stir in the tomato paste, harissa, coriander, paprika, cinnamon, cumin, salt, and pepper. Add the water, stirring to blend, then stir in the couscous until well combined. Stir in the chickpeas and add a little more water if the stuffing is too dry. Taste and adjust the seasoning, if needed.

3. Lightly pack the stuffing into the peppers and arrange the peppers upright in the slow cooker. Pour hot water into the cooker to come about ½ inch up the sides of the peppers. Cover and cook on Low until the peppers are fork-tender but still hold their shape, about 4 hours. Serve hot, sprinkled with the parsley.

Quinoa-Stuffed Bell Peppers

One recipe tester described these peppers as a "flavor explosion," and a quick look through the ingredient list tells you why. Nutty quinoa combines with tangy artichoke hearts and lemon juice, bold sun-dried tomatoes and red onion, sweet baby peas, and seasonings, all cooked slowly inside peppers to meld the flavors.

SERVES 4

SLOW COOKER SIZE:
5- TO 6-QUART

COOK TIME:
4 HOURS ON LOW

GLUTEN-FREE

SOY-FREE

4 large bell peppers (any color or a combination)
2 teaspoons olive oil (optional)
1 large red onion, minced
⅓ cup minced oil-packed sun-dried tomatoes
½ teaspoon dried marjoram
1 (8-ounce) jar marinated artichoke hearts, drained and chopped
1 cup thawed frozen baby green peas
2 cups cooked quinoa
½ cup chopped fresh flat-leaf parsley leaves
2 teaspoons freshly squeezed lemon juice
Salt and freshly ground black pepper

1. Slice off the tops of the peppers and remove and discard the seeds and membranes. Remove the stems and chop the pepper tops; set aside.

2. For the best flavor, heat the oil in a large skillet over medium-high heat. Add the onion and sauté until softened, about 5 minutes. Add the chopped pepper tops and sauté for 3 minutes longer. Stir in the sun-dried tomatoes and marjoram. Alternatively, omit the oil and sauté these ingredients in a few tablespoons of water or combine them in a microwave-safe bowl with a little water, cover, and microwave for 2 minutes.

3. Transfer the onion mixture to a bowl. Add the artichoke hearts, peas, quinoa, parsley, lemon juice, and salt and pepper to taste, and mix well. Spoon the stuffing into the peppers, packing lightly. Arrange the peppers upright in the slow cooker. Pour hot water into the cooker to come about ½ inch up the sides of the peppers. Cover and cook on Low until the peppers are tender but still hold their shape, about 4 hours. Serve hot.

Chestnut- and Apple-Stuffed Squash

One of life's cold-weather pleasures is roasted chestnuts, usually available fresh in markets for only a short time each year. For preparation instructions, see page 176. For more convenient year-round choices, shelled chestnuts can be found at well-stocked supermarkets and gourmet shops, but they can be quite expensive. If you live near an Asian market, look for shelled roasted chestnuts in shelf-stable bags—that's where I get mine for about a dollar a bag.

For the best results, the bread cubes should be dried before using them in the stuffing. To do this, preheat the oven to 225°F. Spread the bread cubes in a single layer on baking pans and bake for about 30 minutes, then set aside to cool. Alternatively, set the bread cubes out at room temperature for a day or two to dry out. Use gluten-free bread to make this recipe gluten-free.

1 large kabocha or buttercup squash
2 teaspoons olive oil (optional)
1 large yellow onion, minced
1 celery rib, minced
1 teaspoon ground sage
½ teaspoon dried thyme
4 cups cubed bread, dried (see headnote)
1 large Granny Smith apple, peeled, cored, and chopped
1 cup coarsely chopped cooked chestnuts
3 tablespoons minced fresh flat-leaf parsley

SERVES 4 TO 6

SLOW COOKER SIZE:
4- TO 6-QUART

COOK TIME:
5 TO 7 HOURS ON LOW

GLUTEN-FREE OPTION

SOY-FREE

1 teaspoon salt

¼ teaspoon freshly ground black pepper

1 cup vegetable broth, or as needed

1. If you can fit two squash halves in your slow cooker, cut the squash in half and scoop out the seeds. Use a sharp knife to make a flat bottom on the two halves so they sit evenly. If you can fit only the whole squash in your slow cooker, slice off the top of the squash and scrape out the seeds. Set aside.

2. For the best flavor, heat the oil in a large skillet over medium-high heat. Add the onion and celery and sauté for 5 minutes. Stir in the sage and thyme; set aside. Alternatively, omit the oil and sauté these ingredients in a few tablespoons of water or combine them in a microwave-safe bowl with a little water, cover, and microwave for 2 minutes.

3. Transfer the onion mixture to a large bowl. Add the dried bread, apple, chestnuts, parsley, salt, and pepper. Stir in just enough broth to moisten, and mix well.

4. Lightly pack the stuffing mixture into the squash and place the squash inside the slow cooker. If cooking the squash whole, place the top back on the squash. Pour hot water into the slow cooker to come about ½ inch up the sides of the squash.

5. Cover and cook on Low until the squash is tender, 5 to 7 hours. Serve hot.

How to Prepare Fresh Chestnuts

Pierce the flat side of the chestnut shells with a sharp knife and make an "x." Boil the chestnuts or arrange them in a single layer in a baking dish and roast them at 350°F until the shells curl back. For easier peeling, remove the outer shell and inner skin with a sharp paring knife while the chestnuts are still hot. The chestnuts are now ready to eat or use in recipes. (Alternatively, shelled roasted chestnuts are available in well-stocked supermarkets and Asian markets.)

Moroccan-Inspired Stuffed Winter Squash

Combine your favorite cooked grain with vegetables, fruits, nuts, and spices to make a fragrant stuffing for squash. To making cutting the squash easier, place it in the microwave for a minute or so, then let it sit for another minute.

1 large kabocha or buttercup squash
2 teaspoons olive oil (optional)
1 large yellow onion, minced
2 celery ribs, minced
1 carrot, peeled and minced
2 garlic cloves, minced
2 tablespoons tomato paste
1½ teaspoons ground coriander
1 teaspoon dried thyme
1 teaspoon ground cinnamon
½ teaspoon ground allspice
½ teaspoon paprika
¼ teaspoon cayenne pepper
½ cup hot water
1 cup chopped dried apricots or golden raisins
½ cup chopped toasted slivered almonds
2 cups cooked rice, couscous, or quinoa
¼ cup minced fresh flat-leaf parsley leaves
1 tablespoon freshly squeezed lemon juice
Salt and freshly ground black pepper

SERVES 4

SLOW COOKER SIZE:
5½- TO 6-QUART

COOK TIME:
5½ TO 7 HOURS
ON LOW

GLUTEN-FREE

SOY-FREE

1. If you can fit two squash halves in your slow cooker, cut the squash in half and scoop out the seeds. Use a sharp knife to make a flat bottom on the two halves so they sit evenly. If you can fit only the whole squash in your slow cooker, slice off the top of the squash and scrape out the seeds. Set aside.

2. For the best flavor, heat the oil in a large skillet over medium-high heat. Add the onion, celery, carrot, and garlic and sauté until softened, about 5 minutes.

Alternatively, omit the oil and sauté these ingredients in a few tablespoons of water or combine them in a microwave-safe bowl, cover, and microwave for 2 to 3 minutes. Stir in the tomato paste, coriander, thyme, cinnamon, allspice, paprika, and cayenne and cook, stirring, for 1 minute longer. Add the water, stirring to mix well.

3. Transfer the onion mixture to a large bowl. Add the apricots, almonds, rice, parsley, and lemon juice. Season to taste with salt and pepper and mix well. Taste and adjust the seasonings, if needed.

4. Lightly pack the stuffing into the squash and place the squash inside the slow cooker. If cooking the squash whole, place the top back on the squash. Pour hot water into the slow cooker to come about ½ inch up the sides of the squash. Cover and cook on Low until the squash is tender, 5½ to 7 hours. Serve hot.

Three Sisters Squash

Large, orange-fleshed squash with dark green skin, such as kabocha or buttercup, are best for stuffing because they have a large cavity to hold more of the delicious ingredients. A 6-quart oval slow cooker is the best size and shape to fit the squash halves inside. Otherwise, choose a squash that fits in your cooker whole and slice off the top few inches so you can scoop out the seeds and stuff it. If you like gravy on your stuffed squash, try the Fat-Free Mushroom Gravy on page 183.

SERVES 4 TO 6

SLOW COOKER SIZE:
6-QUART

COOK TIME:
6 HOURS ON LOW

GLUTEN-FREE

SOY-FREE

1 large kabocha or buttercup squash
2 teaspoons olive oil (optional)
1 medium-size yellow onion, minced
2 garlic cloves, minced
1 minced chipotle chile in adobo
1 teaspoon ground cumin
1 teaspoon ground coriander
1 teaspoon dried thyme

2 cups cooked brown rice

1½ cups cooked pinto beans (page 104) or 1 (15-ounce) can beans, rinsed and drained

1 cup fresh or thawed frozen corn kernels

2 tablespoons minced fresh flat-leaf parsley

Salt and freshly ground black pepper

1. If you can fit two squash halves in your slow cooker, cut the squash in half and scoop out the seeds. Use a sharp knife to make a flat bottom on the two halves so they sit evenly. If you can fit only the whole squash in your slow cooker, slice off the top of the squash and scrape out the seeds. Set aside.

2. For the best flavor, heat the oil in a medium-size skillet over medium-high heat. Add the onion and sauté until softened, about 5 minutes. Stir in the garlic, chipotle chile, cumin, coriander, and thyme and cook for 1 minute longer. Alternatively, omit the oil and sauté these ingredients in a few tablespoons of water or combine them in a microwave-safe bowl with a little water, cover, and microwave for 2 minutes.

3. Transfer the onion mixture to a large bowl. Add the rice, beans, corn, parsley, and salt and pepper to taste. Mix well, then taste and adjust the seasonings, if needed.

4. Lightly pack the stuffing into the squash and place the squash inside the slow cooker. If cooking the squash whole, place the top back on the squash. Pour hot water into the bottom of the slow cooker to come about ½ inch up the sides of the squash. Cover and cook on Low until the squash is tender, about 6 hours. Serve hot.

Great Scot Stuffed Squash

In my previous slow cooker book, I included a groundbreaking recipe for vegan haggis wrapped in bean curd skin. I've since realized that there may be people disinclined to make a haggis recipe (vegan or not), so I wanted to use the delicious filling in a recipe that was more approachable. The result is a stuffed winter squash à la Robert Burns, so named because it was inspired by the traditional haggis that is served on January 25—Robert Burns's birthday. For gluten-free, be sure to use certified gluten-free oats; for soy-free, omit the soy sauce and use a soy-free sauce (purchased or homemade, page 35) or add some soy-free vegetable broth base or additional salt.

SERVES 4

SLOW COOKER SIZE:
4- TO 7-QUART

COOK TIME:
4 HOURS ON LOW

GLUTEN-FREE

SOY-FREE OPTION

1 large kabocha or buttercup squash

2 teaspoons olive oil

1 large yellow onion, minced

2 large carrots, peeled and finely shredded

4 ounces white mushrooms, chopped

1¾ cups vegetable broth

¾ cup rolled old-fashioned rolled oats

1½ cups cooked kidney beans (page 104) or 1 (15-ounce) can beans, rinsed and drained, coarsely mashed

⅔ cup chopped walnuts

2 tablespoons minced fresh flat-leaf parsley

2 tablespoons Scotch whisky

1½ tablespoons soy sauce

1½ teaspoons dried thyme

⅛ teaspoon ground nutmeg

⅛ teaspoon cayenne pepper

Salt and freshly ground black pepper

Fat-Free Mushroom Gravy (page 183)

1. If you can fit two squash halves in your slow cooker, cut the squash in half and scoop out the seeds. Use a sharp knife to make a flat bottom on the two halves so they sit evenly. If you can fit only the whole squash in your slow cooker, cut the top of the squash off and remove the seeds. Set aside.

2. Heat the oil in a large saucepan over medium-high heat. Add the onion and carrots and sauté for 5 minutes. Add the mushrooms and broth, then stir in the oats. Reduce the heat to a simmer and cook, stirring occasionally, for 10 minutes.

3. Stir the kidney beans into the oat mixture. Add the nuts, parsley, whisky, soy sauce, thyme, nutmeg, and cayenne and season to taste with salt and black pepper. Mix well to combine.

4. Lightly pack the stuffing mixture into the squash and place the squash inside the slow cooker. If cooking the squash whole, place the top back on the squash. Pour hot water into the bottom of the slow cooker to come about ½ inch up the sides of the squash. Cover and cook on Low until the squash is tender, about 4 hours.

5. A few minutes before serving time, heat the mushroom gravy. To serve, cut each squash half in half again (or cut the whole squash into quarters) and carefully serve each portion with the hot gravy.

NOTE: If your squash is on the smaller side, you may have some stuffing left over. It can be shaped into patties and sautéed in a skillet or spooned into an oiled baking dish, covered, and baked on its own.

Stuffed Zucchini Puttanesca

As with most stuffed vegetable recipes, this one will need a large cooker (preferably oval) in order to accommodate the zucchini. It can be made heartier by adding 1½ cups of your choice of cooked white beans or cooked crumbled vegan sausage to the stuffing mixture, and using an additional zucchini to accommodate the extra stuffing. Use a gluten-free pasta to make this gluten-free.

SERVES 4

SLOW COOKER SIZE:
5½- TO 6-QUART

COOK TIME:
4 HOURS ON LOW

GLUTEN-FREE OPTION

SOY-FREE

2 large or 4 small zucchini
2 teaspoons olive oil (optional)
6 garlic cloves, minced
3 ripe plum tomatoes, chopped
½ teaspoon red pepper flakes
Salt and freshly ground black pepper
⅓ cup pitted green olives, chopped
⅓ cup pitted kalamata olives, chopped
2 tablespoons capers
2 tablespoons minced fresh flat-leaf parsley leaves
2 tablespoons minced fresh basil leaves
1½ cups cooked orzo or other tiny pasta
1 cup marinara sauce

1. If using long zucchini, cut off the ends and cut the zucchini in half lengthwise. If using round zucchini, just cut off the top ½ inch. Scoop out the zucchini flesh, leaving about ¼ inch of the flesh and the shells intact. Chop the scooped-out zucchini flesh. Slice off a tiny bit on the bottom of each zucchini if needed so they sit flat.

2. For the best flavor, heat the oil in a large skillet over medium heat. Add the garlic and chopped zucchini and sauté for 5 minutes, then remove from the heat. Alternatively, omit the oil and sauté these ingredients in a few tablespoons of water or combine them in a microwave-safe bowl with a little water, cover, and microwave for 2 minutes. Stir in the tomatoes and red pepper flakes, and season to taste with salt and pepper. Stir in the green and black olives, capers, parsley, basil, and orzo. Mix well, then taste and adjust the seasonings, if needed.

3. Lightly oil the slow cooker insert or spray it with nonstick cooking spray. Fill the zucchini shells with the stuffing mixture and place them in the cooker. Spoon the marinara sauce on top of the zucchini. Pour a little bit of hot water into the slow cooker just to cover the bottom of the insert and create steam. Cover and cook on Low until the zucchini is tender, about 4 hours.

FAT-FREE MUSHROOM GRAVY

To make a quick broth, dissolve 1 bouillon cube (vegetable or mushroom) in hot water. In addition to being fat-free, this gravy is also gluten- and soy-free.

¼ cup minced yellow onion

1½ cups plus 2 tablespoons vegetable or mushroom broth

2 cups sliced fresh mushrooms

½ teaspoon ground dried thyme

¼ teaspoon ground sage

2 tablespoons dry red or white wine (optional)

Salt and freshly ground black pepper

½ to 1 teaspoon vegan gravy browner (such as Kitchen Bouquet)

MAKES ABOUT 2½ CUPS

1. Combine the onion and the 2 tablespoons of broth in a small saucepan over medium heat and simmer until the onion is soft. Stir in the mushrooms and cook until slightly softened, then stir in the thyme, sage, and wine, if using. Add 1 cup of the remaining broth and bring to a boil. Reduce the heat and simmer for 5 minutes.

2. Transfer the mixture to a high-speed blender or food processor, add the remaining ½ cup broth, and process until very smooth. Transfer the gravy back to the saucepan and season to taste with salt and pepper. Simmer until the gravy is hot and the flavors are blended. If the gravy is too thick, stir in a small amount of additional broth or some unsweetened almond milk.

Eggplant Stuffed with Red Beans and Bulgur

A large oval slow cooker is best for this recipe to accommodate the eggplant. If your slow cooker is too small to accommodate both eggplant halves side by side, you can stack them crisscross. Bulgur, best known for its use in tabbouleh, is a quick-cooking grain made from wheat kernels that have been steamed, dried, and crushed.

SERVES 4

SLOW COOKER SIZE:
5½- TO 6-QUART

COOK TIME:
4 TO 5 HOURS ON LOW

SOY-FREE

1 large eggplant

2 teaspoons olive oil (optional)

1 small onion, minced

½ small green bell pepper, seeded and minced

1 small celery rib, minced

4 garlic cloves, minced

1 jalapeño chile, seeded and minced

1 teaspoon dried thyme

Salt and freshly ground black pepper

1½ cups cooked dark red kidney beans (page 104) or 1 (15-ounce) can beans, rinsed and drained

1 cup cooked bulgur

1 chipotle chile in adobo, finely minced

1 (14.5-ounce) can crushed tomatoes

1 tablespoon chili powder

1 teaspoon dried basil

1. Halve the eggplant lengthwise and scoop out the flesh, leaving ¼ to ⅓ inch of the flesh and the shells intact. Chop the scooped-out eggplant flesh.

2. For the best flavor, heat the oil in a large skillet over medium-high heat. Add the onion, bell pepper, celery, garlic, jalapeño, thyme, and chopped eggplant. Season to taste with salt and pepper and cook, stirring, for 5 minutes. Alternatively, omit the oil and sauté these ingredients in a few tablespoons of water or combine them in a microwave-safe bowl with a little water, cover, and microwave for 2 minutes.

3. Transfer the onion mixture to a large bowl. Add the beans, bulgur, and chipotle chile, mix well, and season to taste with salt and pepper. Fill the eggplant shells with the stuffing mixture and place them in the slow cooker, stacked crisscross if necessary.

4. In the same bowl, combine the tomatoes, chili powder, basil, and salt and pepper to taste. Mix well, then pour the sauce on top of and around the eggplant. Cover and cook on Low until the eggplant shells are tender but still hold their shape, 4 to 5 hours. Serve hot.

Braciole-Inspired Stuffed Eggplant

Braciole is the name given to Italian beef roulades stuffed with a garlicky bread crumb mixture. In this recipe, that same flavorful crumb mixture is used to stuff eggplant. Be sure to choose an eggplant that will fit inside your slow cooker—a large oval slow cooker works best. If your slow cooker is too small to accommodate both eggplant halves side by side, just stack them crisscross. Use gluten-free bread crumbs to make this gluten-free, and leave out the optional cheese to make it soy-free.

1 large eggplant
2 teaspoons olive oil (optional)
5 garlic cloves, minced
6 ounces white mushrooms, finely chopped
Salt and freshly ground black pepper
1 cup dry bread crumbs
⅓ cup nutritional yeast
⅓ cup golden raisins
¼ cup minced fresh flat-leaf parsley leaves
1 cup marinara sauce
2 tablespoons vegan Parmesan cheese (optional)

SERVES 4 TO 6

SLOW COOKER SIZE:
5- TO 7-QUART

COOK TIME:
4 TO 6 HOURS ON LOW

GLUTEN-FREE OPTION

SOY-FREE OPTION

1. Halve the eggplant lengthwise and scoop out the flesh, leaving ¼ to ⅓ inch of the flesh and the shells intact. Chop the scooped-out eggplant flesh.

2. For the best flavor, heat the oil in a large skillet over medium-high heat. Add the chopped eggplant, garlic, mushrooms, and salt and pepper to taste, and cook, stirring, for 5 minutes. Alternatively, omit the oil and sauté these ingredients in a few tablespoons of water or combine them in a microwave-safe bowl with a little water, cover, and microwave for 2 minutes. Remove from the heat and stir in the bread crumbs, nutritional yeast, raisins, and parsley. Mix well, then taste and adjust the seasonings.

3. Fill the eggplant shells with the stuffing mixture and place them in the slow cooker. Spoon the marinara sauce on top of and around the eggplant. Sprinkle with the cheese, if desired. Cover and cook on Low until the eggplant is tender, 4 to 6 hours. Serve hot.

Italian Stuffed Artichokes

Fresh artichokes require a bit of hands-on work to prepare, but the results are worth it. If your artichokes are small, use five or six instead of four—as many as you can fit comfortably in your slow cooker. Use gluten-free bread crumbs to make this gluten-free, and use a soy-free vegan Parmesan to make it soy-free.

SERVES 4

SLOW COOKER SIZE:
5- TO 6-QUART

COOK TIME:
4 HOURS ON LOW

GLUTEN-FREE OPTION

SOY-FREE OPTION

1 tablespoon olive oil (optional)
3 garlic cloves, minced
1 cup chopped mushrooms of your choice
1 cup dry bread crumbs
2 tablespoons nutritional yeast
¼ cup vegan Parmesan cheese
¼ cup chopped fresh flat-leaf parsley
Salt and freshly ground black pepper
Juice of 2 lemons
4 large artichokes

1. For the best flavor, heat the oil in a medium-size skillet over medium heat. Add the garlic and cook until fragrant, about 30 seconds. Stir in the mushrooms and cook for 3 minutes longer. Alternatively, omit the oil and sauté these ingredients in a few tablespoons of water or combine them in a microwave-safe bowl with a little water, cover, and microwave for 2 minutes. Remove from the heat and stir in the bread crumbs, nutritional yeast, vegan Parmesan, and parsley. Season to taste with salt and black pepper. Mix well. If the mixture is too dry, drizzle in a few teaspoons of water. Set aside.

2. Pour half of the lemon juice into a large bowl of cold water and set aside. Slice off the stem end of each artichoke so that they sit upright. Use a serrated knife to cut off about 1 inch from the top of each artichoke and, with scissors, snip off the sharp tips from the leaves. Gently spread open the center leaves of the artichokes and use a small knife to scrape out the fuzzy leaves in the middle. Place the cut artichokes in the bowl of lemon water as you work.

3. Spread the leaves of each artichoke as much as possible and spoon the stuffing mixture in between the artichoke leaves, pressing it in with your fingers.

Stand the stuffed artichokes upright in the slow cooker. Pour hot water into the bottom of the cooker to come about ½ inch up the sides of the artichokes. Drizzle each artichoke with the remaining lemon juice.

4. Cover and cook on Low until the leaves pull off easily and are tender, about 4 hours. Serve hot or at room temperature.

Sweet and Sour Stuffed Cabbage Rolls

This Eastern European comfort food classic is an ideal candidate for a slow cooker. It enables the cabbage to cook to a tender doneness while keeping the filling nice and moist. Instead of brown rice or barley, you could substitute quinoa in this recipe. (For gluten-free, do not use barley.) Similarly, you can use reconstituted TVP or finely chopped seitan instead of the tempeh, if you prefer (but if you use seitan, then it won't be gluten-free).

1 large head green cabbage, cored
2 teaspoons olive oil (optional)
1 medium-size yellow onion, minced
8 ounces steamed tempeh, finely chopped
1 teaspoon natural sugar
½ teaspoon ground coriander
½ teaspoon dried thyme
¼ teaspoon ground allspice
¼ teaspoon ground cinnamon
Salt and freshly ground black pepper
2½ cups cooked brown rice or barley
¼ cup golden raisins (optional)
2 tablespoons minced fresh flat-leaf parsley leaves
2 teaspoons freshly squeezed lemon juice
1 (14.5-ounce) can crushed tomatoes
⅓ cup dark brown sugar
¼ cup cider vinegar

SERVES 4 TO 6

SLOW COOKER SIZE:
5- TO 6-QUART

COOK TIME:
6 TO 8 HOURS ON LOW

GLUTEN-FREE

1. Steam the cabbage in a large covered pot with a steamer rack until the first few layers of leaves are softened, about 10 minutes. Remove from the pot and set aside to cool (keep the pot on the heat).

2. For the best flavor, heat the oil in a large skillet over medium-high heat. Add the onion and sauté for 5 minutes. Alternatively, omit the oil and sauté the onion in a few tablespoons of water or place the onion in a microwave-safe bowl with a little water, cover, and microwave for 2 minutes. Add the tempeh, sugar, coriander, thyme, allspice, cinnamon, and salt and pepper to taste and mix well. Remove from the heat, stir in the rice, raisins (if using), parsley, and lemon juice, and mix well. Taste and adjust the seasonings, if needed.

3. Remove as many of the cabbage leaves as are soft and lay them out on a flat surface, rib side down. Trim any thick ribs and the bottom end of the leaves. Place about ⅓ cup of the stuffing mixture on each leaf, at the stem end. Roll up each leaf around the stuffing, tucking in the sides as you roll. Repeat the process until the mixture is used up, steaming more cabbage leaves to soften as necessary. Place the filled cabbage rolls in the slow cooker, seam side down, stacking them if necessary.

4. In a bowl, combine the tomatoes, brown sugar, and vinegar and season to taste with salt and pepper. Pour the tomato sauce over the cabbage rolls. Cover and cook on Low until the rolls are tender, 6 to 8 hours. If some of the cabbage rolls are not covered in sauce while cooking, rotate them gently at some point during the cooking time, if possible. Serve hot.

Stuffed Collard Rolls

A smoky black-eyed pea and rice stuffing wrapped with large, bright green collard leaves is a novel way to enjoy the flavors of a Southern New Year's Day tradition, hoppin' John. Top with a soy-free vegan sour cream to make this recipe soy-free.

1 large bunch collard greens, stems removed (about 8 large leaves)

2 teaspoons olive oil (optional)

1 large yellow onion, minced

3 garlic cloves, minced

1 teaspoon dried thyme

1 chipotle chile in adobo, minced (optional)

1½ cups cooked brown rice

1½ cups cooked black-eyed peas (page 104) or 1 (15-ounce) can black-eyed peas, rinsed and drained

1 teaspoon liquid smoke

Salt and freshly ground black pepper

1 cup vegetable broth

Vegan sour cream, purchased or homemade (page 57), for serving

Tabasco sauce, for serving

SERVES 4 TO 6

SLOW COOKER SIZE:
5- TO 6-QUART

COOK TIME:
6 TO 8 HOURS ON LOW

GLUTEN-FREE

SOY-FREE OPTION

1. Steam the collard leaves in a large covered pot with a steamer rack until just soft enough to be pliable, 5 to 8 minutes. Remove the leaves from the pot and set aside to cool.

2. For the best flavor, heat the oil in a medium-size skillet over medium-high heat. Add the onion and sauté until softened, about 5 minutes. Add the garlic, thyme, and chipotle chile, if using, and cook for 1 minute longer. Alternatively, omit the oil and sauté these ingredients in a few tablespoons of water or combine them in a microwave-safe bowl with a little water, cover, and microwave for 2 minutes.

3. In a bowl, combine the onion mixture with the rice, black-eyed peas, liquid smoke, and salt and pepper to taste. Mix well.

4. Arrange the collard leaves on a flat surface. Cut off the thick part of the ribs near the base of the leaves so that the leaves will roll up easily. Place about ⅓ cup of the stuffing mixture near the stem end of each leaf. Beginning from the bottom of the leaf, roll it up around the stuffing, folding in the sides as you roll. Repeat the process until the stuffing and leaves are used up. Arrange the filled collard rolls in the slow cooker, seam side down, stacking them if necessary. Pour the broth over the rolls. Cover and cook on Low until tender, 6 to 8 hours. If some of the rolls are not submerged in the broth, rotate them gently at some point during the cooking time, if possible. Serve hot, passing vegan sour cream and Tabasco sauce at the table.

Corned Seitan and Cabbage Rolls

Liven up your next Saint Patrick's Day dinner with these cabbage rolls stuffed with a seitan mixture reminiscent of corned beef. They taste so good that you'll want to make them throughout the year.

SERVES 4 TO 6

SLOW COOKER SIZE:
5- TO 6-QUART

COOK TIME:
6 TO 8 HOURS ON LOW

SOY-FREE

1 large head green cabbage, cored

2 teaspoons olive oil

1 medium-size yellow onion, minced

1 small carrot, peeled and grated

3 large Yukon Gold potatoes; 1 peeled and grated, 2 peeled and cut into ½-inch dice

8 ounces seitan (purchased or homemade, page 136), chopped

1 teaspoon ground coriander

¼ teaspoon ground allspice

Salt and freshly ground black pepper

3 tablespoons brown mustard

¼ cup cider vinegar

2 tablespoons light brown sugar

1½ teaspoons pickling spices

1 cup vegetable broth

1. Steam the cabbage in a large covered pot with a steamer rack until the first few layers of leaves are softened, about 10 minutes. Remove from the pot and set aside to cool (keep the pot on the heat).

2. Heat the oil in a large skillet over medium-high heat. Add the onion and carrot and sauté for 5 minutes. Add the grated potato to the skillet and cook for 1 minute longer. Stir in the seitan and cook for 1 minute longer. Remove from the heat, and add the coriander, allspice, ½ teaspoon salt, and ¼ teaspoon black pepper. Stir in 1 teaspoon of the mustard and 1 teaspoon of the vinegar. Mix well to combine.

3. In a small bowl, combine the remaining mustard and vinegar with the brown sugar and pickling spices, stirring to blend. Slowly add the vegetable broth, stirring until smooth. Set aside.

4. Remove as many of the cabbage leaves as are soft and lay them out on a flat surface, rib side down. Trim any thick ribs and the bottom end of the leaves. Place about ⅓ cup of the stuffing mixture in the center of each leaf. Roll up the leaf around the stuffing, folding in the sides as you roll. Repeat until the stuffing mixture is used up, steaming more cabbage leaves to soften if necessary.

5. Arrange the filled cabbage rolls in the slow cooker, seam side down, stacking them if necessary. Arrange the diced potatoes around the rolls in the cooker. Pour the broth mixture over the rolls and potatoes and season to taste with salt and pepper. Cover and cook on Low until tender, 6 to 8 hours.

Seitan Roulade

This delicious roast makes enough to serve a crowd and is especially good with mashed potatoes and roasted vegetables. It makes an ideal main dish for holiday dinners. Serve with the Fat-Free Mushroom Gravy (page 183) or your favorite brown gravy or sauce. If you prefer not to use wine in the seitan mixture, just use additional water or broth.

STUFFING:

2 teaspoons olive oil (optional)

3 shallots, minced

3 garlic cloves, minced

2 cups finely minced cremini mushrooms

1 teaspoon fresh thyme or ½ teaspoon dried thyme

1 teaspoon fresh minced sage or ½ teaspoon dried crumbled sage

1 (10-ounce) package frozen chopped spinach, thawed and squeezed dry

1 jarred roasted red bell pepper, minced

Salt and freshly ground black pepper

1 recipe Slow-Cooked Vegan Sausage Links (page 157) or purchased vegan sausage, crumbled or coarsely chopped (optional)

SERVES 8

SLOW COOKER SIZE:
6-QUART

COOK TIME:
6 TO 8 HOURS ON LOW

SEITAN:

2 cups vital wheat gluten

2 tablespoons chickpea flour

2 tablespoons tapioca flour

1 teaspoon onion powder

1 teaspoon dried thyme

½ teaspoon ground sage

½ teaspoon salt

¼ teaspoon black pepper

3 tablespoons dry red wine

2 tablespoons soy sauce

1¼ cups water or vegetable broth, plus more as needed

1. For the stuffing: For the best flavor, heat the oil in a large skillet over medium-high heat. Add the shallots and sauté for 3 minutes. Stir in the garlic, mushrooms, thyme, and sage and cook for 2 minutes longer. Add the spinach and bell pepper and season to taste with salt and pepper. Cook for 2 minutes longer. Alternatively, omit the oil and sauté these ingredients in a few tablespoons of water or combine them in a microwave-safe bowl with a little water, cover, and microwave for 2 minutes. Remove from the heat. Stir in the sausage, if using, and mix well. Taste and the adjust seasonings, if needed. Set aside.

2. For the seitan: In a bowl, combine the vital wheat gluten, chickpea flour, tapioca flour, onion powder, thyme, sage, salt, and pepper. Stir in the wine, soy sauce, and water and mix well to combine, adding up to ¼ cup additional water if the mixture is too dry. You should end up with a soft dough. Knead the dough for a few minutes with your hands, then roll out the seitan on a work surface between two sheets of parchment paper, aluminum foil, or plastic wrap into a 9 x 12-inch rectangle.

3. Transfer the seitan to a large sheet of aluminum foil. Spread the reserved stuffing evenly on top of the seitan, leaving about a 1-inch border all the way around. Beginning at the shorter side, carefully roll up the seitan to enclose the filling. Place the rolled seitan, seam side down, in the center of the foil and close up the foil around the roulade to enclose it.

4. Place the foil-wrapped roulade in the slow cooker, seam side up. Pour hot water into the slow cooker to come about ½ inch up the sides of the roulade. Cover and cook on Low until firm, 6 to 8 hours.

5. Carefully remove the roulade from the slow cooker and open the foil. Let stand for 10 minutes before slicing. Use a serrated knife to cut the roulade into ½-inch-thick slices. Serve hot.

Vegetable Love

While a slow cooker may not be ideal for cooking delicate produce, it's a great way to prepare sturdier vegetables such as potatoes, carrots, parsnips, beets, and winter squash, as well as celery, tomatoes, cabbage, and onions. Slow cooking allows the flavor of the vegetables to intensify without drying out or dissipating their natural juices. This chapter includes a variety of slow-simmered vegetable dishes such as Classic Ratatouille, Citrus-Braised Beets, and Italian-Style Tomatoes and Zucchini.

The slow cooker can also be used to slow-steam or "bake" vegetables such as corn, artichokes, and potatoes—a boon during the hot summer months when you don't want to heat up the kitchen.

Some of these recipes, like Potatoes with Tomatoes and Butter Beans, can be enjoyed as main dishes, while others, like the Sweet and Sour Cabbage, make ideal side dishes.

Slow-Steamed Artichokes

Four small to medium-size artichokes (or six baby artichokes) will fit in a 4-quart slow cooker. For larger artichokes (or more of them), you will need to use a larger cooker.

SERVES 4

SLOW COOKER SIZE:
4- TO 6-QUART

COOK TIME:
6 TO 8 HOURS ON LOW

GLUTEN-FREE

SOY-FREE

4 artichokes
3 cups hot water
Juice of 1 lemon

1. Slice off the stem end of each artichoke so that they sit upright. Use a serrated knife to cut off about 1 inch from the top of each artichoke and, with scissors, snip off the sharp tips from the leaves. Stand the artichokes upright in the slow cooker.

2. Pour the water into the bottom of the cooker, and drizzle the lemon juice over the tops of the artichokes. Cover and cook on Low until the artichokes are tender, 6 to 8 hours.

3. Serve hot or at room temperature.

Citrus-Braised Beets

Orange marmalade and lemon and lime juice combine to infuse the beets with citrus sweetness. For a shortcut, use purchased orange marmalade. Use the smallest beets you can find for the best flavor. The size of the beets will dictate the length of cooking time needed.

SERVES 4

SLOW COOKER SIZE:
4- TO 5-QUART

COOK TIME: 6 TO 8
HOURS ON LOW

GLUTEN-FREE

SOY-FREE

3 tablespoons Orange Marmalade with a Twist of Lemon (page 237)
Juice of 1 lemon
Juice of 1 lime
2 teaspoons olive oil
8 to 10 small beets, trimmed and halved, or 4 large beets, trimmed and quartered
Salt and freshly ground black pepper

1. In a small bowl, combine the marmalade, lemon juice, and lime juice. Add the oil, stirring to blend.

2. Place the beets in the slow cooker and add the citrus mixture, stirring to coat. Season to taste with salt and pepper. Cover and cook on Low until the beets are tender, 6 to 8 hours, stirring once halfway through if possible.

3. Before serving, remove the beet peels (they should slip off easily) and discard. Transfer the beets to a serving bowl. Pour the citrus mixture over the beets and serve.

Braised Brussels Sprouts and Chestnuts

Brussels sprouts and chestnuts have a natural flavor affinity—and, conveniently, they're about the same shape and size, too. Seasoned with a sweet and sour braising liquid, the combination makes a flavorful autumn side dish. If you are using the optional vegan bacon, check to see that it's gluten-free or soy-free if necessary.

2 teaspoons olive oil (optional)
3 shallots, thinly sliced lengthwise
1½ pounds Brussels sprouts, trimmed and halved lengthwise, if large
3 tablespoons vegetable broth
2 tablespoons pure maple syrup
1 tablespoon cider vinegar
Salt and freshly ground black pepper
1 cup roasted shelled chestnuts (page 176)
3 slices vegan bacon, sautéed and chopped (optional)

SERVES 4

SLOW COOKER SIZE:
4-QUART

COOK TIME:
4 HOURS ON LOW

GLUTEN-FREE

SOY-FREE

1. For the best flavor, heat the oil in a small skillet over medium-high heat. Add the shallots and sauté until softened, about 3 minutes. Alternatively, omit the oil and sauté the shallots in a few tablespoons of water or place them in a microwave-safe bowl with a little water, cover, and microwave for 1 to 2 minutes.

2. Generously oil the insert of the slow cooker or spray it with nonstick cooking spray. Transfer the shallots to the cooker and add the Brussels sprouts, broth, maple syrup, vinegar, and salt and pepper to taste. Cover and cook on Low until the Brussels sprouts are tender, 3½ to 4 hours.

3. About 20 minutes before the end of the cooking time, stir in the chestnuts. Just before serving, stir in the bacon, if using. Serve hot.

Sweet and Sour Cabbage

The slow-cooked flavor of this cabbage makes it an ideal side dish for a cold-weather supper. Turn it into an entrée by browning vegan sausage links in a skillet and adding them to the cabbage when ready to serve. Use gluten-free flour to make this dish gluten-free.

SERVES 6

SLOW COOKER SIZE:
4- TO 5-QUART

COOK TIME:
5 TO 6 HOURS ON LOW

GLUTEN-FREE OPTION

SOY-FREE

2 teaspoons olive oil
1 yellow onion, minced
½ teaspoon caraway seeds
2 tablespoons unbleached all-purpose flour
¼ cup water
3 tablespoons cider vinegar
3 tablespoons light brown sugar or granulated natural sugar
1 (2-pound) head green cabbage, cored and shredded
Salt and freshly ground black pepper

1. Heat the oil in a small skillet over medium-high heat. Add the onion and sauté for 5 minutes to soften. Add the caraway seeds and flour and cook, stirring, for 1 minute. Add the water, stirring until smooth.

2. Transfer the onion mixture to the slow cooker and stir in the vinegar and sugar. Add the cabbage and season to taste with salt and pepper. Stir to combine. Cover and cook on Low until the cabbage is tender, 4 to 6 hours.

3. Taste to adjust the seasonings, if needed. Serve hot.

Sicilian-Style Cauliflower

This flavorful side dish can also be enjoyed as a topping for pasta. To do so, either mash some of the cauliflower to make it "saucier" or stir in a tablespoon of tomato paste to thicken the broth, then season to taste. A few shakes of red pepper flakes are a good addition as well.

2 teaspoons olive oil (optional)
1 medium-size yellow onion, minced
3 garlic cloves, minced
1 large head cauliflower, trimmed, cored, and cut into small florets
1 (14.5-ounce) can diced tomatoes, drained
⅓ cup golden raisins
1 tablespoon capers
⅓ cup white wine or vegetable broth
Salt and freshly ground black pepper
3 tablespoons toasted pine nuts, for garnish
2 tablespoons minced fresh flat-leaf parsley or basil, for garnish

SERVES 6

SLOW COOKER SIZE:
4- TO 5-QUART

COOK TIME:
3 HOURS ON LOW

GLUTEN-FREE

SOY-FREE

1. For the best flavor, heat the oil in a medium-size skillet over medium-high heat. Add the onion and sauté until softened, about 5 minutes. Add the garlic and cook for 1 minute longer. Alternatively, omit the oil and sauté these ingredients in a few tablespoons of water or combine them in a microwave-safe bowl with a little water, cover, and microwave for 2 minutes.

2. Transfer the onion mixture to the slow cooker. Add the cauliflower, tomatoes, raisins, capers, wine, and salt and pepper to taste. Cover and cook on Low until the cauliflower is tender, about 3 hours.

3. Serve hot, sprinkled with the pine nuts and parsley.

Braised Manchurian-Style Cauliflower

Now you can enjoy the amazing flavor of the popular Indian appetizer Gobi Manchurian in one easy step. Best of all, it's braised, not fried. If you miss that crunch from the fried version, sprinkle it with the optional crushed peanuts. To make this recipe soy-free, omit the soy sauce and use a soy-free sauce (purchased or homemade, page 35) or add some soy-free vegetable broth base or additional salt.

SERVES 6

SLOW COOKER SIZE:
4-QUART

COOK TIME:
4 TO 5 HOURS ON LOW

GLUTEN-FREE

SOY-FREE OPTION

2 teaspoons vegetable oil (optional)
1 small yellow onion, chopped
4 garlic cloves, minced
1 teaspoon grated fresh ginger
1 teaspoon ground coriander
½ teaspoon cayenne pepper
½ cup ketchup
1 tablespoon tapioca starch or cornstarch
½ cup vegetable broth
2 tablespoons soy sauce
2 teaspoons rice vinegar
¼ teaspoon red pepper flakes
Salt
1 head cauliflower, trimmed, cored, and cut into small florets
¼ cup minced scallions, for garnish
¼ cup minced fresh cilantro, for garnish
3 tablespoons crushed dry-roasted peanuts (for garnish; optional)

1. For the best flavor, heat the oil in a small skillet over medium-high heat. Add the onion and sauté until softened, about 5 minutes. Add the garlic and ginger and cook for 1 minute longer. Add the coriander and ¼ teaspoon of the cayenne, stirring to coat the vegetables. Alternatively, omit the oil and sauté these ingredients in a few tablespoons of water or combine them in a microwave-safe bowl with a little water, cover, and microwave for 2 minutes.

2. In a small bowl, combine the remaining ¼ teaspoon cayenne, ketchup, tapioca, broth, soy sauce, 1 teaspoon of the vinegar, and the red pepper flakes, stirring to blend, then stir it into the onion mixture. Season to taste with salt.

3. Lightly oil the insert of the slow cooker or spray it with nonstick cooking spray. Place the cauliflower in the cooker and pour the sauce over and around the cauliflower. Cover and cook on Low until the cauliflower is tender, 4 to 5 hours. Gently stir in the remaining 1 teaspoon vinegar about 1 hour before the cauliflower is done, if possible.

4. Taste and add more salt, if needed. Serve hot, garnished with a sprinkling of scallions and cilantro, and the peanuts, if using.

Braised Collards with "Pot Likker"

discovered the wonder of collard greens after moving down South in the early 1980s. Typically, collards are cooked for hours on top of the stove to make them tender and flavorful. A slow cooker does an even better job of cooking the greens, since you don't have to watch the pot, and there's no danger of cooking off all that delicious braising liquid known as "pot likker" (or "liquor"). Be sure to wash the collards well before using to remove any sand. A touch of liquid smoke, vinegar, and red pepper flakes add a nice depth of flavor to the collards. For a hearty meal, stir in cooked black-eyed peas and serve over rice, passing Tabasco sauce and vegan sour cream at the table.

1½ pounds collard greens, trimmed of thick stems
2 teaspoons olive oil (optional)
1 small yellow onion, chopped
3 large garlic cloves, minced
¼ teaspoon red pepper flakes
Salt and freshly ground black pepper
1 cup vegetable broth
1 tablespoon cider vinegar
1 teaspoon liquid smoke

SERVES 4

SLOW COOKER SIZE:
4-QUART

COOK TIME:
4 TO 6 HOURS ON LOW

GLUTEN-FREE

SOY-FREE

1. Stack a few of the collard leaves at a time and roll them up tightly. Cut the rolls crosswise into thin strips. Repeat until all the collards are cut. You should end up with 8 to 10 cups. Set aside.

2. For the best flavor, heat the oil in a small skillet over medium-high heat. Add the onion and sauté until softened, about 5 minutes. Stir in the garlic and cook for 1 minute longer. Alternatively, omit the oil and sauté these ingredients in a few tablespoons of water or combine them in a microwave-safe bowl with a little water, cover, and microwave for 2 minutes.

3. Transfer the onion mixture to the slow cooker. Add the reserved collards, then sprinkle with the red pepper flakes and salt and pepper to taste. Pour in the vegetable broth. Cover and cook on Low until the collards are tender, 4 to 6 hours.

4. Just before serving, stir in the vinegar and liquid smoke. Taste and adjust the seasonings, if needed.

Creamy Creamed Corn

Yes, canned "creamed" corn is vegan—there is no cream in it, despite the name. This rich, comforting side dish is great as is or, for extra zing, add some minced canned green chiles or chipotles in adobo. To make this recipe soy-free, use a soy-free vegan cream cheese and a soy-free nondairy milk.

2 teaspoons vegetable oil or vegan butter (optional)
1 medium-size yellow onion, minced
2 pounds fresh or thawed frozen corn kernels
1 (16-ounce) can creamed corn
Salt and freshly ground black pepper
½ cup vegan cream cheese, purchased or homemade (page 31), at room temperature
1 tablespoon cornstarch or tapioca starch
1 cup plain unsweetened nondairy milk

SERVES 6 TO 8

SLOW COOKER SIZE:
4-QUART

COOK TIME:
3 HOURS ON LOW

GLUTEN-FREE

SOY-FREE OPTION

1. For the best flavor, heat the oil in a small skillet over medium-high heat. Add the onion and sauté until softened, about 5 minutes. Alternatively, omit the oil and sauté the onion in a few tablespoons of water or place it in a microwave-safe bowl with a little water, cover, and microwave for 2 minutes.

2. Generously oil the insert of the slow cooker or spray it with nonstick cooking spray. Transfer the onion to the cooker. Add the corn kernels and the creamed corn. Season to taste with salt and pepper.

3. In a bowl, combine the cream cheese, cornstarch, and nondairy milk, stirring until smooth and well blended. Transfer the mixture to the slow cooker, stirring to combine. Cover and cook on Low for 3 hours.

4. Taste and adjust the seasonings, if needed. Use an immersion blender to blend a portion of the corn right in the slow cooker to thicken, or scoop out 2 to 3 cups of the corn and puree in a blender or food processer, then stir the puree back into the corn in the slow cooker. Serve hot.

Surprise Package Corn on the Cob

Because corn on the cob is usually in season in the heat of summer, slow cooking can come in handy when you don't want to heat up the kitchen to cook your corn. You can either wrap the shucked corn in foil or leave the green husks on and place fresh herbs inside, allowing the flavor of the herbs to infuse the corn while it gently cooks. You can also omit the herbs if you prefer plain corn on the cob.

SERVES 4

SLOW COOKER SIZE:
5½- TO 7-QUART

COOK TIME:
2 TO 4 HOURS ON LOW

GLUTEN-FREE

SOY-FREE

8 ears corn

8 to 16 sprigs thyme, rosemary, basil, or other fresh herbs or softened vegan butter blended with your choice of minced chipotle chile, lime juice, or your favorite spice blend

1 cup hot water

1. Set the ears of corn inside the slow cooker to make sure they fit. If using a shallow oval cooker, lay the corn on its side. If using a tall round cooker, stand the corn upright. Trim the ends or break the ears in half if necessary.

2. If using foil, shuck the corn. Tear off 8 sheets of aluminum foil (just large enough to fit an ear of corn inside) and place an ear of corn on each sheet. Divide the fresh herbs and/or other seasonings among the 8 ears of corn (you can use as many or as few different herbs and seasonings as you wish). Wrap each ear of corn tightly in its foil package to enclose the herbs or other seasonings with the corn.

   Alternatively, if cooking the corn in the husk, pull back the husk, remove the corn silk, place the herbs or seasonings on the corn, then pull the husk back up to enclose the herbs with the corn.

3. Place the corn in the slow cooker. Add the hot water, cover, and cook on Low until the corn is tender, 2 to 4 hours. Serve hot.

Lemony Edamame
and Potatoes with Chard

make it a point to use up whatever food is in the house before going to the supermarket. One time, these ingredients included some potatoes, frozen edamame, and a lone lemon, and the result was this light and lovely stew. This makes a hearty side dish as is. To transform it into a more substantial dish, add some sautéed seitan strips or baked diced tempeh. For a soy-free version, substitute lima beans for the edamame. Cooked cannellini beans also work well in this dish.

2 teaspoons olive oil (optional)

1 large yellow onion, chopped

3 garlic cloves, minced

1 teaspoon dried oregano

½ cup dry white wine

2 bay leaves

1½ pounds small white or red-skinned potatoes, scrubbed and halved or quartered if larger than 1 inch

3 cups fresh or thawed frozen shelled edamame

½ cup vegetable broth

1 teaspoon salt

¼ teaspoon freshly ground black pepper

2 tablespoons freshly squeezed lemon juice

8 ounces fresh Swiss chard, stemmed and coarsely chopped

¼ teaspoon red pepper flakes (optional)

3 tablespoons minced fresh flat-leaf parsley, for garnish

1 lemon, cut into wedges, for serving

SERVES 4

SLOW COOKER SIZE:
4- TO 6-QUART

COOK TIME:
6 HOURS ON LOW

GLUTEN-FREE

SOY-FREE OPTION

1. For the best flavor, heat the oil in a medium-size skillet over medium-high heat. Add the onion and sauté until softened, about 5 minutes. Stir in the garlic, oregano, and wine and cook for 2 minutes longer. Alternatively, omit the oil and sauté these ingredients in a few tablespoons of water or combine them in a microwave-safe bowl with a little water, cover, and microwave for 2 minutes.

2. Transfer the onion mixture to the slow cooker. Add the bay leaves, potatoes, edamame, and broth. Add the salt and black pepper. Cover and cook on Low until the vegetables are tender, about 5 hours.

3. Stir in the lemon juice, then taste and adjust the seasonings, if needed.

4. Place the chard in a large bowl, cover with plastic wrap, and microwave for 2 to 3 minutes to wilt. Stir the chard and red pepper flakes, if using, into the slow cooker to combine. Sprinkle with the parsley and serve hot, with the lemon wedges on the side.

Moroccan Eggplant and Artichokes

This flavorful dish is ideal served over couscous. It will serve 6 as a side dish or 4 as a main dish. If using as a main dish, consider adding 1½ to 2 cups cooked chickpeas to the mixture for added protein.

SERVES 6

SLOW COOKER SIZE:
5- TO 6-QUART

COOK TIME:
4 TO 5 HOURS ON LOW

GLUTEN-FREE

SOY-FREE

2 teaspoons olive oil (optional)
1 medium-size yellow onion, minced
4 garlic cloves, minced
1½ teaspoons grated fresh ginger
1 large eggplant, peeled and cut into ½-inch dice
Salt and freshly ground black pepper
1½ teaspoons ground coriander
1 teaspoon sweet paprika
½ teaspoon ground cumin
¼ teaspoon ground cinnamon
¼ teaspoon ground allspice or cardamom
¼ teaspoon cayenne pepper, optional
1½ cups thawed frozen artichoke hearts or 1 (14-ounce) can artichoke hearts, drained and halved
1 large red bell pepper, seeded and cut into ½-inch dice
½ cup pitted and halved kalamata olives
½ cup golden raisins or chopped dried apricots

½ cup vegetable broth

1 tablespoon freshly squeezed lemon juice

¼ cup chopped fresh flat-leaf parsley or cilantro, for garnish

1 teaspoon grated lemon zest, for garnish

1. For the best flavor, heat the oil in a large skillet over medium-high heat. Add the onion and sauté until softened, about 5 minutes. Add the garlic and ginger and cook until fragrant, 1 minute longer. Add the eggplant and season to taste with salt and pepper. Cook, stirring, for 5 minutes. Sprinkle on the coriander, paprika, cumin, cinnamon, allspice, and cayenne (if using), and stir to combine. Alternatively, omit the oil and sauté these ingredients in a few tablespoons of water or combine them in a microwave-safe bowl with a little water, cover, and microwave for 2 minutes.

2. Transfer the onion mixture to the slow cooker. Add the artichokes, bell pepper, olives, and raisins. Stir in the broth and season to taste with salt and pepper. Cover and cook on Low until the vegetables are tender, 4 to 5 hours.

3. Taste and adjust the seasonings, if needed. Serve hot, sprinkled with the lemon juice, parsley, and lemon zest.

Classic Ratatouille

Slow cooking brings out the flavors of the vegetables in this consummate summer vegetable mélange inspired by the classic Provençal dish. If you have a lot of fresh tomatoes on hand, you can use them in this recipe; otherwise, canned tomatoes will do nicely. Ratatouille can be enjoyed as a main dish when you add cooked white beans and serve it over cooked grains, polenta, or pasta. It's also a wonderful side dish or can be enjoyed as a bruschetta topping—hot, warm, or cold.

SERVES 6

SLOW COOKER SIZE:
5- TO 7-QUART

COOK TIME:
4 TO 5 HOURS ON LOW

GLUTEN-FREE

SOY-FREE

2 teaspoons olive oil (optional)

1 medium-size yellow onion, chopped

3 garlic cloves, minced

½ teaspoon dried marjoram

½ teaspoon dried basil

1 large eggplant, peeled and cut into ½-inch dice

4 small zucchini, cut into ½-inch dice

1 bell pepper (any color), seeded and cut into ½-inch dice

6 ripe red tomatoes, peeled and diced, or 1 (28-ounce) can diced tomatoes, drained

Salt and freshly ground black pepper

¼ cup chopped fresh basil or flat-leaf parsley

1. For the best flavor, heat the oil in a medium-size skillet over medium-high heat. Add the onion and sauté until softened, about 5 minutes. Add the garlic, marjoram, and dried basil and cook for 1 minute longer. Alternatively, omit the oil and sauté these ingredients in a few tablespoons of water or combine them in a microwave-safe bowl with a little water, cover, and microwave for 2 minutes.

2. Transfer the onion mixture to the slow cooker. Add the eggplant, zucchini, bell pepper, and tomatoes. Season to taste with salt and pepper. Cover and cook on Low until the vegetables are tender, 4 to 5 hours.

3. Just before serving, stir in the fresh basil. Taste and adjust the seasonings, if needed.

VARIATION

Golden Ratatouille: Use a yellow bell pepper, substitute yellow summer squash for the zucchini, and substitute fresh yellow tomatoes (peeled and diced) for the red tomatoes. For a vibrant garnish, sprinkle with sliced pitted kalamata olives.

Country French Green Beans and Tomatoes

These green beans simmered in a fragrant mixture of tomatoes, onions, and garlic are delicious as a side dish or as a topping for pasta, rice, or baked potatoes.

2 teaspoons olive oil (optional)

4 garlic cloves, minced

1 pound green beans, trimmed and cut into 1-inch pieces

4 or 5 ripe plum tomatoes, chopped, or 1 (14.5-ounce) can diced tomatoes, drained

Salt and freshly ground black pepper

2 tablespoons minced fresh basil

SERVES 4

SLOW COOKER SIZE:
4- TO 5-QUART

COOK TIME:
4 TO 5 HOURS ON LOW

GLUTEN-FREE

SOY-FREE

1. For the best flavor, heat the oil in a small skillet over medium heat. Add the garlic and cook until fragrant, about 1 minute. Alternatively, omit the oil and sauté the garlic in a few tablespoons of water or place the garlic in a microwave-safe bowl with a little water, cover, and microwave for 1 minute.

2. Lightly oil the insert of the slow cooker or spray it with nonstick cooking spray. Transfer the garlic to the cooker. Add the green beans and tomatoes, season to taste with salt and pepper, and stir to combine. Cover and cook on Low until the beans are tender, 4 to 5 hours. Sprinkle with the basil when ready to serve.

Green Bean Casserole Revisited

The sauce, made with vegan cream cheese, is very rich and can be made with white beans or tofu if you prefer. You can top the casserole with canned fried onions as a nod to the original or use toasted bread crumbs instead. For added flavor, stir half of the fried onions into the cooked casserole, and use the rest as the topping. For gluten-free, omit the fried onions or bread crumbs and top with ¼ cup ground toasted walnuts or almonds. Be sure to use a soy-free vegan cream cheese to make this casserole soy-free.

SERVES 4 TO 6

SLOW COOKER SIZE:
4- TO 5-QUART

COOK TIME:
4 TO 5 HOURS ON LOW

GLUTEN-FREE OPTION

SOY-FREE OPTION

2 teaspoons olive oil (optional)
1 small yellow onion, chopped
2 garlic cloves, minced
8 ounces vegan cream cheese, purchased or homemade (page 31)
¾ cup vegetable broth
½ teaspoon salt, plus more as needed
¼ teaspoon freshly ground black pepper
1½ pounds green beans, trimmed and cut into 1-inch pieces
8 ounces white mushrooms, sliced
1 (6-ounce) can French-fried onions or ¼ cup toasted panko bread crumbs

1. For the best flavor, heat the oil in a small skillet over medium-high heat. Add the onion and sauté until softened, about 5 minutes. Add the garlic and cook for 1 minute longer. Alternatively, omit the oil and sauté these ingredients in a few tablespoons of water or combine them in a microwave-safe bowl with a little water, cover, and microwave for 2 minutes.

2. Transfer the onion mixture to a blender or food processor. Add the cream cheese, broth, salt, and pepper and process until smooth. Taste and adjust the seasonings—you may need to add more salt depending on the saltiness of your broth.

3. Lightly oil the insert of the slow cooker or spray it with nonstick cooking spray. Combine the green beans and mushrooms in the cooker and pour the

sauce over them, making sure the vegetables are covered with the sauce. Cover and cook on Low until the green beans are tender, 4 to 5 hours.

4. When ready to serve, if using the fried onions, stir half into the green bean mixture and sprinkle the rest on top. If using toasted bread crumbs, sprinkle them all on top.

Colcannon

Making colcannon in the slow cooker is especially convenient for a St. Patrick's Day party because you can make and serve it in the same (crock)pot. Of course, you don't need to wait until March 17 to enjoy this delicious combo of potatoes and kale. Instead of kale, you may substitute chard, spinach, or even cabbage. Use a soy-free vegan butter or olive oil to make this recipe soy-free.

2 pounds Yukon Gold or russet potatoes, peeled and cut into 1-inch chunks
½ cup vegetable broth
Salt
8 ounces kale, stemmed and finely chopped
2 tablespoons vegan butter or olive oil
½ cup plain unsweetened nondairy milk, warmed
Freshly ground black pepper

SERVES 4

SLOW COOKER SIZE:
4- TO 5-QUART

COOK TIME:
4 TO 5 HOURS ON LOW

GLUTEN-FREE

SOY-FREE OPTION

1. Generously oil the insert of the slow cooker or spray it with nonstick cooking spray. Add the potatoes, broth, and ¾ to 1 teaspoon salt (depending on the saltiness of your broth). Cover and cook on Low until the potatoes are soft, 4 to 5 hours.

2. While the potatoes are cooking, steam the kale over boiling water on the stovetop until tender, 5 to 7 minutes. Set aside.

3. Use a potato masher to mash the potatoes right in the cooker. Use a wooden spoon to stir in the reserved kale, vegan butter, warm nondairy milk, and pepper to taste. Taste and adjust the seasonings, if needed. Serve hot.

Slow-Baked Taters and Sweets

Foil-wrapped potatoes create their own steam as they cook gently in the slow cooker. The size and shape of the potatoes will determine the length of cooking time needed, and the size of your slow cooker will determine how many you can cook at one time. You can also cook all of one kind of potato instead of both kinds. Typically, russet potatoes take longer to cook than sweet potatoes. If cooking both kinds, or if some potatoes are smaller than others, check each one for doneness after 4 hours of cooking.

SERVES 4

SLOW COOKER SIZE:
5- TO 6-QUART

COOK TIME:
4 TO 6 HOURS ON LOW

GLUTEN-FREE

SOY-FREE

2 to 4 russet or other baking potatoes
2 to 4 medium-size sweet potatoes

1. Wash all of the potatoes well, but do not dry them. Prick the russet potatoes with a fork and wrap each one in a sheet of aluminum foil. Wrap the sweet potatoes individually in foil as well.

2. Arrange the potatoes in a single layer in the slow cooker. Cover and cook on Low until tender, 4 to 6 hours.

Garlic Mashed Potatoes with Sour Cream and Chives

Mashed potatoes are easy to make in the slow cooker—and convenient, too, since you can cook and serve them in the same container. They also hold well on the Keep Warm setting if they finish cooking before the rest of the meal. The addition of sour cream and chives adds an extra flavor boost, but you can omit them (as well as the garlic) for more basic mashers. For soy-free, use soy-free vegan butter, vegan sour cream, and nondairy milk.

3 garlic cloves, crushed

2 pounds Yukon Gold or russet potatoes, peeled and cut into 1-inch chunks (about 6 cups)

2 cups water or vegetable broth

Salt and freshly ground black pepper

2 tablespoons vegan butter, plus more if needed (optional)

½ cup vegan sour cream, purchased or homemade (page 57)

2 tablespoons minced fresh chives or 1 tablespoon dried chives

¼ cup plain unsweetened nondairy milk, heated (optional)

SERVES 4

SLOW COOKER SIZE:
4- TO 5-QUART

COOK TIME:
3 TO 4 HOURS ON HIGH

GLUTEN-FREE

SOY-FREE OPTION

1. Combine the garlic and potatoes in the slow cooker. Add enough of the water to cover the potatoes. Season to taste with salt and pepper. (If using water, you'll need to add about 1 teaspoon salt.) Cover and cook on High until the potatoes are soft, 3 to 4 hours.

2. Carefully remove the insert of the slow cooker and drain the potatoes, then return the potatoes to the slow cooker. Add the vegan butter (if using) and the sour cream and mash the potatoes right in the slow cooker. Stir in the chives, then taste and adjust the seasonings, if needed. Add more vegan butter or a little warm nondairy milk, if needed for desired consistency. Serve hot.

Layered Tapenade Potatoes

A bold green olive, tomato, and artichoke tapenade combines with buttery Yukon Gold potatoes for a nice change from the usual potato dishes. Plan to make the tapenade the day before to save time when assembling this recipe. To make this recipe gluten-free, use gluten-free bread crumbs instead of panko.

SERVES 4 TO 6

SLOW COOKER SIZE:
4- TO 5-QUART

COOK TIME:
6 HOURS ON LOW

GLUTEN-FREE OPTION

SOY-FREE

1 (9-ounce) jar marinated artichoke hearts, drained
½ cup pitted green olives
¼ cup oil-packed or reconstituted sun-dried tomatoes, chopped
1½ tablespoons capers
2 teaspoons olive oil (optional)
1 small yellow onion, chopped
3 garlic cloves, minced
½ teaspoon dried basil
½ teaspoon dried thyme
2 pounds Yukon Gold potatoes, peeled and cut into ⅛-inch-thick slices
Salt and freshly ground black pepper
3 tablespoons toasted panko bread crumbs, for garnish
2 tablespoons minced fresh flat-leaf parsley, for garnish

1. In a food processor, combine the artichoke hearts, olives, sun-dried tomatoes, and capers. Pulse to finely mince the tapenade ingredients. If making ahead, transfer to a container, cover, and refrigerate. Allow to come to room temperature before using.

2. For the best flavor, heat the oil in a small skillet over medium-high heat. Add the onion and sauté until softened, about 5 minutes. Stir in the garlic, basil, and thyme and cook for 1 minute longer. Alternatively, omit the oil and sauté these ingredients in a few tablespoons of water or combine them in a microwave-safe bowl with a little water, cover, and microwave for 2 minutes. Set aside.

3. Lightly oil the insert of the slow cooker or spray it with nonstick cooking spray. Arrange half of the potatoes in the bottom of the insert. Season with salt and pepper and top with half of the onion mixture, followed by half of the tapenade. Top with a layer of the remaining potatoes and season to taste with salt and pepper. Spread the remaining onion mixture on top, followed by the remaining tapenade. Cover and cook on Low until the potatoes are tender, about 6 hours.

4. Sprinkle the toasted bread crumbs and parsley over the top and serve.

Granny Apple Sweet Potatoes

Sweet potatoes and Granny Smith apples complement each other in this terrific side dish that's ideal for holiday meals. Not only is it a great change from the overly sweet marshmallow-topped sweet potato casserole, but it's also more practical because it's made in a slow cooker, so it frees up oven and stove space for the rest of your dinner. Use more or less sugar, according to your personal preference. For a soy-free version, use a soy-free vegan butter.

¼ to ⅓ cup packed light brown sugar
¼ teaspoon ground cinnamon
¼ teaspoon salt
3 large sweet potatoes (about 2 pounds), peeled and thinly sliced
2 or 3 large Granny Smith apples, peeled, cored, and sliced
1 tablespoon vegan butter
1 tablespoon freshly squeezed lemon juice

SERVES 4

SLOW COOKER SIZE:
4- TO 6-QUART

COOK TIME:
5 TO 6 HOURS ON LOW

GLUTEN-FREE

SOY-FREE OPTION

1. In a small bowl, combine the brown sugar, cinnamon, and salt.

2. Lightly oil the insert of the slow cooker or spray it with nonstick cooking spray. Arrange a layer of sweet potato slices, followed by a layer of apple slices, sprinkling each layer with some of the sugar mixture. Continue layering until the ingredients are used up. Dot the top layer with the vegan butter and sprinkle with lemon juice. Cover and cook on Low until the potatoes and apples are tender, 5 to 6 hours.

Scalloped Potatoes

As Melissa Chapman said after testing these potatoes, they're obviously not a diet food. What they are is delicious, rich, and creamy—so good, in fact, that Melissa's family couldn't stop raving about them. For soy-free, use a soy-free vegan cream cheese, nondairy milk, and vegan cheese.

SERVES 4 TO 6

SLOW COOKER SIZE:
4- TO 5-QUART

COOK TIME:
5 TO 6 HOURS ON LOW

GLUTEN-FREE

SOY-FREE OPTION

2 teaspoons vegan butter or olive oil

1 small onion, minced

3 garlic cloves, minced

½ teaspoon dried thyme

1 cup vegan cream cheese, purchased or homemade (page 31)

2 tablespoons cornstarch or potato starch

1 cup plain unsweetened nondairy milk

1 teaspoon Dijon mustard

Salt and freshly ground black pepper

1 cup vegetable broth, or as needed

2 pounds russet potatoes, peeled and cut into ⅛-inch-thick slices

½ cup shredded vegan mozzarella cheese (such as Daiya), optional

1. For the best flavor, melt the butter in a small skillet over medium-high heat. Add the onion and sauté until softened, about 5 minutes. Add the garlic and thyme and cook for 1 minute longer. Alternatively, omit the butter and sauté these ingredients in a few tablespoons of water or combine them in a microwave-safe bowl with a little water, cover, and microwave for 2 minutes.

2. In a blender or food processor, combine the onion mixture with the cream cheese, cornstarch, nondairy milk, mustard, and salt and pepper to taste. Add as much of the broth as needed to make a smooth sauce.

3. Generously oil the insert of the slow cooker or spray it with nonstick cooking spray. Spread a thin layer of the sauce in the bottom of the cooker. Arrange a layer of potatoes over the sauce, add a light sprinkling of vegan cheese, if using, and sprinkle with salt and pepper. Top with a layer of sauce, and continue layering until all of the potatoes, cheese, and sauce are used, ending with a layer of sauce and a final sprinkle of cheese, if using. Cover and cook on Low until the potatoes are tender, 5 to 6 hours.

Potatoes with Tomatoes and Butter Beans

This side dish can be made with either fresh or canned tomatoes. Or, serve it with a salad as a delicious main dish. As a variation, omit the potatoes and use the tomato and butter bean mixture as a topping for baked potatoes, pasta, or spaghetti squash. To make this recipe soy-free, omit the soy sauce and use a soy-free sauce (purchased or homemade, page 35) or add some soy-free vegetable broth base or additional salt.

2 teaspoons olive oil (optional)

4 garlic cloves, minced

1 tablespoon tomato paste

1 tablespoon soy sauce

½ teaspoon dried basil

½ teaspoon dried marjoram

¼ teaspoon red pepper flakes (optional)

1½ pounds Yukon Gold potatoes, peeled and thinly sliced

Salt and freshly ground black pepper

2 cups cooked butter beans (page 104) or 1 (15-ounce) can beans, rinsed and drained (see Note)

1½ pounds ripe tomatoes, diced, or 1 (14.5-ounce) can diced tomatoes, drained

2 tablespoons chopped fresh basil or flat-leaf parsley, for garnish

SERVES 4

SLOW COOKER SIZE:
4- TO 6-QUART

COOK TIME:
4 TO 4½ HOURS
ON LOW

GLUTEN-FREE

SOY-FREE OPTION

1. For the best flavor, heat the oil in a small skillet over medium heat. Add the garlic and sauté until softened, about 1 minute. Stir in the tomato paste, soy sauce, basil, marjoram, and red pepper flakes, if using. Alternatively, omit the oil and sauté these ingredients in a few tablespoons of water or combine them in a microwave-safe bowl with a little water, cover, and microwave for 1 minute. Set aside.

2. Lightly oil the insert of the slow cooker or spray it with nonstick cooking spray. Arrange half of the potatoes evenly in the bottom of the insert, seasoning each layer with salt and pepper. Top the potatoes with half each of the beans, the tomatoes, and the garlic mixture. Top with the remaining

potatoes, seasoning each layer with salt and pepper. Add the remaining garlic mixture and beans, and end with a layer of tomatoes. Cover and cook on Low until the vegetables are tender, about 4 hours.

3. Serve hot, sprinkled with the fresh basil.

NOTE: If dried butter beans are unavailable, substitute dried gigante beans, large lima beans, or cannellini beans. If using fresh butter beans, cook them in a saucepan of boiling water for 10 minutes before adding them to the slow cooker.

Maple-Dijon Glazed Root Vegetables

This recipe is a good way to serve root vegetables to your family. I like to use more carrots because they're popular and colorful, with a lesser amount of turnips and parsnips, but you can change the ratio however you like. Slow cooking combined with maple syrup brings out the natural sweetness of root vegetables, while the mustard adds just a touch of piquancy.

SERVES 4

SLOW COOKER SIZE:
4-QUART

COOK TIME:
6 TO 8 HOURS ON LOW

GLUTEN-FREE

SOY-FREE

4 large carrots, peeled and cut into 1-inch chunks
1 medium-size turnip, peeled and cut into 1-inch cubes
1 large parsnip, peeled and cut into 1-inch pieces
4 shallots, halved
2 teaspoons olive oil
3 tablespoons maple syrup
2 tablespoons water
1 tablespoon Dijon mustard
Salt and freshly ground black pepper

1. Lightly oil the insert of the slow cooker or spray it with nonstick cooking spray. Combine the carrots, turnip, parsnip, and shallots in the cooker.

2. In a small bowl, combine the oil, maple syrup, water, and mustard, stirring to blend, then pour it over the vegetables. Season to taste with salt and pepper and stir to combine.

3. Cover and cook on Low until the vegetables are soft, 6 to 8 hours. Stir once about halfway through the cooking time, if possible.

Chimichurri Spaghetti Squash

An abundance of garlic, parsley, and oregano creates a bold, fresh taste in the Argentine chimichurri sauce that enlivens the delicate squash strands. To transform this side dish into a main dish, add sautéed seitan strips or vegan sausage, or cooked white beans. Not only is it easier to cook a spaghetti squash in a slow cooker, but it also tastes better—the long and slow cooking results in a better texture and deeper flavor. A large oval slow cooker works best for this recipe. Make sure to buy a squash that will fit, whole, inside your slow cooker.

1 spaghetti squash (any size that fits inside your slow cooker)
2 cups water
4 or 5 garlic cloves, crushed
1 small bunch fresh flat-leaf parsley, coarsely chopped (about 1½ cups)
1½ teaspoons fresh oregano or ½ teaspoon dried oregano
Pinch of sugar
¾ teaspoon salt
½ teaspoon freshly ground black pepper
¼ teaspoon red pepper flakes
2 tablespoons red wine vinegar
¼ cup olive oil

SERVES 4

SLOW COOKER SIZE:
5- TO 7-QUART

COOK TIME:
7 TO 9 HOURS ON LOW

GLUTEN-FREE

SOY-FREE

1. Pierce the squash several times with a large fork or metal skewer. Place the squash in the slow cooker and add the water. Cover and cook the squash on Low until soft when pierced, 7 to 9 hours.

2. In a food processor, combine the garlic, parsley, oregano, sugar, salt, black pepper, and red pepper flakes and process to a paste. Add the vinegar and oil and process until smooth. Taste and adjust the seasonings, if needed.

3. Once the squash is cooked, turn off the slow cooker, remove the lid, and let the squash cool for 15 minutes, then cut in half and scoop out the seeds. Drag a fork through the squash flesh to separate it into strands and transfer to a serving bowl. Add as much of the sauce as desired (depending on how much squash you have) and toss gently to coat. Serve immediately.

Winter Squash with Garlic and Ginger

I enjoy making this dish for the lovely aroma it shares with the house while it cooks. Butternut squash is used in this recipe because it peels more easily than other winter squashes. However, you can use an unpeeled kabocha or buttercup squash if you prefer—just scrub the outside well. To make this recipe soy-free, omit the soy sauce and use a soy-free sauce (purchased or homemade, page 35) or add some soy-free vegetable broth base or additional salt.

SERVES 4

SLOW COOKER SIZE:
3½ - TO 4-QUART

COOK TIME:
6 HOURS ON LOW

GLUTEN-FREE

SOY-FREE OPTION

2 teaspoons olive oil (optional)
4 garlic cloves, thinly sliced
1½ teaspoons grated fresh ginger
2 tablespoons water
1 tablespoon soy sauce
1 large butternut squash, peeled, seeded, and cut into 2-inch chunks
1 tablespoon light brown sugar
Salt and freshly ground black pepper

1. For the best flavor, heat the oil in a small skillet over medium heat. Add the garlic and ginger and sauté until fragrant, about 1 minute. Alternatively, omit the oil and sauté these ingredients in a few tablespoons of water or combine them in a microwave-safe bowl with a little water, cover, and microwave for 1 minute.

2. Lightly oil the insert of the slow cooker or spray it with nonstick cooking spray. Transfer the garlic mixture to the cooker. Stir in the water and soy sauce.

3. Add the squash chunks to the slow cooker, sprinkle with the sugar, and season to taste with salt and pepper. Stir to coat the squash with the other ingredients. Cover and cook on Low until the squash is tender, 5 to 6 hours.

4. Taste and adjust the seasonings, if needed. Serve hot.

Italian-Style Tomatoes and Zucchini

This is a great way to enjoy those two prolific summer crops, tomatoes and zucchini. Plum tomatoes will yield less watery results. To reduce the liquid in the cooker, remove the cooked vegetables with a slotted spoon, turn the cooker to High, and let the liquid reduce. At this point, you can also stir in a tablespoon of cornstarch slurry (page 14) to thicken it further, if you wish. To make this a main dish, add 1½ cups cooked or canned beans (cannellini are a good choice), then toss with cooked pasta.

2 teaspoons olive oil (optional)
1 medium-size yellow onion, minced
3 garlic cloves, minced
2 pounds zucchini, diced
2 pounds ripe plum tomatoes, diced
1 teaspoon dried basil
¾ teaspoon salt
⅛ teaspoon freshly ground black pepper
2 tablespoons minced fresh flat-leaf parsley or basil, for garnish

SERVES 6

SLOW COOKER SIZE:
5- TO 7-QUART

COOK TIME:
5 TO 6 HOURS ON LOW

GLUTEN-FREE

SOY-FREE

1. For the best flavor, heat the oil in a small skillet over medium heat. Add the onion and garlic and sauté until softened, about 4 minutes. Alternatively, omit the oil and sauté these ingredients in a few tablespoons of water or combine them in a microwave-safe bowl with a little water, cover, and microwave for 2 minutes.

2. Transfer the onion and garlic to the slow cooker and add the zucchini and tomatoes. Sprinkle with the dried basil, salt, and pepper, then stir gently to combine. Cover and cook on Low until the vegetables are tender, 4 to 6 hours.

3. Serve hot, garnished with the parsley.

Braised Vegetables with Beans and Barley

Barley is added to this simple vegetable braise to unify the other ingredients and give it a more substantial and homey feel. It also helps absorb the natural juices (and flavor) exuded by the vegetables as they cook.

SERVES 4

SLOW COOKER SIZE:
4- TO 5-QUART

COOK TIME:
3 HOURS ON HIGH

SOY-FREE

2 teaspoons olive oil (optional)
1 medium-size onion, minced
2 garlic cloves, minced
1 large carrot, thinly sliced
1 celery rib, thinly sliced
1 small red bell pepper, seeded and chopped
1 medium-size zucchini, chopped
1 small fennel bulb, thinly sliced crosswise
½ cup uncooked pearl barley
1 cup vegetable broth
1½ cups cooked cannellini beans (page 104) or 1 (15-ounce) can beans, rinsed and drained
Salt and freshly ground black pepper
1 cup cherry tomatoes, halved
½ cup thawed frozen green peas
¼ cup chopped fresh sage, basil, or marjoram

1. For the best flavor, heat the oil in a medium-size skillet over medium-high heat. Add the onion and sauté until softened, about 5 minutes. Add the garlic and cook for 1 minute longer. Alternatively, omit the oil and sauté these ingredients in a few tablespoons of water or combine them in a microwave-safe bowl with a little water, cover, and microwave for 2 minutes.

2. Transfer the onion mixture to the slow cooker. Add the carrot, celery, bell pepper, zucchini, fennel, barley, broth, and beans. Season to taste with salt and pepper and stir to combine. Cover and cook on High for 2 hours.

3. Add the tomatoes and peas and continue cooking until the vegetables and barley are tender, about 1 hour.

4. When ready to serve, taste and adjust the seasonings, if needed. Stir in the sage and serve hot.

Balsamic Vegetable Crock

More often than not, I come home from the farmers' market with more produce than my refrigerator can hold. I sometimes solve the storage problem by combining some of everything in a slow cooker. I especially enjoy using the slow cooker in the summer to avoid heating up the kitchen. The trick to keeping the just-picked flavor in these vegetables is cooking them on High until just tender. Feel free to mix and match with other vegetables and herbs. When ready to serve, a light drizzle of balsamic reduction provides the finishing touch.

2 teaspoons olive oil (optional)
3 shallots, halved
3 garlic cloves, minced
6 ounces green beans, trimmed and halved
1 red or yellow bell pepper, seeded and cut into ¼-inch strips
8 ounces mushrooms (any kind), halved, quartered, or sliced
3 small zucchini, halved lengthwise and cut into ¼-inch slices
2 small yellow summer squash, halved lengthwise and cut into ¼-inch slices
Salt and freshly ground black pepper
1½ cups cherry tomatoes, halved
3 tablespoons chopped fresh basil
2 tablespoons chopped fresh flat-leaf parsley
Balsamic Reduction (recipe follows)

SERVES 4

SLOW COOKER SIZE:
4- TO 5-QUART

COOK TIME:
2 HOURS ON HIGH

GLUTEN-FREE

SOY-FREE

1. For the best flavor, heat the oil in a small skillet over medium-high heat. Add the shallots and sauté until softened, about 3 minutes. Add the garlic and cook for 1 minute longer. Alternatively, omit the oil and sauté these ingredients in a few tablespoons of water or combine them in a microwave-safe bowl with a little water, cover, and microwave for 2 minutes.

2. Transfer the shallot mixture to the slow cooker. Add the green beans, bell pepper, mushrooms, zucchini, and yellow squash. Season to taste with salt and pepper. Cover and cook on High until the vegetables are tender, about 2 hours.

3. Stir the vegetables gently. Taste and adjust the seasonings, if needed. Add the tomatoes, basil, and parsley. Cover and cook for 10 minutes longer. Serve hot, drizzled with some of the balsamic reduction according to taste.

BALSAMIC REDUCTION

1 cup balsamic vinegar
1 to 2 tablespoons brown sugar (optional)
1 teaspoon olive oil or vegan butter (optional)

Bring the vinegar to a boil in a small saucepan over medium heat. Turn the heat to low and let it simmer until it is reduced to ½ cup, about 10 minutes, then stir in the sugar, if using. Simmer until the reduction becomes syrupy and coats the back of a wooden spoon, about 5 minutes longer. You should end up with between 1/3 and ½ cup. For richer flavor, stir in the optional olive oil (or, if using vegan butter, stir until melted). Store any leftover reduction in an airtight container in the refrigerator, where it will keep for several weeks.

chapter

9

Condiments
from the Crock

I f you've ever cooked a jam, chutney, or fruit butter on top of the stove, you know that it requires careful monitoring and lots of stirring to prevent it from scorching. When you use a slow cooker to make such condiments, those problems virtually disappear. Just load your slow cooker, turn it on, and walk away. Now *that's* convenience!

Made with a cornucopia of fresh produce, the flavorful condiments in this chapter include a luscious Butternut Butter that is great spread on toast or a bagel—or even on pancakes—and a variety of zesty chutneys guaranteed to make you swear off the expensive store-bought stuff. You'll also find slow-cooker favorites such as applesauce, apple butter, orange marmalade, and cranberry sauce on these pages, along with homemade ketchup, stone fruit jam, and a tangy barbecue sauce.

Butternut Butter

The savory yet slightly sweet flavor of this spread is great on toast, English muffins, or bagels. It's also great slathered on pancakes or waffles, followed by a drizzle of maple syrup. This butter benefits from a good stirring about halfway through the cooking process, if possible.

1 large butternut squash, peeled, seeded, and diced (about 6 cups)
1 cup apple juice
1 cup packed light brown sugar or granulated natural sugar
¼ cup maple syrup
½ teaspoon ground cinnamon
¼ teaspoon ground allspice
⅛ teaspoon ground nutmeg
⅛ teaspoon ground ginger
½ teaspoon salt

MAKES ABOUT 3 CUPS

SLOW COOKER SIZE:
4-QUART

COOK TIME:
6 TO 8 HOURS ON LOW,
PLUS 30 MINUTES ON
HIGH IF NEEDED

GLUTEN-FREE

SOY-FREE

1. Lightly oil the slow cooker insert or spray it with nonstick cooking spray. Combine all of the ingredients in the slow cooker, stirring to mix well. Cover and cook on Low until the squash is very soft, 6 to 8 hours.

2. Remove the lid and stir the mixture. If it is at all watery, turn the cooker to High and continue to cook, uncovered, for an additional 30 minutes or more.

3. Turn off the slow cooker and allow to cool completely. When cool, use an immersion blender to puree it until smooth, or transfer the mixture to a food processor or blender and process until smooth. The butternut butter will keep in an airtight container in the refrigerator for up to 6 weeks.

Slow-Cooked Apple Butter

Apple butter requires a long, slow cooking process, making it ideal for a slow cooker, especially since it can easily scorch if left unattended on the stovetop. Unpeeled apples are used because the pectin contained in the skin helps to thicken the apple butter, so buy organic apples if possible. You might want to make this overnight since it takes so long to cook. When you wake up, your house will smell like apple pie. The cooking time will depend on how juicy your apples are, and the amount of sugar used depends on how sweet you like your apple butter. It's great spread on toast or waffles or spooned into hot oatmeal.

MAKES ABOUT 4 CUPS

SLOW COOKER SIZE:
4- TO 6-QUART

COOK TIME:
8 HOURS ON LOW PLUS
2 TO 4 HOURS ON HIGH

GLUTEN-FREE

SOY-FREE

2½ to 3 pounds cooking apples (I prefer McIntosh or Stayman for this recipe), washed, cored, and thickly sliced

1¼ cups natural sugar, or more to taste

⅓ cup apple juice

Juice of 1 lemon

1 tablespoon ground cinnamon

¼ teaspoon ground allspice

¼ teaspoon ground nutmeg

¼ teaspoon ground ginger

¼ teaspoon ground cloves

1. Combine all of the ingredients in the slow cooker. Cover and cook on Low until the apples are very soft, about 8 hours.

2. Remove the lid, turn the heat to High, and stir the mixture. Continue to cook, uncovered, until the mixture thickens, 2 to 4 hours. When the apple butter has reached the thickness you prefer, turn off the slow cooker, remove the lid, and allow to cool completely. When cool, transfer the mixture to a food processor or blender and process until smooth. Alternatively, you can process the apples through a food mill to remove the bits of peel.

3. The apple butter will keep in an airtight container in the refrigerator for up to 2 months.

Cinnamon Applesauce

Living in "apple country" in the Shenandoah Valley of Virginia, we get our pick of great apples. This applesauce is delicious made with a single variety of apple, but I prefer the complexity of combining a few different varieties. My favorites for applesauce are listed below. We love our applesauce spiced with cinnamon (the house smells like apple pie when this is cooking), but if you're not a cinnamon fan, just leave it out.

2 ½ pounds apples, such as Rome Beauty, Pink Lady, or McIntosh, peeled, cored, and diced

⅓ cup granulated natural sugar

1 to 1½ teaspoons ground cinnamon, to your taste

Pinch of salt

½ cup apple juice

1 tablespoon freshly squeezed lemon juice

MAKES ABOUT 3 CUPS

SLOW COOKER SIZE:
4- TO 5-QUART

COOK TIME:
3 TO 4 HOURS ON LOW

GLUTEN-FREE

SOY-FREE

1. Combine all of the ingredients in the slow cooker. Cover and cook on Low until the apples are very soft, 3 to 4 hours.

2. Turn off the slow cooker, remove the lid, and use a potato masher to mash the apples if they are still too chunky. Taste and adjust the seasonings, if needed. Serve warm or at room temperature. If not serving right away, allow to cool completely. The applesauce will keep in an airtight container in the refrigerator for up to 1 week.

Ginger Cran-Apple Chutney

This chutney combines tart cranberries and sweet apples with zesty ginger for a luscious condiment that can be enjoyed in place of cranberry sauce around the holidays. The combination of fresh and crystallized ginger adds depth of flavor. If crystallized ginger is unavailable, you may simply omit it.

MAKES ABOUT 4 CUPS

SLOW COOKER SIZE:
4- TO 5-QUART

COOK TIME:
4 TO 5 HOURS ON LOW

GLUTEN-FREE

SOY-FREE

1 (12-ounce) bag fresh cranberries, rinsed and picked over
½ cup sweetened dried cranberries
2 large apples, cored and finely chopped
2 shallots, minced
1½ teaspoons grated fresh ginger
1 teaspoon chopped crystallized ginger (optional)
1¼ cups packed light brown sugar or granulated natural sugar
¼ cup cider vinegar
Grated zest of 1 lemon or orange

1. Combine all of the ingredients in the slow cooker, stirring to combine. Cover and cook on Low until the chutney becomes jam-like, about 4 hours.

2. Remove the lid, then taste and adjust the seasonings, if needed. Continue to cook, uncovered, until any liquid is evaporated and the chutney thickens, about 30 minutes. Taste and adjust the seasonings, if needed. Turn off the slow cooker and allow to cool completely.

3. The chutney will keep in an airtight container in the refrigerator for up to 2 months. Serve chilled or at room temperature.

Mixed Fruit Chutney

This spicy-sweet chutney combines fresh and dried fruit, making it easy to adapt to whatever fruit you prefer or have on hand. You can mix and match the types of dried fruit, using a single variety or two, such as dried apricots and pears, or a mix of several. For fresh fruit, use your choice of apples, pears, peaches, or pineapple. In addition to serving with Indian food, this chutney is great on veggie burgers and makes a delicious accompaniment to Mom-Style Vegan Meatloaf (page 148) or roasted vegetables.

5 large apples or just-ripe pears, peeled, cored, and coarsely chopped, or 5 or 6 large underripe peaches, peeled (see Note), pitted, and diced
2 cups dried fruit (any kind), chopped
⅓ cup golden raisins
2 shallots, minced
1 cup granulated natural sugar
½ cup cider vinegar
2 teaspoons grated fresh ginger
¼ teaspoon salt
¼ teaspoon red pepper flakes

MAKES ABOUT 4 CUPS

SLOW COOKER SIZE:
4- TO 5-QUART

COOK TIME:
4 HOURS ON HIGH

GLUTEN-FREE

SOY-FREE

1. Combine all of the ingredients in the slow cooker, stirring to combine. Cover and cook on High until the chutney becomes jam-like, about 3½ hours.

2. Remove the lid, then taste and adjust the seasonings, if needed. Continue to cook, uncovered, until the liquid is evaporated and the chutney thickens, about 30 minutes. Taste and adjust the seasonings, if needed. Turn off the slow cooker and allow to cool completely.

3. The chutney will keep in an airtight container in the refrigerator for up to 3 months. Serve chilled or at room temperature.

NOTE: To peel peaches, simply plunge them into boiling water for about 15 seconds and then into ice water—the skins will slip off easily.

Granny Apple–Green Tomato Chutney

Green tomatoes and Granny Smith apples combine for a luscious chutney that is as at home with Indian meals as it is with a veggie burger, vegan meatloaf, or roasted vegetables.

**MAKES ABOUT
3½ CUPS**

SLOW COOKER SIZE:
4-QUART

COOK TIME:
4½ HOURS ON HIGH

GLUTEN-FREE

SOY-FREE

5 large green tomatoes, peeled (see Note), seeded, and chopped
2 large Granny Smith apples, peeled, cored, and chopped
2 shallots, chopped
1 cup raisins
¾ cup granulated natural sugar
¼ cup cider vinegar
2 teaspoons grated fresh ginger
1 teaspoon salt
¼ teaspoon ground cloves or allspice
¼ teaspoon red pepper flakes

1. Combine all of the ingredients in the slow cooker. Cover and cook on High until the chutney becomes jam-like, about 4 hours.

2. Remove the lid, then taste and adjust the seasonings, if needed. Continue to cook, uncovered, until any liquid is evaporated and the chutney thickens, about 30 minutes. Taste and adjust the seasonings, if needed. Turn off the slow cooker and allow to cool completely.

3. The chutney will keep in an airtight container in the refrigerator for up to 2 months. Serve chilled or at room temperature.

NOTE: To peel tomatoes, simply plunge them into boiling water for about 15 seconds and then into ice water—the skins will slip off easily.

Peach and Dried Blueberry Chutney

When you need a tasty accompaniment to your meal, chutney may be just the thing. This one, made with fresh peaches and dried blueberries, is a terrific accompaniment for many seitan or tempeh recipes, as well as grain and bean dishes.

5 or 6 large underripe peaches, peeled (see Note), pitted, and chopped
¾ cup dried blueberries
3 tablespoons minced onion
1 cup packed light brown sugar or granulated natural sugar
⅓ cup cider vinegar
1 teaspoon grated fresh ginger
½ teaspoon salt
¼ teaspoon red pepper flakes (optional)

**MAKES ABOUT
3½ CUPS**

SLOW COOKER SIZE:
4-QUART

COOK TIME:
4½ HOURS ON HIGH

GLUTEN-FREE

SOY-FREE

1. Combine all of the ingredients in the slow cooker. Cover and cook on High until the chutney becomes jam-like, about 4 hours.

2. Remove the lid, then taste and adjust the seasonings, if needed. Continue to cook, uncovered, until any liquid is evaporated and the chutney thickens, about 30 minutes. Taste and adjust the seasonings, if needed. Turn off the slow cooker and allow to cool completely.

3. The chutney will keep in an airtight container in the refrigerator for up to 3 weeks. Serve chilled or at room temperature.

NOTE: To peel peaches, simply plunge them into boiling water for about 15 seconds and then into ice water—the skins will slip off easily.

Mango Chutney with Dates and Lime

Mangoes and dates have a natural affinity. The addition of lime (rind and all) makes this one delicious chutney. Since you are using the entire lime, including the peel, try to buy organic limes. Enjoy this chutney with your favorite Indian food, or use it to enliven even a simple meal of rice and beans.

MAKES ABOUT 3 CUPS

SLOW COOKER SIZE:
4-QUART

COOK TIME:
4½ HOURS ON HIGH

GLUTEN-FREE

SOY-FREE

3 large ripe mangoes, peeled, pitted, and chopped
8 ounces pitted dates, chopped
2 large shallots, minced
2 limes, washed, quartered, and chopped
2 teaspoons grated fresh ginger
1 cup firmly packed light brown sugar or granulated natural sugar
½ cup cider vinegar
½ teaspoon ground coriander
½ teaspoon ground cinnamon
½ teaspoon red pepper flakes

1. Combine all of the ingredients in the slow cooker. Cover and cook on High until the chutney becomes jam-like, about 4 hours.

2. Remove the lid, then taste and adjust the seasonings, if needed. Continue to cook, uncovered, until any liquid is evaporated and the chutney thickens, about 30 minutes. Taste and adjust the seasonings, if needed. Turn off the slow cooker and allow to cool completely.

3. The chutney will keep in an airtight container in the refrigerator for up to 3 weeks. Serve chilled or at room temperature.

Pear Confit

This delicious condiment is equally good served with sweet or savory foods. Serve it on vegan ice cream or a slice of cake or tea bread for an easy dessert, or on toast or a bagel for breakfast. It can also be used instead of a chutney or other relish, or to accompany Seitan Pot Roast (page 126).

6 to 8 underripe pears, peeled, cored, and chopped (about 3 pounds)
½ cup golden raisins
1 cup packed light brown sugar
1 teaspoon grated fresh ginger
½ teaspoon ground cinnamon
Pinch of salt
1 cup apple juice
Juice and zest of 2 lemons

MAKES ABOUT 3 CUPS

SLOW COOKER SIZE:
4-QUART

COOK TIME:
6 TO 8 HOURS ON LOW
PLUS 1 HOUR ON HIGH

GLUTEN-FREE

SOY-FREE

1. Combine the pears, raisins, brown sugar, ginger, cinnamon, salt, apple juice, and lemon zest in the slow cooker. Cover and cook on Low until the pears are soft and the texture is jam-like, 6 to 8 hours.

2. Remove the lid and turn the setting to High. Continue to cook, uncovered, until thick, about 1 hour, stirring occasionally.

3. Stir in the lemon juice, then taste and adjust the seasonings, if needed. Turn off the slow cooker and allow to cool completely. Serve chilled or at room temperature. The confit will keep in an airtight container in the refrigerator for up to 2 weeks.

Easiest Cranberry Sauce

Just three ingredients and two hours in the slow cooker result in a great-tasting cranberry sauce that thickens as it cools. This makes a fairly tart cranberry sauce, so if you prefer it sweeter, use more sugar and/or less lemon juice.

MAKES ABOUT 2 CUPS

SLOW COOKER SIZE:
4- TO 6-QUART

COOK TIME:
2 HOURS ON HIGH

GLUTEN-FREE

SOY-FREE

1 (12-ounce) bag fresh cranberries, rinsed and picked over
1 cup natural sugar
1 tablespoon freshly squeezed lemon, lime, or orange juice
Finely grated zest of 1 lemon, lime, or orange

1. Combine the cranberries, sugar, and juice in the slow cooker, stirring to mix. Cover and cook on High until the cranberries have popped, about 2 hours.

2. Stir in the zest, then taste and adjust the seasonings, if needed. Turn off the slow cooker, remove the lid, and allow to cool completely. Serve chilled or at room temperature. The cranberry sauce will keep in an airtight container in the refrigerator for up to 2 weeks.

Stone Fruit Jam

This luscious fruit jam combines two of my summertime favorites—peaches and apricots. But you may also use plums, pluots, or plucots—they're all welcome additions, so feel free to mix and match your favorites, or use just one kind of fruit. If you can use locally grown fruit at the peak of its season, it will make this jam even more special. The jam needs to cool and then chill in the refrigerator in order for it to thicken nicely.

MAKES ABOUT 4 CUPS

SLOW COOKER SIZE:
4- TO 5-QUART

COOK TIME:
5 HOURS ON HIGH
(2 HOURS COVERED;
3 HOURS UNCOVERED)

GLUTEN-FREE

SOY-FREE

2 pounds fresh firm peaches, peeled (see Note), pitted, and chopped
1 pound fresh firm apricots, peeled (see Note), pitted, and chopped
3 tablespoons freshly squeezed lemon juice
1 (1.75-ounce) package pectin
3 cups sugar, or to taste

1. Combine the peaches, apricots, and lemon juice in the slow cooker, stirring to mix. For a less chunky jam, crush the fruit with a potato masher. Sprinkle on the pectin and let stand for 20 minutes, then stir in the sugar. Cover and cook on High for 2 hours, stirring once about halfway through.

2. Remove the lid and continue to cook until the jam reaches your preferred consistency, about 3 hours. Turn off the slow cooker and allow to cool completely. Ladle the jam into jars or other containers with tight-fitting lids and refrigerate until chilled and thickened, at least 4 hours. The jam will keep in an airtight container in the refrigerator for up to 8 weeks or in the freezer for up to 3 months.

NOTE: To peel peaches and apricots, simply plunge them into boiling water for about 15 seconds and then into ice water—the skins will slip off easily.

Orange Marmalade with a Twist of Lemon

The addition of lemon juice and zest adds a nice twist to this flavorful marmalade. Orange marmalade can be used in lots of recipes, including the Artisanal Sweet and Spicy Wiener Balls (page 36) and the Citrus-Braised Beets (page 196). It's best to use organic oranges since you'll be including the peel in this recipe—and be sure to wash the oranges well.

4 Valencia or navel oranges (about 2 pounds), washed
3½ cups water
4 cups sugar
Juice and zest of 1 lemon

MAKES ABOUT 4 CUPS

SLOW COOKER SIZE:
4- TO 5-QUART

COOK TIME:
6 TO 7 HOURS ON HIGH

GLUTEN-FREE

SOY-FREE

1. Using a vegetable peeler or sharp paring knife, remove just the colored part of the peel from the oranges. Cut the strips of peel crosswise into very fine shards. Quarter the oranges and remove and discard any seeds and as much white pith as you can.

2. Transfer the orange pieces to a food processor and pulse until chopped. Transfer the oranges and peel to the slow cooker. Add the water, sugar, and lemon zest. Stir to combine. Cover and cook on High, stirring occasionally, until the peel becomes translucent, about 4 hours.

3. Remove the lid, stir in the lemon juice, and continue to cook, uncovered, until the mixture reduces and becomes syrupy, 2 to 3 hours.

4. Turn off the slow cooker and allow to cool completely; the marmalade will thicken more as it cools. The marmalade will keep in an airtight container in the refrigerator for up to 2 months.

Handcrafted Ketchup

Making your own ketchup elevates this all-purpose condiment from average to awesome. In addition to having a bright, fresh flavor (even when made with canned puree), this ketchup contains far less sodium and none of the high-fructose sweeteners that can be found in many store-bought brands. Note that the higher water content of fresh tomatoes necessitates the longer cooking time for that version.

MAKES ABOUT 3 CUPS

SLOW COOKER SIZE:
4-QUART

COOK TIME:
3 HOURS ON HIGH
(FOR TOMATO PUREE)
OR 4½ HOURS ON HIGH
(FOR FRESH
TOMATOES)

GLUTEN-FREE

SOY-FREE

1 small yellow onion, quartered

⅓ cup packed light brown sugar or granulated natural sugar

⅓ cup cider vinegar

2 (28-ounce) cans tomato puree or 4 pounds ripe tomatoes, peeled, seeded, and diced

½ teaspoon dry mustard

¼ teaspoon ground cinnamon

¼ teaspoon ground ginger

¼ teaspoon ground allspice

¼ teaspoon ground cloves or mace

Salt and freshly ground black pepper

1. Process the onion in a food processor until finely minced. Add the sugar and vinegar and process until smooth. Transfer the mixture to the slow cooker. Add the remaining ingredients and stir to combine. Cover and cook on High, stirring occasionally, for 2½ hours.

2. Remove the lid and cook until the ketchup thickens, about 30 minutes longer if using puree or about 2 hours longer if using fresh tomatoes. Taste and adjust the seasonings, adding more salt or sugar, if needed.

3. Turn off the slow cooker and allow to cool completely. The ketchup will keep in an airtight container in the refrigerator for several weeks.

Better Barbecue Sauce

This recipe makes a lot, but the sauce keeps well in the refrigerator or freezer. Since the flavor of the seasonings may dissipate after long cooking, you may need to add more spices near the end of the cooking time. This recipe can be made soy-free by omitting the soy sauce and Worcestershire sauce and using a soy-free sauce (purchased or homemade, page 35) or adding some soy-free vegetable broth base or additional salt.

2 teaspoons olive oil (optional)
1 medium-size yellow onion, minced
2 garlic cloves, minced
1 chipotle chile in adobo, minced
1 (8-ounce) can tomato sauce
1 cup ketchup
3 tablespoons light brown sugar
1 tablespoon vegan Worcestershire sauce
1 tablespoon soy sauce
1 teaspoon smoked paprika
½ teaspoon ground cumin
½ teaspoon chili powder
½ teaspoon ground coriander
¼ teaspoon dry mustard
¼ teaspoon cayenne pepper
Salt and freshly ground black pepper

MAKES ABOUT 3 CUPS

SLOW COOKER SIZE:
4-QUART

COOK TIME:
4 HOURS ON LOW

GLUTEN-FREE

SOY-FREE OPTION

¼ cup water
⅓ cup apple cider vinegar
1 teaspoon liquid smoke

1. For the best flavor, heat the oil in a medium-size skillet over medium-high heat. Add the onion and sauté until softened, about 5 minutes. Add the garlic and cook for 1 minute longer. Alternatively, omit the oil and sauté these ingredients in a few tablespoons of water or combine them in a microwave-safe bowl, cover, and microwave for 2 to 3 minutes.

2. Transfer the onion mixture to the slow cooker. Add the chipotle, tomato sauce, ketchup, brown sugar, Worcestershire sauce, soy sauce, paprika, cumin, chili powder, coriander, mustard, cayenne, and salt and pepper to taste. Stir in the water. Cover and cook on Low for 4 hours.

3. Stir in the vinegar and liquid smoke. Taste and adjust the seasonings, if needed. If a thicker sauce is desired, remove the lid, turn the setting to High, and continue to cook, stirring occasionally, until it is reduced to the desired consistency, about 30 minutes. Taste and adjust the seasonings, if needed.

4. Use an immersion blender to puree the mixture until smooth, or allow it to cool in the slow cooker, then transfer to a blender or food processor and process until smooth. When completely cool, transfer to an airtight container and store in the refrigerator for up to 8 weeks or in the freezer for up to 3 months.

Don't Forget Dessert

While you may expect a slow cooker to be useful for making bread puddings or even baked apples, you may be surprised to learn that you can also make cobblers, cakes, and even cheesecakes—all without turning on the oven. I like to see people's expressions when I tell them that the cheesecake they're enjoying not only contains no dairy, but was also "baked" in a slow cooker.

There are several advantages to making desserts in a slow cooker. For one thing, it's more economical than heating your oven, which, in the summer, provides the added advantage of keeping the kitchen cool. "Baking" in a slow cooker produces moist cakes and other desserts without the worry of scorching or burning, as the steamy heat of the cooker gently transforms ingredients into tasty treats.

Because many people have only one slow cooker—and it's usually either a 4-quart or a 6-quart—I've done my best to provide options for making these desserts using either size. Some desserts, such as puddings, are best made directly in the slow cooker insert, while other desserts, such as cakes, are best "baked" in pans that are set inside the slow cooker. Even so, instructions are provided to prepare most of these recipes either way.

If you plan to make a dessert using a baking pan, be sure you have a pan that fits inside your slow cooker. For example, a 7-inch springform pan will fit inside a 6-quart slow cooker. You should also be able to find small cake pans, glass or ceramic baking dishes, or aluminum pans that will work. (Some people even use coffee cans for breads.) Also available are baking pans that are made to fit inside slow cookers.

Some of these recipes call for a rack or trivet to suspend the pan above a small amount of water in the bottom of the cooker. For this purpose, you may use virtually any heatproof object, including a ring made of crumpled aluminum foil or a small heatproof bowl. Special racks designed to fit inside your slow cooker may also be available from the manufacturer.

Whether you "bake" your cakes and other desserts directly in the slow cooker or in a pan set inside the cooker, you may want to place a piece of parchment paper, cut to fit, in the bottom of your pan or slow cooker insert for easy removal of your dessert. When baking cakes inside a slow cooker, I recommend draping a clean kitchen towel over the cooker before putting on the lid in order to prevent water condensation droplets from dripping onto the cake as it bakes.

Applesauce-Walnut Cake

This flavorful old-fashioned treat can be made either directly in the insert of a 4-quart round cooker or in a small baking pan set inside a 6-quart oval cooker.

SERVES 6 TO 8

SLOW COOKER SIZE:
4-QUART OR 6-QUART

COOK TIME:
2 HOURS ON HIGH FOR
4-QUART; 3 HOURS ON
HIGH FOR 6-QUART

SOY-FREE

1¾ cups unbleached all-purpose flour

⅔ cup packed light brown sugar or granulated natural sugar

1 teaspoon baking powder

½ teaspoon baking soda

½ teaspoon salt

1½ teaspoons ground cinnamon

¼ teaspoon ground allspice

¼ teaspoon ground nutmeg

⅛ teaspoon ground cloves

1 cup unsweetened applesauce

1 tablespoon freshly squeezed lemon juice

1 teaspoon pure vanilla extract

¼ cup vegetable oil

½ cup chopped walnuts

1. If using a 4-quart slow cooker, place a round of parchment paper, cut to fit, in the bottom of the slow cooker insert. Coat the parchment and sides of the insert with nonstick cooking spray. If using a 6-quart slow cooker, place a rack, trivet, or a ring of crumpled aluminum foil in the bottom of the insert. Lightly oil a baking pan that will fit in the cooker and set aside. If using a springform pan, wrap the outside bottom and sides of the pan with foil to prevent leakage.

2. In a large bowl, combine the flour, sugar, baking powder, baking soda, salt, cinnamon, allspice, nutmeg, and cloves. Mix well.

3. In a separate bowl, combine the applesauce, lemon juice, vanilla, and oil. Mix well. Stir the wet mixture into the dry mixture, mixing until smooth and well blended. Fold in the walnuts.

4. If using a 4-quart slow cooker, transfer the batter directly into the slow cooker, spreading evenly. Drape a clean kitchen towel over the cooker, put on the lid, and cook on High until a tester inserted in the center of the cake comes out clean, about 2 hours. Remove the lid and towel, turn off the cooker, and allow the cake to cool completely before serving.

If using a 6-quart slow cooker, transfer the batter to the prepared baking pan. Pour about 1 inch of hot water into the bottom of the insert and place the pan on the rack inside the slow cooker. Drape a clean kitchen towel over the cooker, put on the lid, and cook on High until a tester inserted in the center of the cake comes out clean, about 3 hours. Remove the pan from the cooker and set aside to cool completely before serving.

Fat-Free Apple Crock Cake

Apple cakes are so delicious that I thought I'd include two versions. Whereas the previous recipe is made with applesauce, nuts, and oil, this one uses fresh apples and eliminates the oil and nuts. Many thanks to recipe tester Barbara Bryan for testing this cake several times to get the texture just right while making it deliciously fat-free. This can be made either directly in the insert of a 4-quart round cooker or in a small baking pan set inside a 6-quart oval cooker.

1¾ cups unbleached all-purpose flour
1 teaspoon baking powder
1 teaspoon baking soda
½ teaspoon salt
1 teaspoon ground cinnamon
¼ teaspoon ground allspice
¼ teaspoon ground nutmeg
Pinch of ground cloves
1 cup packed light brown sugar or granulated natural sugar
1 tablespoon freshly squeezed lemon juice

SERVES 6 TO 8

SLOW COOKER SIZE:
4-QUART OR 6-QUART

COOK TIME:
2 TO 2½ HOURS ON
HIGH FOR 4-QUART;
3 HOURS ON HIGH
FOR 6-QUART

SOY-FREE

1 teaspoon pure vanilla extract
½ cup unsweetened applesauce
2 Granny Smith or Stayman apples, peeled, cored, and chopped (about 2 cups)
Confectioners' sugar

1. If using a 4-quart slow cooker, place a round of parchment paper, cut to fit, in the bottom of the slow cooker insert. Coat the parchment and sides of the insert with nonstick cooking spray. If using a 6-quart slow cooker, place a rack, trivet, or a ring of crumpled aluminum foil in the bottom of the insert. Lightly oil a baking pan that will fit in the cooker and set aside. If using a springform pan, wrap the outside bottom and sides of the pan with foil to prevent leakage.

2. In a large bowl, combine the flour, baking powder, baking soda, salt, cinnamon, allspice, nutmeg, and cloves.

3. In a separate bowl, combine the sugar, lemon juice, vanilla, and applesauce and mix well. Add the apples and stir to coat. Stir the wet mixture into the dry mixture, mixing until well blended.

4. If using a 4-quart slow cooker, transfer the batter directly into the slow cooker, spreading evenly. Drape a clean kitchen towel over the cooker, put on the lid, and cook on High until a tester inserted in the center of the cake comes out clean, 2 to 2½ hours. Remove the lid and towel, turn off the cooker, and allow to cool completely. Dust the top with confectioners' sugar just before serving.

   If using a 6-quart slow cooker, transfer the batter to the prepared baking pan. Pour about 1 inch of hot water into the bottom of the insert and place the pan on the rack inside the slow cooker. Drape a clean kitchen towel over the cooker, put on the lid, and cook on High until a tester inserted in the center of the cake comes out clean, about 3 hours. Remove the pan from the cooker and set aside to cool completely. Dust the top with confectioners' sugar just before serving.

Piña Colada Cake

If you like piña coladas—or the flavor of creamy coconut and sweet pineapple with a hint of rum—you'll love this cake. This recipe can be made either directly in the insert of a 4-quart round cooker or in a small baking pan set inside a 6-quart oval cooker. To make this recipe soy-free, use a soy-free vegan butter or vegetable oil.

2 cups unbleached all-purpose flour

⅓ cup packed light brown sugar or granulated natural sugar

¼ cup unsweetened shredded coconut, plus more for garnish (optional)

1½ teaspoons baking powder

½ teaspoon baking soda

½ teaspoon salt

1 cup cream of coconut

3 tablespoons vegan butter, softened, or vegetable oil

¾ cup finely chopped fresh or canned pineapple, well drained, juice reserved

⅓ cup plus 2 tablespoons pineapple juice from the chopped pineapple, plus more if needed (add purchased pineapple juice if necessary to yield the required amount)

1 tablespoon dark rum or 1 teaspoon rum extract

½ teaspoon coconut extract

1 teaspoon apple cider vinegar

1 cup confectioners' sugar

SERVES 6

SLOW COOKER SIZE:
4-QUART OR 6-QUART

COOK TIME:
2 HOURS ON HIGH
FOR 4-QUART;
3½ TO 4 HOURS ON
HIGH FOR 6-QUART

SOY-FREE OPTION

1. If using a 4-quart slow cooker, place a round of parchment paper, cut to fit, in the bottom of the slow cooker insert. Coat the parchment and sides of the insert with nonstick cooking spray. If using a 6-quart slow cooker, place a rack, trivet, or a ring of crumpled aluminum foil in the bottom of the insert. Lightly oil a baking pan that will fit in the cooker and set aside. If using a springform pan, wrap the outside bottom and sides of the pan with foil to prevent leakage.

2. In a large bowl, combine the flour, sugar, ¼ cup shredded coconut, baking powder, baking soda, and salt and stir to combine.

3. In a separate bowl, combine the cream of coconut, vegan butter, chopped pineapple, ⅓ cup of the reserved pineapple juice, rum, coconut extract, and

vinegar. Add the wet mixture to the dry mixture about a third at a time, mixing well after each addition.

4. If using a 4-quart slow cooker, transfer the batter directly into the slow cooker, spreading evenly. Drape a clean kitchen towel over the cooker, put on the lid, and cook on High until a tester inserted in the center of the cake comes out clean, about 2 hours. (Check the cake at 1 hour and 45 minutes if your cooker runs hot.) Remove the lid and towel, turn off the cooker, and allow the cake to cool completely.

   If using a 6-quart slow cooker, transfer the batter to the prepared baking pan, spreading it evenly. Pour about 1 inch of hot water into the bottom of the insert and place the pan on the rack inside the slow cooker. Drape a clean kitchen towel over the cooker, put on the lid, and cook on High until a tester inserted in the center of the cake comes out clean, 3 to 4 hours. Remove the pan from the cooker and set aside to cool completely.

5. Once the cake is cool, place the confectioners' sugar in a small bowl. Stir in the remaining 2 tablespoons pineapple juice and continue stirring until it is a well-blended glaze, adding additional pineapple juice a teaspoon at a time if the glaze is too thick. Pour the glaze onto the cake, spreading with a spatula, if needed, to cover the top. Sprinkle the top with additional coconut, if desired. Serve immediately or refrigerate for 20 minutes to set the glaze.

Spiced Pumpkin Cake

The daughter of one of the recipe testers who made this cake said that if she could bake autumn, this is what it would taste like. This cake can be made either directly in the insert of a 4-quart round cooker or in a small baking pan set inside a 6-quart oval cooker. The chocolate frosting on page 250 is wonderful on this cake.

1¾ cups unbleached all-purpose flour
¾ cup packed light brown sugar or granulated natural sugar
1½ teaspoons baking powder

½ teaspoon salt

1 teaspoon ground cinnamon

½ teaspoon ground allspice

½ teaspoon ground nutmeg

¼ teaspoon ground cloves

1 cup canned solid-pack pumpkin

¼ cup unsweetened almond milk

¼ cup vegetable oil

1 teaspoon pure vanilla extract or rum extract

½ cup chopped pecans (optional)

SERVES 6

SLOW COOKER SIZE:
4-QUART OR 6-QUART

COOK TIME:
2½ HOURS ON HIGH
FOR 4-QUART;
3½ HOURS ON HIGH
FOR 6-QUART

SOY-FREE

1. If using a 4-quart slow cooker, place a round of parchment paper, cut to fit, in the bottom of the slow cooker insert. Coat the parchment and sides of the insert with nonstick cooking spray. If using a 6-quart slow cooker, place a rack, trivet, or a ring of crumpled aluminum foil in the bottom of the insert. Lightly oil a baking pan that will fit in the cooker. If using a springform pan, wrap the outside bottom and sides of the pan with foil to prevent leakage.

2. In a large bowl, combine the flour, sugar, baking powder, salt, cinnamon, allspice, nutmeg, and cloves. Mix well.

3. In a separate bowl, combine the pumpkin, almond milk, oil, and vanilla. Mix well. Stir the wet mixture into the dry mixture, mixing until smooth and well blended. Fold in the pecans, if using.

4. If using a 4-quart slow cooker, transfer the batter directly into the slow cooker, spreading evenly. Drape a clean kitchen towel over the cooker, put on the lid, and cook on High until a tester inserted in the center of the cake comes out clean, about 2½ hours. (Check the cake at 2 hours if your cooker runs hot.) Remove the lid and towel, turn off the cooker, and allow the cake to cool completely before serving.

   If using a 6-quart slow cooker, transfer the batter to the prepared baking pan, spreading it evenly. Pour about 1 inch of hot water into the bottom of the insert and place the pan on the rack inside the slow cooker. Drape a clean kitchen towel over the cooker, put on the lid, and cook on High until a tester inserted in the center of the cake comes out clean, about 3½ hours. Remove the pan from the cooker and set aside to cool completely before serving.

Chocolate Truffle Cake

This dense chocolate cake is rich and fudgy, so even a small piece will satisfy. This recipe can be made either directly in the insert of a 4-quart round cooker or in a small baking pan set inside a 6-quart oval cooker. For soy-free, use a soy-free vegan butter and soy-free nondairy milk.

SERVES 6 TO 8

SLOW COOKER SIZE:
4-QUART OR 6-QUART

COOK TIME:
1½ HOURS ON HIGH
FOR 4-QUART;
3 TO 4 HOURS ON
HIGH FOR 6-QUART

SOY-FREE OPTION

CAKE:
1½ cups unbleached all-purpose flour
¼ cup unsweetened cocoa powder
1½ teaspoons baking powder
¼ teaspoon baking soda
¼ teaspoon salt
3 tablespoons vegan butter, softened
⅔ cup granulated natural sugar
1 cup nondairy milk
1 teaspoon pure vanilla extract
½ teaspoon cider vinegar

FROSTING:
¼ cup unsweetened cocoa powder
2 tablespoons vegan butter, melted
1 teaspoon pure vanilla extract
3 tablespoons nondairy milk, plus more if needed
1½ cups confectioners' sugar, plus more if needed

1. If using a 4-quart slow cooker, place a round of parchment paper, cut to fit, in the bottom of the slow cooker insert. Coat the parchment and sides of the cooker with nonstick cooking spray. If using a 6-quart slow cooker, place a rack, trivet, or a ring of crumpled aluminum foil inside the slow cooker. Lightly oil a baking pan that will fit in the cooker. If using a springform pan, wrap the outside bottom and sides of the pan with foil to prevent leakage.

2. For the cake: In a medium-size bowl, combine the flour, cocoa powder, baking powder, baking soda, and salt. Set aside.

3. In the bowl of an electric mixer, cream together the vegan butter and granulated sugar on high speed until blended. Beat in the nondairy milk, vanilla, and vinegar until blended. Add the flour mixture and incorporate on low speed until evenly mixed.

4. If using a 4-quart slow cooker, transfer the batter directly into the slow cooker, spreading evenly. Drape a clean kitchen towel over the cooker, put on the lid, and cook on High until a tester inserted in the center of the cake comes out clean, about 1½ hours. Remove the lid and towel, turn off the cooker, and allow to cool completely.

   If using a 6-quart slow cooker, transfer the batter to the prepared baking pan, spreading it evenly. Pour about 1 inch of hot water into the bottom of the insert and place the pan on the rack inside the slow cooker. Drape a clean kitchen towel over the cooker, put on the lid, and cook on High until a tester inserted in the center of the cake comes out clean, about 3 hours. Remove the pan from the cooker and set aside to cool completely.

5. While the cake is cooling, make the frosting. Stir the cocoa into the melted vegan butter until well combined. Stir in the vanilla and nondairy milk and mix until smooth. Slowly stir in the confectioners' sugar until well blended. If the frosting is too thin, add more confectioners' sugar. If it's too thick, add more nondairy milk, 1 teaspoon at a time, until it reaches the desired consistency. Refrigerate the frosting for at least 1 hour before using, then frost the cake and serve.

Carrot Cake with Pineapple

Carrot cake is a personal favorite that I make year-round. In the summer, I like to use freshly dug carrots from my garden and make it in the slow cooker so that I don't heat up the kitchen.

This cake can be made either directly in the insert of a 4-quart round cooker or in a small baking pan set inside a 6- to 7-quart oval cooker. Enjoy it plain or with a light dusting of confectioners' sugar, or whip up a vegan cream cheese frosting (recipe follows).

SERVES 6

SLOW COOKER SIZE:
4-QUART OR 6-QUART

COOK TIME:
2 HOURS ON HIGH FOR
4-QUART; 3 HOURS ON
HIGH FOR 6-QUART

SOY-FREE

1½ cups unbleached all-purpose flour

¾ cup packed light brown sugar or granulated natural sugar

1½ teaspoons baking powder

½ teaspoon salt

1 teaspoon ground cinnamon

¼ teaspoon ground nutmeg

2 carrots, peeled and finely shredded (1 cup packed)

⅓ cup finely chopped fresh or canned pineapple, well drained, juice reserved

½ cup pineapple juice from the chopped pineapple, plus more if needed (add water, unsweetened almond milk, or purchased pineapple juice if necessary to yield ½ cup)

¼ cup vegetable oil

½ cup chopped macadamia nuts (optional)

1. If using a 4-quart slow cooker, place a round of parchment paper, cut to fit, in the bottom of the slow cooker insert. Coat the parchment and sides of the insert with nonstick cooking spray. If using a 6-quart slow cooker, place a rack, trivet, or a ring of crumpled aluminum foil inside the slow cooker. Lightly oil a baking pan that will fit in the cooker. If using a springform pan, wrap the outside bottom and sides of the pan with foil to prevent leakage.

2. In a large bowl, combine the flour, sugar, baking powder, salt, cinnamon, and nutmeg. Mix well.

3. In a separate bowl, combine the carrots, chopped pineapple, ½ cup reserved pineapple juice, and oil. Mix well. Stir the wet mixture into the dry mixture,

mixing until well blended. If the batter is too dry, add a little more pineapple juice, a tablespoon or two at a time. Fold in the macadamias, if using.

4. If using a 4-quart slow cooker, transfer the batter directly into the slow cooker, spreading evenly. Drape a clean kitchen towel over the slow cooker, put on the lid, and cook on High until a tester inserted in the center of the cake comes out clean, about 2 hours. Remove the lid and towel, turn the cooker off, and allow to cool completely before serving.

   If using a 6-quart slow cooker, transfer the batter to the prepared baking pan, spreading it evenly. Pour about 1 inch of hot water into the bottom of the insert and place the pan on the rack inside the slow cooker. Drape a clean kitchen towel over the slow cooker, put on the lid, and cook on High until a tester inserted in the center of the cake comes out clean, about 3 hours. Remove the pan from the cooker and set aside to cool before frosting or serving.

QUICK CREAM CHEESE FROSTING

1 cup vegan cream cheese, purchased or homemade (page 31), at room temperature

½ cup vegan butter, at room temperature

1½ cups confectioners' sugar

1 teaspoon pure vanilla extract

Combine all of the ingredients in a food processor and process until smooth and well blended.

MAKES ABOUT 2½ CUPS

Orange-Topped Italian Polenta Cake

Polenta cake is popular throughout Italy. There are many variations, including those that are fragrant with orange and almonds. This recipe can be made either directly in the insert of a 4-quart round cooker or in a small baking pan set inside a 6-quart oval cooker. For a shortcut version, use purchased orange marmalade. For soy-free, use a soy-free vegan butter.

SERVES 6

SLOW COOKER SIZE:
4-QUART OR 6-QUART

COOK TIME:
2 TO 3 HOURS ON HIGH

SOY-FREE OPTION

⅔ cup plus 1 tablespoon natural sugar

1 navel orange, peeled and sliced into ⅛-inch-thick rounds

1¼ cups all-purpose flour

⅓ cup fine-ground cornmeal

¼ cup finely ground almonds

1½ teaspoons baking powder

¾ teaspoon salt

¼ cup vegan butter, softened

⅓ cup plus 2 tablespoons Orange Marmalade with a Twist of Lemon (page 237)

1 teaspoon pure vanilla extract

1 cup unsweetened almond milk

1. If using a 4-quart slow cooker, arrange two 3-inch-wide strips of parchment paper in a crisscross pattern across the bottom and up the sides of the slow cooker insert. Place a round of parchment paper, cut to fit, on top of the crisscross. Coat the parchment and sides of the insert with cooking spray.

   If using a 6-quart slow cooker, place a rack, trivet, or a ring of crumpled aluminum foil inside the cooker. Generously grease and flour a 7-inch springform pan or round cake pan. If using a springform pan, place it on a sheet of aluminum foil and bring up the sides of the foil to prevent leakage.

2. Sprinkle 1 tablespoon of the sugar onto the parchment circle or the bottom of the prepared pan. Arrange the orange slices on top of the sugar in a circular pattern, overlapping slightly, if necessary.

3. In a bowl, combine the flour, cornmeal, almonds, baking powder, and salt.

4. In a separate large bowl, combine the remaining ⅔ cup sugar, vegan butter, ⅓ cup of the marmalade, and vanilla, and beat until well blended. Slowly beat in the almond milk, then gradually stir in the dry ingredients until smooth.

5. If using a 4-quart slow cooker, transfer the batter directly into the slow cooker, spreading evenly and being careful not to dislodge the orange slices. Drape a clean kitchen towel over the slow cooker, put on the lid, and cook on High until a tester inserted in the center of the cake comes out clean, about 2 hours. Remove the lid and towel, turn off the cooker, and allow the cake to cool completely. Carefully lift the cake out of the cooker, using the four ends of the parchment strips to help dislodge the cake, and invert onto a plate.

   If using a 6-quart slow cooker, transfer the batter to the prepared baking pan, spreading evenly and being careful not to dislodge the orange slices. Pour about 1 inch of hot water into the bottom of the insert and place the pan on the rack inside the slow cooker. Drape a clean kitchen towel over the slow cooker, put on the lid, and cook on High until a tester inserted in the center of the cake comes out clean, 2 to 3 hours. Remove the lid and the towel, turn off the cooker, and let cool for 10 minutes, then remove the pan from the cooker and set aside to cool completely. When cool, carefully remove the sides from the springform pan, if using, and invert the cake onto a plate.

6. Heat the remaining 2 tablespoons marmalade in a saucepan over low heat or in the microwave in a heatproof bowl until warm. Stir until smooth. Brush the top of the cake with the warm marmalade. Allow the marmalade to cool completely before serving.

Chocolate–Peanut Butter Cheesecake

If I had to name a favorite dessert combination, chocolate and peanut butter would be at the top of the list. For the best results, this recipe requires a 7-inch springform pan and a 6-quart slow cooker. For a gluten-free cheesecake, use gluten-free chocolate cookies.

SERVES 6 TO 8

SLOW COOKER SIZE:
6- TO 7-QUART

COOK TIME:
2½ TO 3 HOURS
ON HIGH

GLUTEN-FREE OPTION

1½ cups crushed vegan chocolate cookies

3 tablespoons vegan butter, melted

16 ounces vegan cream cheese, purchased or homemade (page 31)

8 ounces silken tofu, drained

½ cup creamy peanut butter, at room temperature

¾ cup natural sugar

¼ cup unsweetened cocoa powder

2 tablespoons nondairy milk

Chocolate Curls (below), for garnish (optional)

1. Place a rack, trivet, or a ring of crumpled aluminum foil inside the cooker. Lightly oil a 7-inch springform pan that will fit in the cooker. Place it on a sheet of aluminum foil and bring up the sides of the foil to prevent leakage.

2. To make the crust, combine the chocolate crumbs and melted vegan butter in a bowl, stirring with a fork to moisten. Spread the crumb mixture in the springform pan and press evenly into the bottom and up the sides of the pan.

3. In a food processor, combine the cream cheese and tofu and blend until smooth. Add the peanut butter, sugar, cocoa powder, and nondairy milk, and process until smooth and well blended. Scrape the batter evenly into the prepared pan. Pour about 1 inch of hot water into the bottom of the insert and place the pan on the rack inside the slow cooker. Drape a clean kitchen towel over the slow cooker, put on the lid, and cook on High until firm, 2½ to 3 hours.

4. Remove the pan from the cooker and set aside to cool completely. Once cool, cover and refrigerate for several hours or overnight. To serve, remove the sides of the pan, using a knife to loosen it if necessary. Decorate the top of the cheesecake with the chocolate curls, if desired.

Chocolate Curls

To make chocolate curls, warm a piece of chocolate (at least 1 ounce) in your hands for a few minutes to soften it. Slowly drag a vegetable peeler across a flat side of the chocolate to make curls. For smaller curls, drag the peeler across the thinner sides of the chocolate. Refrigerate the curls until ready to use so they can firm up.

Black and Blue Broundies

What's a "broundie"? It's my name for these round brownies that are as fun to eat as they are to pronounce. I make these in four 1-cup soufflé cups, then cut them in half horizontally for 8 large brownies. You could, instead, make them in two or three 1-pint straight-sided canning jars, or go the traditional route and use a small rectangular baking pan (just make sure it will fit inside your slow cooker). Top with vegan ice cream, chocolate syrup, and fresh berries.

1 cup cooked black beans (page 104) or 1 cup canned beans, rinsed, drained, and blotted dry

½ cup natural sugar

½ cup blueberry jam

½ cup unsweetened cocoa powder

1 teaspoon pure vanilla extract

¾ cup unbleached all-purpose flour

1½ teaspoons baking powder

SERVES 8

SLOW COOKER SIZE:
4- TO 7-QUART

COOK TIME:
2 HOURS ON HIGH
FOR 4-QUART;
3 HOURS ON HIGH
FOR 5- TO 7-QUART

SOY-FREE

1. If using a large slow cooker, generously grease the insides of four 1-cup soufflé cups or spray them with nonstick cooking spray. Set aside. If using a 4-quart slow cooker, you can make 1 large broundie by placing a round of parchment paper, cut to fit, in the bottom of the cooker. Then coat the parchment and sides of the 4-quart cooker with nonstick cooking spray.

2. In a food processor, combine the beans, sugar, jam, cocoa powder, and vanilla and blend until smooth. Add the flour and baking powder, and pulse to combine.

3. If using a large slow cooker and soufflé cups, scrape the batter into the prepared cups. Cover the tops of the cups with aluminum foil, making several holes in the foil for steam to escape. Pour about ½ inch of hot water into the bottom of the insert and place the cups in the cooker, stacking them if necessary. Drape a clean kitchen towel over the cooker, put on the lid, and cook on High until a tester inserted in the center of the cups comes out clean, about 3 hours. Remove the cups from the slow cooker, remove the foil, and

set aside to cool. Use a knife or thin metal spatula to help loosen the broundies from the sides of the cups, then carefully remove the broundies and transfer to a wire rack to cool completely. To serve, cut the broundies horizontally into 2 rounds each.

If making 1 large broundie in a 4-quart slow cooker, spread the batter into the prepared cooker. Drape a clean kitchen towel over the cooker, put on the lid, and cook on High until a tester inserted in the center comes out clean, about 2 hours. Remove the lid and the towel, turn off the cooker, and allow to cool completely before serving.

Pumpkin-Oatmeal Bars

If you don't have a rectangular baking pan that will fit inside your slow cooker, you can make these bars directly in the cooker insert. They'll need less time to cook and you'll have to cut them into wedges instead of bars. For gluten-free bars, be sure to use certified gluten-free oats.

SERVES 8 TO 10

SLOW COOKER SIZE:
4- TO 6-QUART

COOK TIME:
2 TO 3 HOURS ON HIGH

GLUTEN-FREE

2 cups old-fashioned rolled oats
½ cup packed light brown sugar or granulated natural sugar
2 teaspoons ground cinnamon
¼ teaspoon ground nutmeg
¼ teaspoon ground allspice
1½ teaspoons baking powder
1 teaspoon salt
6 ounces soft or silken tofu, drained and crumbled
⅔ cup canned solid-pack pumpkin
1 cup nondairy milk
1 teaspoon pure vanilla extract
½ cup chopped toasted pecans
½ cup sweetened dried cranberries
Confectioners' sugar, for serving (optional)

1. If using a 4-quart slow cooker, lightly oil the insert or spray it with nonstick cooking spray. If using a 6-quart slow cooker, place a rack, trivet, or a ring of crumpled aluminum foil in the bottom of the cooker insert. Lightly oil or spray a 7 x 9-inch baking pan or other pan that will fit inside your slow cooker.

2. In a large bowl, combine the oats, sugar, cinnamon, nutmeg, allspice, baking powder, and salt.

3. In a blender or food processor, combine the tofu, pumpkin, nondairy milk, and vanilla and process until smooth. Add the wet ingredients to the dry ingredients and mix well to combine. Stir in the pecans and cranberries.

4. If using a 4-quart slow cooker, spread the mixture in the prepared crock. Drape a clean kitchen towel over the cooker, put on the lid, and cook on High until a tester inserted in the center comes out clean, about 2 hours. Remove the lid, turn off the cooker, and allow to cool completely before cutting into wedges. Enjoy as is or sprinkle with a little confectioners' sugar to serve.

   If using a 6-quart slow cooker, spread the pumpkin mixture evenly in the prepared baking pan. Pour about 1 inch of hot water into the bottom of the insert and place the pan on the rack inside the slow cooker. Drape a clean kitchen towel over the slow cooker, put on the lid, and cook on High until a tester inserted in the center comes out clean, about 3 hours. Remove the pan from the slow cooker and set aside to cool completely before cutting into bars. Enjoy as is or sprinkle with a little confectioners' sugar to serve.

Tutti-Frutti Cobbler

In addition to being the title of an old rock-and-roll song, *tutti-frutti* also means "all fruit" in Italian, making it an apt name for this cobbler, which can include as many varieties of fruit as you like. It's great made with a variety of berries or stone fruits such as peaches and plums. One of my favorite combinations includes blueberries, blackberries, peaches, and apricots. You may also use harder fruit, such as apples or pears, but you'll need to cut the pieces smaller and possibly cook the cobbler longer in order for the fruit to soften. Use this recipe as a guide (you'll need 5 to 6 cups total berries and/or cut fruit) to include your own favorites. The slow cooker is a great way to make cobblers during the heat of summer, when fresh fruit is abundant but you don't want to turn on the oven. Instead of fresh fruit, thawed frozen fruit or canned fruit pie filling may be substituted. For a gluten-free cobbler, use a gluten-free flour.

SERVES 4 TO 6

SLOW COOKER SIZE:
4-QUART

COOK TIME:
3 HOURS ON HIGH

GLUTEN-FREE OPTION

SOY-FREE

2 large ripe peaches, peeled (see Note), pitted, and sliced
2 ripe apricots, peeled (see Note), pitted, and sliced
1 cup fresh blueberries, rinsed and picked over
1 cup fresh blackberries, rinsed and picked over
¾ cup natural sugar
1½ tablespoons tapioca starch or cornstarch
1¼ cups unbleached all-purpose flour
1 teaspoon baking powder
¼ teaspoon ground cinnamon
¼ teaspoon salt
½ cup unsweetened almond milk
1 tablespoon vegetable oil
½ teaspoon pure vanilla extract

1. Lightly oil the insert of the slow cooker or spray it with nonstick cooking spray. Add all of the fruit and ½ cup of the sugar. Sprinkle with the tapioca and stir to combine. Set the slow cooker on High, cover, and cook for 2 hours.

2. In a bowl, combine the flour, the remaining ¼ cup sugar, baking powder, cinnamon, and salt. Stir in the almond milk, oil, and vanilla, stirring until just combined to form a soft dough.

3. Stir the fruit in the slow cooker, then spread the dough evenly over the fruit mixture. Cover and continue to cook on High until the topping is cooked and a tester inserted in the center comes out clean, about 1 hour.

4. Remove the lid, turn off the cooker, and let the cobbler sit for 15 minutes before serving.

NOTE: To peel peaches and apricots, simply plunge them into boiling water for about 15 seconds and then into ice water—the skins will slip off easily.

Pear-Mincemeat Crisp

No meat or suet in this mincemeat—just delicious pears and a whole lot of fragrant spices. This comforting, intensely flavored crisp, with its crumbly granola topping, is best served warm accompanied by vegan vanilla ice cream for a harmonious combination of texture, temperatures, and flavors. I prefer Bosc pears for this recipe, but you may use another variety if you prefer. Be sure to remove the pith from the orange when peeling it to avoid any bitter taste. If you prefer not to include the brandy, simply omit it. To make this gluten-free, use gluten-free granola.

SERVES 6

SLOW COOKER SIZE:
4-QUART

COOK TIME:
5 HOURS ON HIGH

SOY-FREE

GLUTEN-FREE OPTION

1 large orange
4 firm ripe Bosc pears, peeled, cored, and chopped
1 cup raisins (dark, golden, or a combination)
1 cup chopped dried apples, pears, or apricots, or a combination
1½ cups apple juice
½ cup packed dark brown sugar or granulated natural sugar
¼ cup brandy or 1 teaspoon brandy extract
2 tablespoons cider vinegar
½ teaspoon ground cinnamon
½ teaspoon ground nutmeg
½ teaspoon ground allspice
¼ teaspoon ground cloves
Pinch of salt
1¼ cups granola of your choice
2 tablespoons pure maple syrup or agave nectar

1. Remove 2 tablespoons of zest from the orange and place it in a food processor. Peel and seed the orange and cut it into quarters. Remove and discard any white pith. Add the peeled and seeded orange quarters to the food processor and pulse until chopped, then transfer to the slow cooker.

2. Add the pears, raisins, dried apples, juice, sugar, brandy, vinegar, cinnamon, nutmeg, allspice, cloves, and salt. Stir to combine, then cover and cook on High for 2 hours.

3. Remove the lid, stir the mixture, then continue to cook, uncovered, until the mixture thickens, about 2 hours.

4. In a bowl, combine the granola and maple syrup, stirring to coat. Stir the fruit mixture, then sprinkle the granola mixture over the top. Cover and cook for 1 hour longer. Serve warm, spooned into dessert dishes.

Banana Brown Betty

Bananas stand in for apples in this unusual take on the classic apple brown Betty dessert. In the words of recipe tester Jonathan Shanes, "Move over, bananas Foster!" This really does taste like bananas Foster—maybe it should be called Banana Brown Betty Foster? Whatever you call it, it's positively divine when topped with vegan vanilla ice cream. For gluten-free, use a gluten-free bread.

⅓ cup pure maple syrup
¼ cup unsweetened almond milk
½ teaspoon ground cinnamon
¼ teaspoon ground ginger
¼ teaspoon ground nutmeg
⅛ teaspoon salt
6 cups cubed white bread
4 ripe bananas, peeled and chopped
⅓ cup chopped toasted pecans
⅓ cup packed light brown sugar or granulated natural sugar
2 tablespoons brandy or rum or 1 teaspoon brandy or rum extract

SERVES 4

SLOW COOKER SIZE:
4-QUART

COOK TIME:
1½ TO 2 HOURS
ON HIGH

GLUTEN-FREE OPTION

SOY-FREE

1. In a large bowl, combine the maple syrup, almond milk, cinnamon, ginger, nutmeg, and salt and mix well. Add the bread cubes and stir to coat.

2. In a separate bowl, combine the bananas, pecans, sugar, and brandy, stirring to mix.

3. Lightly oil the slow cooker insert or spray it with nonstick cooking spray. Spread half of the bread mixture in the bottom of the cooker, followed by half of the banana mixture. Repeat the layering, then cover and cook on High until firm, 1½ to 2 hours. Serve hot.

Three-Way Pumpkin Bread Pudding

'[I]'ve been a fan of pumpkin bread pudding for as long as I can remember, but sometimes the pumpkin flavor can get lost amid all the fragrant spices and boozy sauces. This version puts the "pumpkin" in pumpkin bread pudding because it includes both cubes of pumpkin cake and pumpkin puree and is topped with a lightning-quick pumpkin sauce. Regular white bread may be substituted for the pumpkin cake, if desired—it will still have a delicious pumpkin-y flavor. You may also add ½ cup sweetened dried cranberries to the mixture. For a gluten-free version, use gluten-free cake or bread; for soy-free, use a soy-free nondairy milk.

SERVES 6 TO 8

SLOW COOKER SIZE:
4-QUART

COOK TIME:
3 HOURS ON LOW

GLUTEN-FREE OPTION

SOY-FREE OPTION

BREAD PUDDING:

2 cups cubed Spiced Pumpkin Cake (page 248) or other pumpkin cake or bread

2 cups cubed whole-grain bread (such as oat bread)

1 (16-ounce) can solid-pack pumpkin

¾ cup packed light brown sugar or granulated natural sugar

3 tablespoons rum or bourbon or 1 teaspoon rum extract (optional)

1 teaspoon pure vanilla extract

1½ teaspoons ground cinnamon

¼ teaspoon ground nutmeg

¼ teaspoon ground ginger

¼ teaspoon ground allspice

¼ teaspoon salt

3 cups nondairy milk, warmed

PUMPKIN SAUCE:

½ cup soy creamer or a thick nondairy milk, plus more if needed

¼ cup reserved pumpkin puree (from can used to make bread pudding)

1 teaspoon light brown sugar

⅛ teaspoon ground cinnamon

⅛ teaspoon ground nutmeg

⅛ teaspoon ground ginger

1 tablespoon rum or bourbon or 1 teaspoon rum extract (optional)

1. For the bread pudding: Lightly oil the slow cooker insert or spray it with nonstick cooking spray. Press half each of the cake and bread cubes into the bottom of the cooker.

2. Remove ¼ cup of the pumpkin puree from the can and set aside for the sauce. In a large bowl, combine the remaining pumpkin puree, sugar, rum (if using), vanilla, cinnamon, nutmeg, ginger, allspice, and salt. Blend well, then slowly add the warm nondairy milk, stirring constantly. Carefully pour half of the pumpkin mixture over the cake and bread cubes in the slow cooker, pressing them into the wet mixture to moisten. Repeat with the remaining cake and bread cubes and the rest of the pumpkin mixture. Cover and cook on Low until firm, about 3 hours.

3. Turn off the slow cooker and let the pudding sit, covered, for 20 minutes before serving. In the meantime, make the sauce.

4. For the pumpkin sauce: In a small saucepan, combine all of the ingredients over medium heat and stir to blend well. Cook, stirring, for about 4 minutes to mellow the flavor of the pumpkin and spices. For a thinner sauce, stir in a little more creamer. The sauce can be used warm, or it can be made ahead and chilled before using.

5. To serve, spoon the warm bread pudding into dessert bowls and drizzle with the sauce.

Zabaglione-Inspired Bread Pudding

Zabaglione is a light custard made with Marsala that is traditionally served on its own or as a sauce over cake or fruit. In France it's called *sabayon*. Among the new twists in this recipe, the sauce becomes part of a delicious bread pudding and is topped with berries, with white chocolate added for an extra layer of flavor. The main twist, of course, is that this version is 100 percent vegan. For gluten-free bread pudding, use gluten-free bread.

SERVES 6

SLOW COOKER SIZE:
4-QUART

COOK TIME:
3 HOURS ON LOW

GLUTEN-FREE OPTION

SOY-FREE

½ cup vegan white chocolate chips

3 cups unsweetened almond milk

½ cup packed light brown sugar or granulated natural sugar

½ cup dry Marsala

Pinch of salt

6 cups cubed white bread

2 cups fresh raspberries or sliced strawberries, for serving

1. In a saucepan, combine the white chocolate chips with 1 cup of the almond milk. Cook, stirring, over low heat until the chocolate is melted and the mixture is smooth. Stir in the sugar, Marsala, and salt, then slowly add the remaining almond milk, stirring until well blended.

2. Lightly oil the slow cooker insert or spray it with nonstick cooking spray. Press half of the bread cubes into the bottom of the cooker. Pour half of the Marsala mixture over the bread cubes in the slow cooker, pressing them into the Marsala mixture to moisten. Repeat with the remaining bread and Marsala mixture. Cover and cook on Low until firm, about 3 hours.

3. Turn off the slow cooker and let the pudding rest, covered, for 20 minutes. Serve warm, topped with fresh berries.

Warm and Fudgy Chocolate Bread Pudding

This chocolaty dessert gives you that "warm and fudgy" feeling inside. I highly recommend serving this bread pudding warm with vegan vanilla ice cream. For gluten-free, use gluten-free bread. For soy-free, use a soy-free vegan butter.

2 cups unsweetened almond milk

2 cups vegan semisweet chocolate chips

4 cups white bread cubes

½ cup chopped pecans or walnuts (optional)

¾ cup granulated natural sugar

¼ cup unsweetened cocoa powder

½ teaspoon salt

1 teaspoon pure vanilla extract

1 tablespoon vegan butter

SERVES 6

SLOW COOKER SIZE:
5- TO 6-QUART

COOK TIME:
2½ TO 3 HOURS
ON HIGH

GLUTEN-FREE OPTION

SOY-FREE OPTION

1. Lightly oil the insert of the slow cooker or spray it with nonstick cooking spray. Heat 1½ cups of the almond milk in a saucepan until it is just ready to boil. Take the pan off the heat and stir in 1⅔ cups of the chocolate chips. Stir until the chips are melted, then set aside.

2. Spread the bread cubes in the prepared slow cooker. Sprinkle with the nuts, if using, and the remaining ⅓ cup chocolate chips.

3. Heat the remaining ½ cup almond milk in another saucepan. Add the sugar, cocoa, salt, and vanilla, stirring to dissolve, about 2 minutes. Combine the cocoa mixture with the chocolate chip mixture, then pour it all over the bread in the slow cooker. Press the bread cubes down so that they are submerged in the chocolate mixture. Dot the top of the bread pudding with bits of the vegan butter. Cover and cook on High until a tester inserted in the center comes out clean, 2½ to 3 hours.

4. Remove the lid, turn off the cooker, and let stand for at least 15 minutes before serving. Serve warm or at room temperature.

Coconut Rice Pudding with Mango

A favorite dessert in Thai restaurants, rice pudding with fresh mango is easy to make at home in your slow cooker. If you prefer a sweeter pudding, add up to ¼ cup extra sugar.

SERVES 6

SLOW COOKER SIZE:
4-QUART

COOK TIME:
2 HOURS ON HIGH

GLUTEN-FREE

SOY-FREE

1 cup uncooked jasmine rice
½ cup granulated natural sugar, or more to taste
¼ teaspoon salt
2 (14-ounce) cans unsweetened coconut milk
2 cups unsweetened almond milk, plus more if needed
1 teaspoon coconut extract
1 teaspoon pure vanilla extract
1 large ripe mango, peeled, pitted, and chopped

1. Lightly oil the slow cooker insert or spray it with nonstick cooking spray. Combine the rice, sugar, and salt in the cooker. In a saucepan or the microwave, heat the coconut milk and almond milk just to boiling. Slowly add the heated milks to the slow cooker, stirring to dissolve the sugar. Cover and cook on High until the rice is tender, about 2 hours.

2. Turn off the slow cooker and stir in the coconut and vanilla extracts. Allow to cool, uncovered, for 10 minutes, then stir in the mango. To help thicken the pudding, stir it gently to let it absorb any remaining liquid; it will continue to thicken as it cools. If the pudding is too thick, stir in a little more almond milk until it's the consistency you like. The pudding can be served warm, at room temperature, or chilled. To serve chilled, spoon the pudding into dessert glasses, cover, and refrigerate until cold.

Apricot Tapioca Pudding

To make this homey dessert extra special, garnish each serving with a dollop of vegan whipped cream (soy-free, if desired).

⅓ cup small pearl tapioca
½ cup chopped dried apricots
⅓ cup granulated natural sugar
2½ cups unsweetened almond milk
¼ cup apricot preserves
1 teaspoon pure vanilla extract

1. Lightly oil the slow cooker insert or spray it with nonstick cooking spray. Combine the tapioca, apricots, sugar, and almond milk in the cooker. Stir to combine. Cover and cook on Low until the pudding has thickened and the liquid is absorbed, about 2 hours.

2. In a small bowl, combine the preserves and the vanilla, stirring to blend. Add the mixture to the pudding, stirring to mix well. Cover and continue to cook on Low for 20 minutes longer.

3. Remove the lid, turn off the cooker, and allow to cool. Serve at room temperature or chilled. To serve chilled, spoon the pudding into dessert bowls, cover tightly, and refrigerate until needed.

SERVES 4

SLOW COOKER SIZE:
4-QUART

COOK TIME:
2 HOURS AND
20 MINUTES ON LOW

GLUTEN-FREE

SOY-FREE

Lemon-Ginger Poached Pears

These pears may be enjoyed warm or chilled; I especially like them served at room temperature with a scoop of vegan vanilla ice cream and a slice of vegan pound cake. I prefer Bosc pears in this recipe, although you may use Bartletts instead. Use more or less ginger, depending on your personal preference.

SERVES 4 TO 6

SLOW COOKER SIZE:
4- TO 6-QUART

COOK TIME:
2 HOURS ON LOW PLUS
30 MINUTES ON HIGH

GLUTEN-FREE

SOY-FREE

2½ cups white grape juice
¼ cup natural sugar, plus more if needed
2 to 3 teaspoons grated fresh ginger
4 to 6 strips lemon zest
Pinch of salt
½ cinnamon stick
4 to 6 firm ripe Bosc or Bartlett pears, peeled, halved, and cored
Juice of 1 lemon
Mint sprigs, for garnish (optional)

1. Heat the grape juice, sugar, ginger, lemon zest, and salt in a saucepan on the stove or in a bowl in the microwave until hot, stirring to dissolve the sugar. Transfer to the slow cooker and add the cinnamon stick.

2. Add the pears to the slow cooker. Cover and cook on Low until the pears are just tender, about 2 hours. Do not overcook.

3. Use a slotted spoon to transfer the pears to a shallow bowl and drizzle with the lemon juice. Taste the poaching liquid, adding more sugar if needed. Turn the setting to High and cook, uncovered, to reduce the poaching liquid by half, about 30 minutes. Strain the reduced liquid into a bowl and set aside to cool completely.

4. To serve, arrange the pears in shallow dessert bowls. Drizzle with some of the poaching liquid and garnish with mint sprigs, if using. Serve warm, chilled, or at room temperature.

Baked Cran-Apples

Baked apples are a wonderful autumn treat that fills the house with the fragrance of apple pie as they cook. Healthful and easy to make, these apples, stuffed with sweet-tart cranberries and bits of walnuts or pecans, are best served warm and are especially good paired with a scoop of vegan vanilla ice cream. They can also be enjoyed for breakfast (without the ice cream!) or even as a side dish at dinner. Use as many apples as will fit side by side in your slow cooker; the cooking time will depend on the number and size of the apples used. Because the peels will stay on, try to get organic apples for this recipe.

4 to 6 large firm apples, such as Granny Smith or Rome Beauty, washed
Juice of 1 lemon
⅓ cup packed light brown sugar or granulated natural sugar
⅓ cup sweetened dried cranberries
¼ cup crushed, chopped, or coarsely ground almonds, walnuts, or pecans
½ teaspoon ground cinnamon
½ cup naturally sweetened cranberry juice

SERVES 4 TO 6

SLOW COOKER SIZE:
4- TO 7-QUART

COOK TIME:
2½ TO 4 HOURS
ON HIGH

GLUTEN-FREE

SOY-FREE

1. Core the apples about three-quarters of the way down, leaving enough on the bottom so the stuffing doesn't leak out. Peel a ½-inch band of the peel from the cored apples about one-quarter of the way down from the top. Rub the exposed part of the apples with the lemon juice to avoid discoloration. Lightly oil the slow cooker insert or spray it with nonstick cooking spray, and place the apples upright in a single layer in the cooker.

2. In a small bowl, combine the brown sugar, cranberries, nuts, and cinnamon. Pack the mixture into the cored center of each apple (it's okay if it heaps on top). Pour the cranberry juice into the slow cooker to surround the apples. Cover and cook on High until the apples are soft but not collapsing, 2½ to 4 hours. (If your slow cooker runs hot, check the apples after 2 hours.)

3. Remove the lid and turn off the cooker to allow the apples to cool slightly. Serve warm or at room temperature, drizzled with the cooking liquid.

Maple-and-Rum-Glazed Slow-Baked Apples

This recipe is courtesy of Melissa Chapman, who tested many of the recipes for this book. She developed this luscious glazed apple recipe when she scored loads of locally grown apples at the farmers' market. Use as many apples as will fit side by side in your slow cooker; the cooking time will depend on the number and size of the apples used. Because the peels will stay on, try to get organic apples for this recipe. For gluten-free, be sure to use certified gluten-free oats.

SERVES 6

SLOW COOKER SIZE:
4- TO 7-QUART

COOK TIME:
2 TO 4 HOURS ON HIGH

GLUTEN-FREE

SOY-FREE

4 to 6 tart apples, washed
Juice of 1 lemon

FILLING:
¼ cup old-fashioned rolled oats
⅓ cup packed light brown sugar
¼ cup golden raisins
¼ cup macadamia nut pieces (or your favorite nut)
¼ teaspoon ground nutmeg
½ teaspoon ground cinnamon

GLAZE:
½ cup pure maple syrup
½ cup apple juice
¼ cup dark rum or spiced rum
¼ teaspoon ground nutmeg
¼ teaspoon ground cinnamon

1. Core the apples about three-quarters of the way down, leaving enough on the bottom so the stuffing doesn't leak out. Peel a ½-inch band of the peel from the cored apples about one-quarter of the way down from the top. Rub the exposed part of the apples with the lemon juice to prevent discoloration.

2. For the filling: In a small bowl, combine all of the filling ingredients, stirring to mix well. Pack the mixture into the cored center of each apple (it's okay if it heaps on top).

3. For the glaze: In a small bowl, combine all of the glaze ingredients, stirring to mix well.

4. Arrange the stuffed apples upright in a single layer in the slow cooker and pour the glaze over the apples. Cover and cook on Low until the apples are soft but not collapsing, 2 to 4 hours, basting the apples with the glaze a few times throughout the cooking process.

5. Remove the lid and turn off the cooker to allow the apples to cool slightly. Serve warm or at room temperature, drizzled with the cooking liquid.

Granola-Stuffed Baked Apples

When baked apples are stuffed with granola, it gives them an added dimension of texture and flavor, reminiscent of an apple crisp. Like the previous recipe, these are as good for breakfast as they are for dessert. Use as many apples as will fit side by side in your slow cooker. The cooking time and amount of granola needed will depend on the number and size of the apples used. For gluten-free, use gluten-free granola. For soy-free, use a soy-free vegan butter.

SERVES 4 TO 6

SLOW COOKER SIZE:
4- TO 7-QUART

COOK TIME:
2 TO 4 HOURS ON HIGH

GLUTEN-FREE OPTION

SOY-FREE OPTION

4 to 6 large firm apples, such as Granny Smith or Rome Beauty, washed
Juice of 1 lemon
1 to 1½ cups granola of your choice
2 tablespoons light brown sugar or granulated natural sugar
½ teaspoon ground cinnamon
1½ tablespoons vegan butter, cut into 4 to 6 pieces
½ cup apple juice

1. Core the apples about three-quarters of the way down, leaving enough on the bottom so the stuffing doesn't leak out. Peel a ½-inch band of the peel from the cored apples about one-quarter of the way down from the top. Rub the exposed part of the apples with the lemon juice to prevent discoloration. Lightly oil the slow cooker insert or spray it with nonstick cooking spray, and place the apples upright in a single layer in the cooker.

2. In a small bowl, combine the granola, brown sugar, and cinnamon. Pack the mixture into the cored center of each apple (it's okay if it heaps on top). Dot the tops of the apples with the vegan butter. Pour the apple juice into the slow cooker to surround the apples. Cover and cook on High until the apples are soft but not collapsing, 2 to 4 hours. (If your slow cooker runs hot, check the apples after 1½ hours.)

3. Remove the lid and turn off the cooker to allow the apples to cool slightly. Serve warm or at room temperature, drizzled with the cooking liquid.

chapter

11

Breakfast and Bread

Breakfast—or bread, for that matter—probably isn't the first thing you think of when you consider using a slow cooker. But there are ways to make both in a slow cooker that are convenient alternatives to their conventional cooking methods.

In this chapter, you'll find some breakfast recipes made with nutritious whole grains that can cook overnight so they're ready by morning. Other recipes take only a few hours to cook but can easily be made overnight with the help of an automatic timer. If your slow cooker doesn't have a timer, you can purchase an inexpensive kitchen appliance timer, available at hardware stores, that will allow you to set your slow cooker to begin cooking up to two hours after you go to bed. (Remember, uncooked food should not be left at room temperature for longer than two hours.) Many slow cookers are also equipped with a Keep Warm setting, which can be handy if your breakfast is ready before you are. Another option is to simply make a large batch of oatmeal, for example, ahead of time in the slow cooker, store it in the refrigerator, and then reheat a portion each morning in the microwave.

If cooked grains aren't your thing, this chapter also includes a variety of frittatas and bread puddings that can be enjoyed for breakfast, brunch, or a light supper.

The breads in this chapter can be enjoyed any time of day as well. I call them "slow quick breads," since they are, in fact, quick breads that can be made in a slow cooker.

Slow-Cooker Granola

Making your own granola at home is easy and economical. It tastes better, too, since you make it fresh and can add whatever ingredients you like, substituting different dried fruits or nuts according to taste. To make this granola gluten-free, omit the wheat germ and use certified gluten-free oats.

⅔ cup pure maple syrup
¼ cup vegetable oil
¼ cup packed light brown sugar or granulated natural sugar
3 tablespoons water
1 teaspoon pure vanilla extract
5 cups old-fashioned rolled oats
1 cup slivered blanched almonds
½ cup wheat germ
½ cup sunflower seeds
½ cup unsweetened shredded coconut
½ cup chopped dates or dried apricots
½ cup golden raisins or sweetened dried cranberries

MAKES ABOUT 8 CUPS

SLOW COOKER SIZE:
5- TO 7-QUART

COOK TIME:
1 HOUR ON HIGH PLUS
2 HOURS ON LOW

GLUTEN-FREE OPTION

SOY-FREE

1. Lightly oil the slow cooker insert or spray it with nonstick cooking spray and turn on the setting to High. Add the maple syrup, oil, sugar, water, and vanilla and stir to blend and dissolve the sugar.

2. In a bowl, combine the oats, almonds, wheat germ, sunflower seeds, coconut, and dates, mixing well. Transfer about half of the oat mixture to the slow cooker, stirring to coat with the wet mixture. Add the remaining half of the oat mixture and stir to combine and coat evenly. Cook, uncovered, on High, stirring occasionally, for 1 hour.

3. Reduce the heat to Low, cover, and cook, stirring occasionally, until the granola is crisp and dry, about 2 hours. (If your slow cooker runs hot, it may be done a bit sooner, and be sure to stir occasionally so it doesn't burn if you have a "hot spot.") Stir in the raisins. Remove the lid and allow the granola to cool in the slow cooker, or spread the granola on a baking sheet to cool completely. Store in a tightly covered container at room temperature. The granola will keep well for several weeks, longer if frozen.

Here are some delicious ways to top your bowl of hot oatmeal or other hot breakfast cereal:

- Maple syrup
- Agave nectar
- Fruit jam or preserves
- Dark unsulfured molasses
- Granola
- Toasted chopped nuts or sunflower seeds
- Ground flaxseed
- Toasted sesame seeds
- Chopped fresh apple, pear, and/or peach

- Sliced fresh banana
- Fresh berries
- Dried cranberries, blueberries, or raisins
- Chopped dried plums
- Pitted sliced dates
- Cinnamon and sugar
- Vegan yogurt
- Slow-Cooked Apple Butter (page 228)

Granola Oatmeal

Granola is an easy way to add some sweetness and crunchy texture to your oatmeal. Use the homemade granola on page 277 or your favorite brand from the store. For gluten-free oatmeal, use gluten-free granola and certified gluten-free oats. Rolled oats generally take less time to cook than steel-cut oats.

SERVES 4

SLOW COOKER SIZE:
4-QUART

COOK TIME:
6 TO 8 HOURS ON LOW

GLUTEN-FREE OPTION

SOY-FREE

1¼ cups old-fashioned rolled oats or steel-cut oats
4½ cups water
½ teaspoon salt
1½ teaspoons ground cinnamon
1 cup granola
Unsweetened almond milk, for serving

1. Lightly oil the slow cooker insert or spray it with nonstick cooking spray. Combine the oats, water, salt, and cinnamon in the cooker. Cover and cook on Low until the oats are soft and the oatmeal is thickened, 6 to 8 hours.

2. Stir in the granola, adding more water or almond milk if the oatmeal is too thick. Serve hot, spooned into bowls and drizzled with a little almond milk.

Overnight Apple-Cinnamon Oatmeal

You'll love waking up to this fragrant oatmeal. Turn on your slow cooker just before you go to bed, and it will be ready in the morning. Leftover oatmeal can be reheated in the microwave or saucepan, with a little water or almond milk added to thin out the consistency. Dried chopped apples may be substituted for fresh in this recipe, if desired. For extra flavor, toast the oats in a dry skillet over medium heat, stirring until golden and fragrant, before adding to the slow cooker. For gluten-free oatmeal, be sure to use certified gluten-free oats.

1¼ cups steel-cut oats
3 cups water
2 cups apple juice
2 apples (I like Fuji or Gala in this recipe), peeled, cored, and chopped
½ cup golden raisins or dried cranberries
¼ cup packed light brown sugar or granulated natural sugar, or more to taste
1 tablespoon ground flaxseed (optional)
1 teaspoon ground cinnamon
½ teaspoon salt
Unsweetened almond milk, for serving

SERVES 4

SLOW COOKER SIZE:
4-QUART

COOK TIME:
7 TO 8 HOURS ON LOW

GLUTEN-FREE

SOY-FREE

1. Lightly oil the slow cooker insert or spray it with nonstick cooking spray. Combine all of the ingredients except the almond milk in the slow cooker and mix well. Cover and cook on Low until the oatmeal is thickened and the oats are soft, 7 to 8 hours.

2. Serve hot, drizzled with a little almond milk.

PB & J Oatmeal

Have your peanut butter at room temperature so that it is soft enough to streak into the oatmeal. If the peanut butter is especially firm, it's okay to add it into the oatmeal by the spoonful at any time during the cooking time. For gluten-free oatmeal, be sure to use certified gluten-free oats. Turn on your slow cooker just before going to bed so the oatmeal is ready in the morning.

SERVES 4 TO 6

SLOW COOKER SIZE:
4-QUART

COOK TIME:
7 TO 8 HOURS ON LOW

GLUTEN-FREE

SOY-FREE

1½ cups steel-cut oats
5½ cups water
¾ teaspoon salt
1 teaspoon ground cinnamon
½ cup creamy peanut butter, at room temperature
½ cup strawberry jam or your favorite fruit jelly, jam, or preserves
Unsweetened almond milk, for serving

1. Lightly oil the insert of the slow cooker or spray it with nonstick cooking spray. Combine the oats, water, salt, and cinnamon in the slow cooker. Cover and cook on Low until the oatmeal is thickened and the oats are soft, 7 to 8 hours.

2. Stir the peanut butter into the oatmeal, followed by the jam—do not incorporate it, just streak it in. Serve hot, with drizzles of almond milk to achieve the desired consistency. Alternatively, you can serve the peanut butter and jam separately at the table, to be added as desired.

Amish Oatmeal

Amish oatmeal is usually baked in a casserole, but I like to make it in my slow cooker. It cooks up in 2 hours or less, so it's great for a Sunday brunch. This oatmeal is typically firm and sweet (some say it's like eating an oatmeal cookie for breakfast), but you can add more or less sugar according to taste. Instead of dried cranberries, feel free to substitute raisins or another dried fruit—I especially like this made with dried blueberries, although it does turn the oatmeal a purplish color. For gluten-free oatmeal, be sure to use certified gluten-free oats; for soy-free, use almond milk or soy-free nondairy milk, and vegan butter.

3 cups unsweetened almond milk or other nondairy milk
½ cup packed light brown sugar or maple syrup
2 tablespoons vegan butter, melted
2 teaspoons pure vanilla extract
1½ teaspoons baking powder
1½ teaspoons ground cinnamon
½ teaspoon salt
2½ cups old-fashioned rolled oats
⅔ cup sweetened dried cranberries
½ cup toasted slivered blanched almonds or chopped walnuts

SERVES 6

SLOW COOKER SIZE:
4- TO 6-QUART

COOK TIME:
2 HOURS ON HIGH

GLUTEN-FREE

SOY-FREE OPTION

1. In a large mixing bowl, combine the almond milk, sugar, melted butter, vanilla, baking powder, cinnamon, and salt. Mix well until smooth and well blended. Add the oats, cranberries, and almonds and stir until combined.

2. Generously grease the slow cooker insert or spray it with nonstick cooking spray. Spread the mixture evenly in the cooker. Cover and cook on High until set in the middle, about 2 hours. Serve hot.

Pumpkin Breakfast Quinoa

Wake up to the fragrance of pumpkin pie with this nourishing breakfast featuring protein-rich quinoa. Be sure to rinse the quinoa well before using to remove the bitter outer coating.

SERVES 4

SLOW COOKER SIZE:
4-QUART

COOK TIME:
6 TO 7 HOURS ON LOW

GLUTEN-FREE

SOY-FREE

1 cup quinoa, rinsed and drained
4 cups unsweetened almond milk
½ cup canned solid-pack pumpkin
¼ cup pure maple syrup or agave
1 teaspoon pure vanilla extract
½ teaspoon salt
1 teaspoon ground cinnamon
¼ teaspoon ground ginger
¼ teaspoon ground nutmeg
¼ teaspoon ground allspice
Sweetened dried cranberries, for garnish
Chopped toasted pecans, for garnish

1. Generously oil the slow cooker insert or spray it with nonstick cooking spray. Combine the quinoa, almond milk, pumpkin, maple syrup, vanilla, salt, cinnamon, ginger, nutmeg, and allspice in the cooker. Cover and cook on Low until the quinoa is soft and thickened, 6 to 7 hours.

2. Serve hot, spooned into bowls and sprinkled with cranberries and pecans.

Breakfast Polenta

Long before polenta became a darling of the dinner table, it was known to many as a breakfast food called cornmeal porridge or mush. I think "breakfast polenta" has a nicer ring to it. Instead of the sweet toppings listed below, you could omit the maple syrup and add savory toppings such as vegan bacon bits, cooked crumbled vegan sausage, chopped sun-dried tomatoes, and so on. For soy-free, simply omit the vegan butter or use a soy-free option.

1 cup medium- or coarse-ground polenta or cornmeal
4 cups water
1 teaspoon salt
1 tablespoon vegan butter (optional)
2 tablespoons pure maple syrup, plus more for serving
Fresh berries, sliced bananas, dried cranberries, and/or toasted nuts, for topping (optional)

SERVES 4

SLOW COOKER SIZE:
4-QUART

COOK TIME:
7 TO 8 HOURS ON LOW

GLUTEN-FREE

SOY-FREE OPTION

1. Combine the cornmeal, water, and salt in the slow cooker. Cover and cook on Low, stirring occasionally if possible, until thickened, 7 to 8 hours. Taste and adjust the seasonings, adding more salt if needed.

2. Just before serving, stir in the vegan butter, if using, and the maple syrup. Serve hot, passing additional maple syrup at the table, along with any of the optional toppings.

Indian Pudding

This Native American classic is known for its rich molasses flavor. I've included it in the breakfast chapter because it's an excellent and nutritious option, but really it's probably at its best served warm for dessert with a scoop of vegan vanilla ice cream. For soy-free pudding, use a soy-free vegan butter.

SERVES 6

SLOW COOKER SIZE:
4-QUART

COOK TIME:
3 HOURS ON HIGH OR
6 TO 8 HOURS ON LOW

GLUTEN-FREE

SOY-FREE OPTION

3½ cups unsweetened almond milk
½ cup medium-ground cornmeal
½ teaspoon salt
¼ cup packed light brown sugar
¼ cup molasses
½ teaspoon ground cinnamon
½ teaspoon ground ginger
¼ teaspoon ground nutmeg
⅔ cup chopped dates
1 teaspoon pure vanilla extract
½ teaspoon baking powder
2 tablespoons vegan butter

1. Lightly grease the insert of the slow cooker or spray it with nonstick cooking spray. In a large saucepan, combine 2 cups of the almond milk, the cornmeal, and salt and bring to a boil, stirring constantly. Reduce the heat to medium, and stir in the brown sugar, molasses, cinnamon, ginger, nutmeg, and dates. Remove from the heat and add 1 cup of the almond milk, the vanilla, and the baking powder, stirring until blended.

2. Transfer the mixture to the slow cooker. Pour the remaining ½ cup almond milk on top and dot with the vegan butter. Cover and cook on High for 3 hours or on Low for 6 to 8 hours. Serve warm.

Congee in a Crock

Congee is a bland rice porridge served with a variety of savory toppings. It is enjoyed as a breakfast food in China. Serve it hot in small bowls accompanied by a variety of condiments, to be added according to taste. I use Arborio rice for a creamy texture, but any medium-grain rice may be used instead. Different types of rice require different cooking times. For soy-free congee, omit the soy sauce and use a soy-free sauce (purchased or homemade, page 35) or add some soy-free vegetable broth base or additional salt.

1 cup uncooked Arborio rice
1 small yellow onion, minced
2 teaspoons grated fresh ginger
6 cups hot vegetable broth
1 teaspoon salt
1 tablespoon soy sauce
Chopped scallions, crushed roasted peanuts, soy sauce, sriracha sauce, and/or toasted sesame oil, for serving

SERVES 4 TO 6

SLOW COOKER SIZE:
4- TO 5-QUART

COOK TIME:
4 TO 6 HOURS ON LOW,
PLUS 30 MINUTES ON
HIGH IF NEEDED

GLUTEN-FREE

SOY-FREE OPTION

1. Combine the rice, onion, and ginger in the slow cooker. Stir in the hot broth, salt, and soy sauce. Cover and cook on Low until the texture is thick and creamy, 4 to 6 hours. If it is not done after 6 hours, remove the lid, turn the setting to High, and cook, uncovered, until the liquid is absorbed and the rice is tender, about 30 minutes.

2. Ladle the congee into soup bowls and sprinkle with some scallions and peanuts, with additional to pass at the table, along with bottles of soy sauce, sriracha, and sesame oil for diners to add according to their tastes.

French Toast Bread Pudding

Consider making this luscious bread pudding for a special breakfast or brunch. When Lori Maffei tested this recipe, she remarked that it was so good that she had to force herself to stop eating it right out of the slow cooker to save some for her children. Here's what else she said: "I thought this was just perfect. Delicious and very appealing visually as well, especially with the nuts. I can see using dried fruit or fresh apples, or both, as variations. Did I say how much I love this recipe?!" For a gluten-free version, use a gluten-free bread.

SERVES 4

SLOW COOKER SIZE:
4- TO 6-QUART

COOK TIME:
1½ TO 2 HOURS
ON HIGH

GLUTEN-FREE OPTION

8 cups soft white Italian bread cubes
6 ounces soft or silken tofu, drained
½ cup packed light brown sugar
2 teaspoons pure vanilla extract
1 teaspoon ground cinnamon
¼ teaspoon ground nutmeg
⅛ teaspoon ground allspice
¼ teaspoon salt
2 cups nondairy milk
¼ cup pure maple syrup, plus more for serving
1 tablespoon vegan butter
¼ cup coarsely chopped pecans or walnuts

1. Preheat the oven to 275°F. Spread the bread cubes on a baking sheet and bake for 30 minutes to dry the bread.

2. Generously oil the slow cooker insert or spray it with nonstick cooking spray. Transfer the dried bread to the cooker.

3. In a food processor, combine the tofu, sugar, vanilla, cinnamon, nutmeg, allspice, and salt, and process until well blended. Stir in the milk and maple syrup.

4. Pour the tofu mixture over the bread cubes in the slow cooker, pressing them into the wet mixture to moisten. Dot with bits of the vegan butter and sprinkle the top with the pecans. Cover and cook on High until firm, about 1½ hours. Serve topped with additional maple syrup.

Bananas Foster Bread Pudding

This yummy bread pudding makes a special brunch dish—kind of a combination of bananas Foster and French toast, all in one fragrant and easy-to-make bread pudding. When topped with ice cream, it also makes a great dessert. For a gluten-free version, use a gluten-free bread.

½ cup pure maple syrup
½ cup packed light brown sugar
2 tablespoons vegan butter
3 tablespoons dark rum or brandy (optional)
3 ripe bananas
6 ounces firm silken tofu
1 cup nondairy milk
2 tablespoons cornstarch
1 teaspoon pure vanilla extract
½ teaspoon salt
8 cups cubed white bread
1 cup pecan pieces
⅓ cup dried banana chips

SERVES 4

SLOW COOKER SIZE:
4- TO 5-QUART

COOK TIME:
2 HOURS ON HIGH

GLUTEN-FREE OPTION

1. In a saucepan, combine the maple syrup, sugar, and butter and cook over medium heat, stirring to dissolve the sugar and melt the butter. Stir in the rum, if using, then remove from the heat.

2. In a food processor, combine the bananas, tofu, nondairy milk, cornstarch, vanilla, and salt and process until smooth, scraping down the sides as needed. Add the maple syrup mixture and process to combine.

3. Generously grease the insert of the slow cooker or spray it with nonstick cooking spray. Combine the bread, pecans, and banana chips in the crock, stirring to mix well. Scrape the wet mixture onto the bread mixture, pressing the bread into the wet mixture to moisten. Cover and cook on High for 2 hours. Serve warm.

Sausage 'n' Scramble Casserole

This hearty casserole is ideal for breakfast or brunch, but it also makes a great main dish for a light supper.

SERVES 4 TO 6

SLOW COOKER SIZE:
4- TO 5-QUART

COOK TIME:
2 HOURS ON HIGH

2 teaspoons olive oil (optional)

1 medium-size yellow onion, minced

3 garlic cloves, minced

1 red or green bell pepper, seeded and chopped

2 cups sliced white mushrooms

½ teaspoon dried basil

½ teaspoon ground fennel seed

¼ teaspoon red pepper flakes, or more to taste

2 cups crumbled cooked vegan sausage, purchased or homemade (page 157)

1 pound firm tofu, drained, crumbled, and squeezed dry

1½ cups plain unsweetened nondairy milk

3 tablespoons nutritional yeast

1 tablespoon cornstarch

1 teaspoon yellow mustard

1 teaspoon smoked paprika

¼ teaspoon ground cayenne pepper (optional)

Salt and freshly ground black pepper

6 cups cubed French or Italian bread

½ cup shredded vegan mozzarella cheese (optional)

2 tablespoons chopped fresh flat-leaf parsley or basil, for garnish

1. For the best flavor, heat the oil in a large skillet over medium-high heat. Add the onion and sauté until softened, about 5 minutes. Add the garlic, bell pepper, and mushrooms and cook for 2 minutes longer. Stir in the dried basil, fennel, and red pepper flakes. Alternatively, omit the oil and sauté these ingredients in a few tablespoons of water or combine them in a microwave-safe bowl with a little water, cover, and microwave for 2 minutes. Drain off any liquid. Stir in the crumbled sausage and set aside.

2. In a food processor or blender, combine the tofu, nondairy milk, nutritional yeast, cornstarch, mustard, paprika, and cayenne, if using. Season to taste

with salt and pepper and blend until smooth. Taste and adjust the seasonings, adding more salt if needed.

3. Generously oil the slow cooker insert or spray it with nonstick cooking spray. Spread the bread cubes in the bottom of the slow cooker. Add the reserved sausage mixture, then add the tofu mixture and stir to combine. Spread the mixture out evenly in the slow cooker, and sprinkle the top with the vegan cheese, if using. Cover and cook on High for 2 hours. Serve hot, sprinkled with the parsley.

Cheesy Mushroom-Chorizo Frittata

To save time in the morning, assemble this the night before and then turn on the cooker first thing in the morning for a leisurely brunch main dish. (It also makes a good light supper choice.) Vegan frittatas hold well in the slow cooker and are best prepared in a wide, shallow cooker. It can be a little difficult to remove the first piece of the frittata, but after that, the pieces are easier to get out.

1 pound firm tofu, well drained and lightly pressed
½ cup vegetable broth
¼ cup nutritional yeast
1 tablespoon cornstarch or tapioca starch
½ teaspoon onion powder
½ teaspoon garlic powder
½ teaspoon dried basil
½ teaspoon smoked paprika
Salt and freshly ground black pepper
2 teaspoons olive oil (optional)
5 scallions, minced
8 ounces white mushrooms, chopped
1 cup crumbled vegan chorizo
1 cup Creamy Cheesy Sauce (page 123) or shredded vegan cheese of your choice

SERVES 4

SLOW COOKER SIZE:
4- TO 6-QUART

COOK TIME:
2 TO 3 HOURS ON HIGH

GLUTEN-FREE

1. In a food processor or blender, combine the tofu, broth, nutritional yeast, cornstarch, onion powder, garlic powder, basil, paprika, and salt and pepper to taste. Process until smooth and well blended. Set aside.

2. For the best flavor, heat the oil in a large skillet over medium-high heat. Add the scallions, mushrooms, chorizo, and salt and pepper to taste and cook until the mushrooms release their liquid and it evaporates. Alternatively, omit the oil and sauté these ingredients in a few tablespoons of water or combine them in a microwave-safe bowl with a little water, cover, and microwave for 2 minutes. Drain off any liquid exuded by the mushrooms.

3. Generously oil the slow cooker insert or spray it with nonstick cooking spray. Combine the chorizo mixture and the tofu mixture in the slow cooker, mixing well and spreading evenly. Top with the cheesy sauce (or sprinkle with the shredded cheese). Cover and cook on High until firm, 2 to 3 hours.

4. Cut into wedges and serve hot.

Artichoke and Mushroom Frittata

Studded with pieces of artichoke heart and mushrooms, this frittata is a good choice for a brunch or light supper served with crusty bread. It holds well in the slow cooker and is best prepared in a wide, shallow cooker. It can be a little difficult to remove the first piece of the frittata, but after that, the pieces are easier to get out.

1 pound firm tofu, well drained and lightly pressed

1 cup vegetable broth

3 tablespoons nutritional yeast

1 tablespoon cornstarch or tapioca starch

½ teaspoon onion powder

Salt and freshly ground black pepper

⅓ cup chopped oil-packed sun-dried tomatoes

2 teaspoons olive oil (optional)

5 scallions, minced

8 ounces white mushrooms, thinly sliced or chopped

½ teaspoon dried thyme

½ teaspoon dried basil

2 cups canned or thawed frozen artichoke hearts, chopped

1 teaspoon capers, rinsed and drained, chopped if large

½ cup shredded vegan cheese of your choice (optional)

SERVES 4

SLOW COOKER SIZE:
4- TO 6-QUART

COOK TIME:
3 TO 4 HOURS ON LOW

GLUTEN-FREE

1. In a food processor or blender, combine the tofu, broth, nutritional yeast, cornstarch, onion powder, and salt and pepper to taste. Add 1 tablespoon of the sun-dried tomatoes and process until smooth and well blended. Set aside.

2. For the best flavor, heat the oil in a medium-size skillet over medium-high heat. Add the scallions, mushrooms, thyme, basil, and salt and pepper to taste, and cook for 3 to 4 minutes. Alternatively, omit the oil and sauté these ingredients in a few tablespoons of water or combine them in a microwave-safe bowl with a little water, cover, and microwave for 2 minutes. Drain off any liquid exuded by the mushrooms. Stir in the artichokes, the remaining sun-dried tomatoes, and the capers.

3. Generously oil the insert of the slow cooker or spray it with nonstick cooking spray. Spread the cooked vegetables evenly in the bottom of the cooker. Add the reserved tofu mixture, stirring to combine all of the ingredients, then spread the mixture evenly. Sprinkle on the cheese, if using. Cover and cook on Low until firm, 3 to 4 hours.

4. Cut into wedges and serve hot.

Greek Frittata

Kalamata olives, spinach, and red bell pepper make a colorful topping for this flavorful frittata seasoned with lemon juice, garlic, and herbs.

SERVES 4

SLOW COOKER SIZE:
5- TO 6-QUART

COOK TIME:
2 HOURS ON HIGH

GLUTEN-FREE

2 teaspoons olive oil (optional)

1 small yellow onion, chopped

3 large garlic cloves, crushed

1 teaspoon dried basil

1 teaspoon dried oregano

1 pound firm tofu, well drained and lightly pressed

2 to 3 tablespoons nutritional yeast

1 tablespoon freshly squeezed lemon juice

Salt and freshly ground black pepper

3 cups lightly packed fresh baby spinach

1 jarred roasted red bell pepper, chopped

½ cup pitted kalamata olives, coarsely chopped

1. For the best flavor, heat the oil in a small skillet over medium-high heat. Add the onion and sauté until softened, about 5 minutes. Add the garlic, basil, and oregano and cook until fragrant, 1 minute longer. Alternatively, omit the oil and sauté these ingredients in a few tablespoons of water until softened or combine them in a microwave-safe bowl with a little water, cover, and microwave for 2 minutes.

2. Transfer the onion mixture to a food processor or blender. Add the tofu, nutritional yeast, lemon juice, and salt and pepper to taste, and process until smooth and well blended. Generously oil the slow cooker insert or spray it with nonstick cooking spray. Scrape the tofu mixture into the cooker. Cover and cook on High for 1½ hours.

3. Meanwhile, lightly steam the spinach or microwave it until just wilted. Chop the spinach and place it in a bowl. Add the roasted bell pepper and olives and mix to combine. Spread the spinach and olive mixture on top of the frittata, cover, and cook for an additional 30 minutes, until set. Serve hot.

Autumn Fruit Crock

A satisfying cold-weather breakfast alone or as a topping for oatmeal or other hot cereal, this compote also makes a great dessert. If your pears are ripe, the cooking time may be shorter, so check for doneness about 30 minutes ahead of time to see if it's cooked. If you'd like a little color in your compote, substitute fresh cranberries for dried, although you may need to add a little extra sugar if doing so.

3 large apples, peeled, cored, and cut into 1-inch dice
2 just-ripe pears, peeled, cored, and cut into 1-inch dice
1 cup dried apricots, quartered
½ cup sweetened dried cranberries
½ cup pitted prunes, halved
¼ cup granulated natural sugar
Grated zest and juice of 1 lemon or orange
1 cinnamon stick
¼ cup water

SERVES 8

SLOW COOKER SIZE:
4- TO 5-QUART

COOK TIME:
6 HOURS ON LOW OR
3 HOURS ON HIGH,
PLUS 30 MINUTES ON
HIGH IF NEEDED

GLUTEN-FREE

SOY-FREE

1. Combine all of the ingredients in the slow cooker. Cover and cook on Low until the fruit is soft and the liquid is syrupy, about 6 hours on Low or 3 hours on High. If the liquid needs more reducing, remove the lid and cook uncovered on High for 30 minutes longer.

2. Set aside to cool and thicken. Serve warm or at room temperature. If not using right away, transfer to a bowl, cover, and refrigerate until ready to serve.

Chai-Spiced Breakfast Bread

This fragrant loaf is delicious served warm with hot tea or coffee—or even chai, if you're so inclined. To make soy-free bread, use soy-free vegan butter and soy-free nondairy milk.

MAKES 1 LOAF

SLOW COOKER SIZE:
4-QUART OR 6-QUART

COOK TIME:
1½ HOURS ON HIGH
FOR 4-QUART;
3 HOURS ON HIGH
FOR 6-QUART

SOY-FREE OPTION

1¾ cups unbleached all-purpose flour
2 teaspoons baking powder
½ teaspoon baking soda
½ teaspoon salt
½ teaspoon ground cardamom
¾ teaspoon ground cinnamon
¼ teaspoon ground nutmeg
⅛ teaspoon ground cloves
¾ cup natural sugar
¼ cup vegan butter, melted and cooled
2 tablespoons unsweetened applesauce
¾ cup nondairy milk mixed with ½ teaspoon apple cider vinegar
½ cup double-strength brewed black tea
2 teaspoons pure vanilla extract
2 tablespoons sunflower seeds or chopped walnuts (optional)

1. If using a 4-quart slow cooker, lightly oil the insert of the slow cooker or spray it with nonstick cooking spray. If using a 6-quart slow cooker, place a rack, trivet, or a ring of crumpled aluminum foil in the bottom of the slow cooker insert. Lightly oil a 7 x 9-inch baking pan or other pan that will fit inside the cooker.

2. In a large bowl, combine the flour, baking powder, baking soda, salt, cardamom, cinnamon, nutmeg, and cloves. Mix well.

3. In a separate bowl, combine the sugar and vegan butter and beat until well combined. Add the applesauce, nondairy milk and vinegar mixture, tea, and vanilla, and stir until blended. Add the wet mixture to the dry mixture, stirring to combine with a few quick strokes. Stir in the sunflower seeds, if using.

4. If using a 4-quart slow cooker, transfer the batter to the slow cooker, smoothing evenly. If using a 6-quart slow cooker, transfer the batter to the prepared pan, pour about ½ inch of hot water into the bottom of the cooker, and place the baking pan on the rack inside the slow cooker.

5. Drape a clean kitchen towel over the cooker, put on the lid, and cook on High until the bread is firm and a tester inserted in the center comes out dry, about 1½ hours if cooking directly in the cooker insert or about 3 hours if cooking in a baking pan inside the cooker.

6. Allow the bread to cool, uncovered, before slicing. This bread tastes best served warm, soon after it is made.

Pumpkin–Chocolate Chip Bread

Pumpkin and chocolate have a natural affinity for each other, a fact that is evident in this delicious loaf. It's a great snack to keep on hand during the autumn months, especially around Halloween or Thanksgiving.

1 cup canned solid-pack pumpkin
½ cup packed light brown sugar or granulated natural sugar
¼ cup pure maple syrup
2 tablespoons vegetable oil
1 teaspoon pure vanilla extract
1¾ cups unbleached all-purpose flour
2 teaspoons baking powder
½ teaspoon salt
½ teaspoon ground cinnamon
¼ teaspoon ground nutmeg
¼ teaspoon ground allspice
½ cup semisweet vegan chocolate chips

SERVES 6 TO 8

SLOW COOKER SIZE:
4-QUART OR 6-QUART

COOK TIME:
2 HOURS ON HIGH
FOR 4-QUART;
3 HOURS ON HIGH
FOR 6-QUART

SOY-FREE

1. If using a 4-quart slow cooker, generously oil the insert of the slow cooker crock or spray it with nonstick cooking spray. If using a 6-quart slow cooker,

lightly oil a 7 x 9-inch baking pan or other pan that will fit inside your cooker. Place a rack, trivet, or a ring of crumpled aluminum foil in the bottom of the cooker insert.

2. In a medium-size bowl, combine the pumpkin, sugar, maple syrup, oil, and vanilla and mix well.

3. In a separate large bowl, combine the flour, baking powder, salt, cinnamon, nutmeg, and allspice. Stir the wet ingredients into the dry ingredient, mixing with a few quick strokes. Add the chocolate chips and stir until just combined.

4. If using a 4-quart slow cooker, scrape the batter into the insert, spreading evenly. If using a 6-quart slow cooker, transfer the batter to the prepared pan, pour about ½ inch of hot water into the bottom of the cooker, and place the pan on the rack in the slow cooker.

5. Drape a clean kitchen towel over the cooker and put on the lid. Cook on High until the bread is firm and a tester inserted in the center comes out clean, about 2 hours if cooking directly in the cooker insert or about 3 hours if cooking in a baking pan inside the cooker.

6. Allow the bread to cool, uncovered, before slicing.

Three-Corn Cornbread

In addition to being a great chili accompaniment, cornbread makes a delicious breakfast bread when served warm and slathered with homemade apple butter (page 228) or a little vegan butter.

1¼ cups medium- or coarse-ground cornmeal
1 cup unbleached all-purpose flour
2 teaspoons baking powder
½ teaspoon salt
1 (15-ounce) can creamed corn
½ cup fresh or thawed frozen corn kernels
¼ cup pure maple syrup
2 tablespoons vegetable oil

SERVES 6 TO 8

SLOW COOKER SIZE:
4-QUART OR 6-QUART

COOK TIME:
2 HOURS ON HIGH FOR
4-QUART; 3 HOURS ON
HIGH FOR 6-QUART

SOY-FREE

1. If using a 4-quart slow cooker, generously oil the insert of the cooker. If using a 6-quart slow cooker, lightly oil a 7 x 9-inch baking pan or other pan that will fit inside the cooker, or spray it with nonstick cooking spray. Place a rack, trivet, or a ring of crumpled aluminum foil in the bottom of the slow cooker insert.

2. In a large bowl, combine the cornmeal, flour, baking powder, and salt.

3. In a separate large bowl, combine the creamed corn, corn kernels, maple syrup, and oil. Add the wet ingredients to the dry ingredients and mix well with a few quick strokes.

4. If using a 4-quart slow cooker, scrape the batter into the insert, spreading evenly. If using a 6-quart slow cooker, transfer the batter to the prepared pan, pour about ½ inch of hot water into the bottom of the cooker, and place the pan on the rack.

5. Drape a clean kitchen towel over the top and put on the lid. Cook on High until the bread is firm and a tester inserted in the center comes out clean, about 2 hours if cooking directly in the cooker insert or about 3 hours if cooking in a baking pan inside the cooker.

6. Allow the bread to cool, uncovered, before slicing.

Berry-Banana Breakfast Bread

I like to make this slow cooker bread in the summer when fresh blueberries are abundant, although it can also be made with frozen or dried blueberries. To vary this, leave out the blueberries, or add a different kind of berry or fruit, or add walnuts or chocolate chips.

MAKES 1 LOAF

SLOW COOKER SIZE:
4-QUART OR 6-QUART

COOK TIME:
1½ TO 2 HOURS ON
HIGH FOR 4-QUART;
3 HOURS ON HIGH
FOR 6-QUART

SOY-FREE

⅓ cup unsweetened applesauce
½ cup packed light brown sugar
3 ripe bananas, mashed
1 teaspoon pure vanilla extract
1¾ cups unbleached all-purpose flour
2 teaspoons baking powder
½ teaspoon salt
¾ cup fresh, thawed frozen, or dried blueberries

1. If using a 4-quart slow cooker, generously oil the insert of the cooker or spray it with nonstick cooking spray. If using a 6-quart slow cooker, place a rack, trivet, or a ring of crumpled aluminum foil in the bottom of the cooker insert. Lightly oil a 7 x 9-inch baking pan or other pan that will fit inside the cooker.

2. In a large bowl, combine the applesauce, brown sugar, bananas, and vanilla, and mix well.

3. In a separate bowl, combine the flour, baking powder, and salt. Add the dry ingredients to the wet ingredients and mix well. Gently stir in the blueberries.

4. If using a 4-quart slow cooker, pour the batter into the insert. If using a 6-quart slow cooker, pour the batter into the prepared pan, pour about ½ inch of hot water into the bottom of the cooker, and place the pan on the rack. Drape a clean kitchen towel over the top of the cooker, put on the lid, and cook on High until the bread is firm and a tester inserted in the center comes out dry, 1½ to 2 hours if cooking directly in the cooker insert or about 3 hours if cooking in the baking pan inside the cooker.

5. Allow the bread to cool, uncovered, before slicing.

chapter 12

Hot Drinks

From a steaming crock of spiced cider at a Halloween party to a festive punch on New Year's Eve, hot drinks are a welcome addition to cold-weather gatherings of all kinds. A slow cooker is a great way to keep hot drinks at an ideal serving temperature. You can make and serve your beverage from the same crock and, when turning on the Keep Warm setting, it will do just that throughout the evening. You can set the slow cooker right on the table or countertop, leaving you free from monitoring a simmering pot on top of the stove.

Of course, you don't need a crowd to serve your favorite hot beverages. The Vanilla-Spice Chai or Mexican Hot Chocolate can be enjoyed as your own private indulgence, while the Hot Sangria is a good choice for a cozy evening for two. Whatever your choice, these drinks can be served piping hot directly from the slow cooker into waiting mugs or heatproof punch cups. Since the contents of a slow cooker will remain at a good serving temperature for several hours, it can also be convenient when you go out for an hour or two—to build a snowman, for example—and want to come home to a nice hot drink that's waiting for you. With this varied selection of hot drinks, there's something delicious to warm up everyone in the house.

Blushing Spiced Cider

The first cold nip of autumn is occasion enough to put on a pot of this warming cider. It's a great beverage for a gathering and can be made as a spiked punch by adding a generous splash of vodka or rum to the slow cooker when ready to serve, or to individual servings as desired.

2 cinnamon sticks, broken into pieces
1 teaspoon whole cloves
1 teaspoon allspice berries
2 quarts apple cider
2 cups cranberry juice
½ cup packed light brown sugar
2 tablespoons freshly squeezed lemon juice
1 medium-size orange, unpeeled, sliced

MAKES ABOUT
2 QUARTS

SLOW COOKER SIZE:
4-QUART

COOK TIME:
1 TO 2 HOURS ON LOW

GLUTEN-FREE

SOY-FREE

1. Place the cinnamon, cloves, and allspice in the center of a 6-inch square piece of cheesecloth. Gather the ends of the cloth together and tie with kitchen string to enclose the spices.

2. Combine the apple cider, cranberry juice, and brown sugar in the slow cooker and stir to dissolve the sugar. Stir in the lemon juice and add the spice bag. Cover and cook on Low until hot, 1 to 2 hours.

3. Just before serving, remove and discard the spice bag and float the orange slices on the top. Serve hot. If not serving right away, turn the slow cooker to the Keep Warm setting.

Hot Sangria

Prepare a fun and fruity alternative to mulled wine with the convenience of a slow cooker. Put it together, turn it on, and then forget it. Guests can help themselves, and the wine stays at the perfect serving temperature for hours.

MAKES ABOUT 3 QUARTS

SLOW COOKER SIZE:
4- TO 5-QUART

COOK TIME:
1 HOUR ON HIGH

GLUTEN-FREE

SOY-FREE

2 (750-milliliter) bottles dry red wine
½ cup brandy or orange-flavored liqueur
1 cup sugar
1 cup orange juice
1 cup cranberry juice
1 cup fresh or frozen sliced peaches or cherries
1 orange, unpeeled, halved lengthwise and sliced crosswise
1 lemon, unpeeled, halved lengthwise and sliced crosswise

1. Combine all of the ingredients in the slow cooker. Cover and cook on High for 1 hour.

2. Serve hot, in clear punch cups or heat-resistant glasses, including some of the fruit with each serving. If not serving right away, turn the slow cooker to the Keep Warm setting.

Celebration Punch

Fruit juice seasoned with spices makes for a refreshing alcohol-free punch. For a spiked version, add a splash or two of rum when ready to serve.

3 cinnamon sticks, broken into pieces
1 teaspoon whole cloves
1 cup water
½ cup packed light brown sugar or natural granulated sugar
1 (6-ounce) can frozen lemonade concentrate, thawed
2 cups cranberry juice
1½ quarts apple cider or apple juice
1 navel orange, unpeeled, sliced

**MAKES ABOUT
2 QUARTS**

SLOW COOKER SIZE:
4-QUART

COOK TIME:
2 HOURS ON LOW

GLUTEN-FREE

SOY-FREE

1. Place the cinnamon and cloves in the center of a 6-inch square piece of cheesecloth and tie it with kitchen string to enclose the spices.

2. Combine the water and brown sugar in the slow cooker and stir to dissolve the sugar. Stir in the lemonade concentrate, then add the cranberry juice, stirring to dissolve the lemonade. Add the spice bag and stir in the apple cider. Cover and cook on Low for 2 hours.

3. Just before serving, remove and discard the spice bag and float the orange slices in the punch. Serve hot. If not serving right away, turn the slow cooker to the Keep Warm setting.

Spiced Rum Punch

Spiced rum provides depth and complexity to this bracing and delicious punch. It may well be the hit of your next get-together. Use a soy-free vegan butter for soy-free punch.

SERVES 4

SLOW COOKER SIZE:
1½- TO 4-QUART

COOK TIME:
45 MINUTES TO
1 HOUR ON LOW

GLUTEN-FREE

SOY-FREE OPTION

½ cup packed dark brown sugar
¼ cup vegan butter, at room temperature
¼ cup agave nectar
½ teaspoon ground cinnamon
¼ teaspoon ground nutmeg
¼ teaspoon ground cloves
½ teaspoon pure vanilla extract
1 cup spiced rum
3 cups boiling water
Cinnamon sticks, for garnish

1. Combine the sugar, butter, agave, cinnamon, nutmeg, cloves, and vanilla in the slow cooker and stir until well blended. Add the rum and the boiling water. Stir to blend well. Cover and cook on Low until hot, 45 minutes to 1 hour.

2. Serve hot in mugs and garnish with cinnamon sticks. If not serving right away, turn the slow cooker to the Keep Warm setting.

Hot and Spicy Virgin Mary Sipper

You can spike this with vodka, if desired. With or without, it's a great way to warm up on a cold night! To make this soy-free, omit the Worcestershire sauce and use a soy-free sauce (purchased or homemade, page 35) or add some soy-free vegetable broth base or additional salt.

1 (46-ounce) can blended vegetable juice, such as V8
1½ tablespoons brown sugar
1½ tablespoons freshly squeezed lemon juice
1 to 2 teaspoons horseradish
1 teaspoon vegan Worcestershire sauce
½ teaspoon celery salt
½ teaspoon Tabasco sauce
Celery sticks, for garnish

MAKES ABOUT 6 CUPS

SLOW COOKER SIZE:
4- TO 5-QUART

COOK TIME:
2 HOURS ON HIGH

GLUTEN-FREE

SOY-FREE OPTION

1. Combine the vegetable juice, brown sugar, lemon juice, horseradish, Worcestershire, celery salt, and Tabasco in the slow cooker. Cover and cook on High until hot, about 2 hours.

2. Serve hot, ladled into cups or mugs. Garnish each serving with a celery stick. If not serving right away, turn the slow cooker to the Keep Warm setting.

Hot White Chocolate

If you're a fan of white chocolate like I am, you enjoy it any way you can get it—and this white version of hot chocolate is no exception. Because white chocolate is so sweet, this recipe requires very little additional sweetener.

SERVES 4 TO 6

SLOW COOKER SIZE:
4-QUART

COOK TIME:
2 HOURS ON HIGH

GLUTEN-FREE

SOY-FREE

4 cups unsweetened almond milk
½ cup vegan white chocolate chips
2 tablespoons agave nectar
2 teaspoons pure vanilla extract
Ground nutmeg or unsweetened cocoa powder, for garnish (optional)

1. Combine the almond milk, white chocolate, agave, and vanilla in the slow cooker, stirring to mix well. Cover and cook on High, stirring occasionally, until the chocolate is melted and the mixture is hot, about 2 hours.

2. Stir well before serving in warm cups or mugs. Garnish with a sprinkling of nutmeg or cocoa, if desired. If not serving right away, turn the slow cooker to the Keep Warm setting.

Mocha Affogato

Inspired by an Italian dessert where hot espresso is poured over a scoop of gelato, this decadent concoction is like having coffee and dessert rolled into one—especially if you add the optional scoop of vanilla ice cream to each serving. Add the Kahlúa or not at your own discretion—it's delicious either way. For soy-free, be sure to use soy-free vegan ice cream. This recipe is easily doubled for a crowd.

1 pint vegan chocolate ice cream

4 cups hot brewed coffee

½ cup Kahlúa, or to taste (optional)

1 pint vegan vanilla ice cream (optional)

SERVES 6

SLOW COOKER SIZE:
4-QUART

COOK TIME:
1 TO 2 HOURS ON LOW

GLUTEN-FREE

SOY-FREE OPTION

1. Place the chocolate ice cream in the slow cooker. Pour the hot coffee over the ice cream, stirring to melt. Cover and cook on Low until hot, 1 to 2 hours. If not serving right away, turn the slow cooker to the Keep Warm setting.

2. Just before serving, stir in the Kahlúa, if using. Serve as is in coffee mugs, or place a small scoop of vanilla ice cream in the bottom of each coffee mug before ladling the mocha mixture on top, and serve with a spoon.

Mexican Hot Chocolate

Nothing beats the flavor and aroma of homemade hot chocolate, and this Mexican version, with cinnamon sticks and an optional pinch of cayenne, really hits the spot on a cold day or evening. The addition of vegan whipped cream (soy-free, if desired) makes it extra special.

½ cup semisweet vegan chocolate chips

¼ cup agave nectar

3 cinnamon sticks

Pinch of cayenne pepper (optional)

4 cups unsweetened almond milk

Vegan whipped cream (optional)

SERVES 4

SLOW COOKER SIZE:
4-QUART

COOK TIME:
2 HOURS ON HIGH

GLUTEN-FREE

SOY-FREE

1. Combine the chocolate, agave, cinnamon, and cayenne (if using) in the slow cooker. Add the almond milk, stirring to mix well. Cover and cook on High, stirring occasionally, until the chocolate is melted, about 2 hours. If not serving right away, turn the slow cooker to the Keep Warm setting.

2. Stir well and remove the cinnamon sticks before serving in warm cups or mugs. Top with a dollop of vegan whipped cream, if desired.

Vanilla-Spice Chai

Chai tea can be pricey in coffee shops, and even chai tea concentrate is expensive to buy for making at home. This recipe allows you to have it your way. You can increase or decrease the spices according to your own taste preference. If you don't have a whole vanilla bean, add a little vanilla extract just before serving. If you don't have whole cardamom pods, sprinkle a little ground cardamom into the spice mixture before closing up the cheesecloth.

SERVES 6

SLOW COOKER SIZE:
3½ - TO 4-QUART

COOK TIME: 4 HOURS
AND 15 MINUTES
ON HIGH, PLUS 30
MINUTES ON LOW

GLUTEN-FREE

SOY-FREE

6 (¼-inch-thick) slices fresh ginger
8 whole cloves
½ teaspoon fennel seeds
½ teaspoon cardamom seeds
½ teaspoon whole black peppercorns
4 cinnamon sticks, whole or broken into pieces
1 vanilla bean, whole or cut into pieces
4 cups water
6 black or rooibos tea bags, regular or decaf
4 cups vanilla almond milk
Agave nectar, to taste (optional)

1. Place the ginger, cloves, fennel seeds, cardamom seeds, and peppercorns in the center of a small square of cheesecloth and tie it with kitchen string to enclose the spices. If using pieces of cinnamon sticks and vanilla bean, rather than whole ones, you may add them to the bag, although you may need to make two spice bags for it all to fit.

2. Place the spice bag in the slow cooker along with the whole cinnamon sticks and whole vanilla bean, if using. Add the water, cover, and cook on High for 4 hours.

3. Add the tea bags, cover, and allow to steep for 15 minutes, then turn the setting to Low. Remove the tea bags and the spices. Stir in the almond milk

and agave, if using. Cover and continue to cook for 30 minutes longer to heat the almond milk. Serve hot in mugs. If not serving right away, turn the slow cooker to the Keep Warm setting. (See Note for make-ahead instructions.)

NOTE: To make ahead, do not add the almond milk in step 3. Instead, transfer the chai to a container and refrigerate. When ready to serve, add the almond milk and heat on the stovetop or in the microwave until hot, or serve chilled. Alternatively, you can use the chai mixture as your homemade version of chai concentrate—simply store it in the refrigerator and combine any amount with an equal amount of almond milk. Heat it up or add a few ice cubes for refreshing iced chai.

Measurement Equivalents

Please note that all conversions are approximate.

LIQUID CONVERSIONS

U.S.	METRIC	U.S.	METRIC
1 tsp	5 ml	1 cup + 2 tbs	275 ml
1 tbs	15 ml	1¼ cups	300 ml
2 tbs	30 ml	1⅓ cups	325 ml
3 tbs	45 ml	1½ cups	350 ml
¼ cup	60 ml	1⅔ cups	375 ml
⅓ cup	75 ml	1¾ cups	400 ml
⅓ cup + 1 tbs	90 ml	1¾ cups + 2 tbs	450 ml
⅓ cup + 2 tbs	100 ml	2 cups (1 pint)	475 ml
½ cup	120 ml	2½ cups	600 ml
⅔ cup	150 ml	3 cups	720 ml
¾ cup	180 ml	4 cups (1 quart)	945 ml
¾ cup + 2 tbs	200 ml		(1,000 ml is 1 liter)
1 cup	240 ml		

WEIGHT CONVERSIONS

U.S./U.K	METRIC
½ oz	14 g
1 oz	28 g
1½ oz	43 g
2 oz	57 g
2½ oz	71 g
3 oz	85 g
3½ oz	100 g
4 oz	113 g
5 oz	142 g
6 oz	170 g
7 oz	200 g
8 oz	227 g
9 oz	255 g
10 oz	284 g
11 oz	312 g
12 oz	340 g
13 oz	368 g
14 oz	400 g
15 oz	425 g
1 lb	454 g

OVEN TEMPERATURE

°F	GAS MARK	°C
250	½	120
275	1	140
300	2	150
325	3	165
350	4	180
375	5	190
400	6	200
425	7	220
450	8	230
475	9	240
500	10	260
550	Broil	290

Index